# Unlimited Selling Power

### How to Master Hypnotic Selling Skills

## Dr. Donald J. Moine

## Dr. Kenneth L. Lloyd

PRENTICE HALL

D0199199

**PRENTICE HALL PRESS**
**Published by the Penguin Group**
**Penguin Group (USA) Inc.**
**375 Hudson Street, New York, New York 10014, USA**
Penguin Group (Canada), 90 Eglinton Avenue East, Suite 700, Toronto, Ontario M4P 2Y3, Canada
(a division of Pearson Penguin Canada Inc.)
Penguin Books Ltd., 80 Strand, London WC2R 0RL, England
Penguin Group Ireland, 25 St. Stephen's Green, Dublin 2, Ireland (a division of Penguin Books Ltd.)
Penguin Group (Australia), 250 Camberwell Road, Camberwell, Victoria 3124, Australia
(a division of Pearson Australia Group Pty. Ltd.)
Penguin Books India Pvt. Ltd., 11 Community Centre, Panchsheel Park, New Delhi—110 017, India
Penguin Group (NZ), 67 Apollo Drive, Rosedale, North Shore 0632, New Zealand
(a division of Pearson New Zealand Ltd.)
Penguin Books (South Africa) (Pty.) Ltd., 24 Sturdee Avenue, Rosebank, Johannesburg 2196,
South Africa

Penguin Books Ltd., Registered Offices: 80 Strand, London WC2R 0RL, England

PRINTING HISTORY
Prentice Hall Press trade paperback edition / March 1990

Library of Congress Cataloging-in-Publication Data

Moine, Donald J., [date]
    Unlimited selling power : how to master hypnotic skills / by
Donald J. Moine and Kenneth Lloyd.
        p. cm.
    ISBN 0-13-689126-8
    1. Selling—Psychological aspects.   2. Hypnotism.   I. Lloyd,
Kenneth.   II. Title.
    HF5438.8.P75M653   1990                        89-25500
    658.8'5'019—dc20                               CIP

PRINTED IN THE UNITED STATES OF AMERICA

30   29   28   27   26   25   24   23   22   21

Most Prentice Hall Press books are available at special quantity discounts for bulk purchases for sales
promotions, premiums, fund-raising, or educational use. Special books, or book excerpts, can also be
created to fit specific needs. For details, write: Special Markets, Penguin Group (USA) Inc., 375 Hudson Street, New York, New York 10014.

Dr. Donald J. Moine was co-author of
*Modern Persuasion Strategies: The
Hidden Advantage in Selling,*
Herd, J. & Moine, 1984, Prentice-Hall.

This book is dedicated to
Linda and Roberta

# Contents

## Chapter 3
### PROFITING FROM THE LESSONS OF THE WORLD'S GREATEST HYPNOTIST

## Chapter 4
### BUILDING TRUST AND RAPPORT THROUGH THE POWER OF HYPNOTIC PACING

# Chapter 5
## CREATING SALES PRESENTATIONS THAT MESMERIZE

# Chapter 6
## CAPITALIZING ON THE PERSUASIVE POWERS OF SALES STORIES AND METAPHORS

# Chapter 7
## USING HYPNOTIC SALES QUESTIONS TO GET THE KIND OF INFORMATION YOU NEED TO CLOSE SALES 135

## Chapter 8
### DEVELOPING AND USING SCRIPT BOOKS FOR CONSISTENTLY EFFECTIVE HYPNOTIC SALES PRESENTATIONS     159

## Chapter 9
### CUSTOMIZING YOUR SCRIPT BOOK TO MEET YOUR NEEDS AND THOSE OF YOUR CUSTOMERS     171

## Chapter 10
### MASTERING SALES HYPNOSIS THROUGH STATE-OF-THE-ART TRAINING TECHNOLOGY     183

Chapter **11**

**UNLEASHING THE POWER OF SELF-HYPNOSIS**                        **203**

Chapter **12**

**DEVELOPING AND IMPLEMENTING YOUR ACTION
PLAN FOR SALES SUCCESS**                                        **221**

# Chapter 13
## USING THE SALES MAGIC OF ED McMAHON 231

# Epilog
## SALES HYPNOSIS: THE KEY TO LIFELONG SALES SUCCESS 257

# How This Book Will Help You Put the Power of Sales Hypnosis to Work

In 1983, Tom Olds was struggling to make ends meet. He was months behind in making his car payments. His house was getting dangerously close to foreclosure. *He was in debt to numerous credit card companies.* Then, his girlfriend of three years walked out on him.

Today, Tom lives in a $700,000 house in the Tustin Hills of Southern California. He owns a BMW 733i and bought his new wife a 3-carat diamond ring. His bank accounts are bulging and he has numerous investments. His future is secured.

*What happened in these few short years?* How did Tom turn his life around?

Tom Olds learned the best kept secret of sales superstars: the ability to build immediate trust and command respect and confidence by using gentle forms of conversational hypnosis.

Before you object, let us tell you that Tom has not put anyone to sleep with hypnosis. He hasn't tricked anyone. He never uses deceit or any under-handed methods.

In fact, Tom is a man of high moral standards. He regularly attends and donates to his church, the Crystal Cathedral, and was married by the Reverend Robert Schuller. Tom is a man of great integrity. If you had told him a few years ago that he would find financial freedom and self-confidence through the use of sales hypnosis, he would have scoffed at the notion.

If you had shown the Tom Olds of 1983 the communication techniques Tom now uses daily, he wouldn't have even considered them hypnosis. *The techniques are so subtle, so natural, and so friendly, that few people consciously recognize their hypnotic powers.* No one has any reason to question them or to resist them.

THESE ARE THE TECHNIQUES OF THE "BORN SALESMAN." These are the techniques that were previously considered "unteachable." Either you knew how to sell like a champion or you didn't. *Most of us didn't.*

While the techniques seem like anything but hypnosis, that is exactly what they are: **pure hypnosis.** Scientists who study language patterns have *documented* that top salespeople use forms of conversational hypnosis and that less-successful salespeople don't. In addition, scientists have found that top negotiators use conversational hypnosis, as do the best attorneys and the most charismatic ministers and preachers.

These powerful techniques can now be learned and used, for the first time, by the rest of us.

How it is done is what this book is about: sales hypnosis and its many powers. In reading this book, you will learn the specific techniques which have enabled Tom Olds and thousands of other people to greatly increase their incomes, their self-confidence, and their personal happiness.

Tom Olds was a hard-working and energetic student. After earning his undergraduate degree, he worked his way through two more years of college to get a M.B.A. from the University of Chicago.

Trained and certified as an accountant, Tom got a job with one of the "Big Eight" accounting firms. His career path was mapped out and Tom thought he was set for life—until the boredom set in. Tom realized that while accounting is an honorable profession, he was not cut out to spend the rest of his years pouring over financial statements, computer print-outs, and other pieces of paper. Tom was also frustrated with what seemed to him to be the relatively low pay that the accounting field offered.

Tom searched for another profession. He wanted excitement, adventure, some travel, and good money. After several years, he quit the Big Eight firm and became an in-house accountant with a major airline. He got to travel and see the world. He had a few adventures. The money was a little better, but still not what Tom wanted and it was definitely not as much as he thought he deserved.

Most significantly, Tom was still pouring over numbers on little pieces of paper, day-in and day-out. He couldn't see himself doing this at sixty. Or even at forty.

But what could he do? What other paths were open to him? Tom had no interest in going back to school to learn another profession, such as law or medicine. He'd had all the school he could stand. He couldn't sleep at night, knowing he had to leave the profession he had trained so laboriously for, and not knowing where else to go or what else to do.

In his work for the airline, Tom met a number of salespeople. He envied their relative freedom and was amazed at how much money some of them, *the best of them,* made. He saw in these top salespeople many of the traits he thought he had: the willingness to work hard, a love of people, good verbal skills, and a quick mind. "I can do it," Tom thought. "This is the profession for me!"

As Tom began investigating the different types of sales, he learned he could use his knowledge of accounting to sell certain financial products and services. It seemed like a natural, a slam-dunk. He also learned that financial sales was one of the most highly-paid of all sales specialties.

Having done his homework, Tom quit his job at the airline and signed up with a broker-dealer of financial products. Tom expected the work to be difficult at first, but he had no idea just how arduous it would be. Despite the long hours he put in, his income was meager, and it didn't improve much over the coming year.

Tom lived in Redondo Beach, California, not far from our office in Palos Verdes. When we met him in 1982, he was in the deepest financial trouble he had ever experienced in his life. His savings were completely gone and it looked like few sales would be coming in to replenish them. In addition to his financial problems, the departure of his girlfriend put his personal life in upheaval.

Then Tom read a news article in the *Los Angeles Times* about our work in the new field of sales hypnosis. He read about our research into the trust-building techniques used by top salespeople. He read about the sales superstars we had studied and tape recorded. He read about our findings on how to almost effortlessly dissolve customer resistance. When he called us, Tom was excited about learning the techniques of the "born salesman" and he was highly motivated to practice and apply what he was going to learn.

We introduced Tom to Zond, Inc., one of our client companies. Zond is in the business of selling large wind-turbines in California and is, in fact, the premier company in the nation in that industry. While we arranged the interview with Zond for Tom, he had to sell himself to the company. He did a good job, and was brought on board as a rookie salesman late in 1983.

As he learned the product and how to sell it, he was learning sales hypnosis. In the few remaining months of 1983, he made more money than he had made in all of 1982. By the end of the year, he was the Number 3 salesman in the company.

We had regular meetings with Tom and he studied all of our latest findings on sales hypnosis. He began building a sales script book of his

**own** most powerful hypnotic sales lines *so that he would never forget them.* In a later chapter of this book, you will learn how to build your own **mastermind** sales script book to write your own ticket to sales success.

In early 1984, so that he could learn and practice advanced techniques of influence and persuasion, Tom attended one of the many seminars we do on those subjects. With his new knowledge, and with hard work and discipline, his sales began to soar. *On one very special day in 1984, a day none of us will forget,* Tom sold four giant wind turbines for $720,000 and made $48,000 in personal income from commissions!

His income jumped from approximately $30,000 in 1982 to over $240,000 in 1983. In 1984, Tom took home almost $400,000 and in 1985, he hit the same bulls-eye again!

Can all of Tom's success be attributed to sales hypnosis? Definitely **not.** Tom sells an excellent product and he works very long hours. However, even the best products don't sell themselves. And there are many, many salespeople who work very long hours for excellent companies *and yet they still don't make very much money.*

*"Sales hypnosis is my extra edge,"* Tom says. *"I would be somewhat successful without it, but having mastered it has made me much more powerful and influential as a salesperson."*

Tom's wife, Mary, has an equally exciting story to tell. Tom met Mary when she was working as a receptionist. Mary had worked as a model and modeling was her first love. She wanted to return to modeling but didn't know how she would break back in. When she met Tom, his finances were almost depleted and he could offer her no help.

In 1988, Mary started Mary's Models and began providing in-store models to top department stores and cosmetics stores. Tom and Mary trained their models in non-manipulative techniques of hypnotic selling, and soon their models were setting sales records in the cosmetic, perfume, and personal care product areas.

Mary then began providing models for companies exhibiting at trade shows. As word of the sales power of Mary's models got around, more and more department stores and corporations began calling Mary Olds to hire her specially trained models. Mary's models are not only beautiful—they are powerful communicators!

Today, approximately one year after starting her company, Mary employs over 300 models! She has had to buy a powerful computer system just to take care of the huge weekly payroll and the tax accounting. Several years ago, when she attended our seminars on hypnotic selling techniques, she had no idea she would ever be teaching these techniques to others. Now, as a business owner and business executive, Mary Olds has found that these techniques give her employees, her models, an extra competitive advantage over models provided by any other agency.

This book is about how you can have the same competitive edge—Sales Hypnosis—that has made Tom Olds, Mary Olds, and many other salespeople and business executives more successful than they ever dreamed possible.

**Donald J. Moine**
Rolling Hills Estates, California
**Kenneth L. Lloyd**
Encino, California

# 1

## Unveiling The Best-Kept Secret Of Sales Superstars

It is an indisputable fact that top salespeople use forms of indirect or conversational hypnosis to command attention, build trust, garner respect and confidence, to create unforgettable impressions and to close sales. No one can argue with this fact.

University researchers have studied forms of conversational hypnosis for years. Studies of sales superstars have conclusively shown that they extensively use this powerful form of human communication.

Linguists are professionals who specialize in the study of how human beings use language. If anyone understands how the spoken word affects perception and thinking, it is linguists. *Their research has shown that top salespeople and top negotiators and skilled attorneys all use similar forms of indirect hypnosis.*

With all of the years of research that has been done, with all of the technical reports that have been published, with all of the indisputable proof we have that highly persuasive people do use conversational hypnosis, *why is this finding so little understood and so shocking to the average person?* Why have these techniques been kept secret?

The notion of using hypnosis as part of the sales process brings to mind images of unwary customers being tricked into buying products that they don't need and can't afford. It brings to mind the image of a salesman slowly waving a gold Cross pen in front of the prospect, back and forth, back and forth, until the prospect's eyes glass over, and his hand slowly reaches out for the pen and signs the order.

The above scenario is exactly what this book is not about. And, it is exactly what sales hypnosis is not about.

## Keys that Unlock the Secret of Hypnotic Selling

Scientific studies of sales superstars have been conducted on elite salespeople who earn in excess of $100,000 per year in personal income. In our own studies, which were inaugurated in 1978, we have interviewed, traveled with, worked with and tape-recorded a wide variety of salespeople—ranging from those who are flat broke to those who earn over $800,000 a year in personal income. *Many of these sales champions cannot explain how they do what they do.*

THUS, ONE OF THE REASONS THAT SALES HYPNOSIS HAS NOT BEEN TAUGHT PREVIOUSLY IS THAT THE PEOPLE WHO PRACTICED IT COULD NOT THEMSELVES EXPLAIN HOW IT OPERATED. They could do sales hypnosis, *but they didn't have the tools to break it down and teach it to others.* Apparently, asking masters in the art of sales hypnosis to also be great teachers was akin to asking great athletes to also be great coaches. A great idea, but it is seldom realized.

The job was left to scientific researchers to discover *the structure* of sales hypnosis. The researchers found that highly successful salespeople use communication techniques *which are nearly identical in structure* to the communication techniques used by hypnotists.

The purpose of this book is to explain, for the first time, how sales superstars achieve results that are unattainable by average salespeople. In learning about sales hypnosis, you will discover that this powerful form of communication is ethical and, in fact, *humanistic.* You will learn many hypnotic sales techniques which will allow you to help an even greater number of people by being an even more effective sales professional.

Let's now remove the veil of secrecy that has previously surrounded conversational hypnosis. Let's learn how almost everyone can benefit from using these unique forms of human communication.

## Getting Beyond Popular Conceptions and Misconceptions about Hypnosis

*The proper place to start is to explain exactly what hypnosis is and what it isn't.* As one of the most misunderstood of all human communication processes, hypnosis has been an easy target for sensationalism in movies and on television. Hypnosis has the power to both fascinate and frighten. There are still many well-educated people who erroneously believe that hypnosis is some form of "sleep." While some people use hypnosis as an entertainment medium, *the most widespread use of hypnosis today is in psychotherapy and counseling.* Look under the "H" listings in your local telephone advertising directory to verify that almost every city and town in America now has hypnotists working in private practice. They use hypnosis in everything from helping people lose weight, helping them stop smoking, for stress reduction, and in marriage counseling and psychotherapy. Hypnosis is also used by many dentists for pain control. Someone who is allergic to anesthesia can be hypnotized prior to dental work to block all perceptions of pain.

The most recently discovered area for the application of hypnosis is business, management and sales. *Of these, the specialization experiencing the greatest growth is sales hypnosis. This is the first book about the exciting and rapidly growing field of sales hypnosis.*

The experts still disagree about the one "perfect" definition of hypnosis. *However, there is little disagreement about its key components.* Many of the key components of hypnotic language, you might be surprised to learn, occur naturally in everyday life.

The best way to understand hypnosis is to look at it as a state of greatly increased suggestibility. That is, the hypnotized person is *far more susceptible to influence by messages and images.* Have you been looking for methods to increase your ability to influence others? If so, you will find that hypnosis has many of the techniques you've been seeking.

## Recognizing Hypnosis as a Part of Everyday Life

There are different levels of hypnosis which you can observe everyday in your friends and business associates. In light hypnosis, your body may feel relaxed and you might be aware of "day-dreaming." Anyone who is capable of concentrating for a few minutes can easily enter this state. Light hypnosis is a wonderful altered state of awareness for programming your mind so that you can achieve higher levels of success and have more focused energy.

People who are in a medium-level hypnotic state are not distracted by outside disturbances, and may also have a semi-glazed or unfocused look in their eyes. They may be reading a book or pushing a grocery cart and not even respond to a loud noise a few feet away. Medium-level hypnotic states can also be accompanied by very deep levels of relaxation, or a complete lack of awareness of the body.

In the deepest levels of hypnosis, you may not even be able to remember what has happened during hypnosis. You may have what is known as "hypnotic amnesia." In the deepest levels of hypnosis, the powers of the human imagination are greatly increased. At this level of hypnosis, if a person is given an onion and if that person is told it is a delicious apple, he will eat it as if it were an apple. Root canals, amputations and other operations have been performed on people using only deep hypnosis as the anesthesia. Physical strength can also be significantly increased. Many Olympic-calibre weight lifters and marathon runners use self-hypnosis to increase their abilities to perform and to decrease the perception of pain. While deep hypnosis, or trance hypnosis, is a fascinating subject to study, there is seldom, if ever, any need for this level of hypnosis in sales.

Hypnosis is a constantly changing and fluid state. Within five minutes, you or a customer might momentarily drop to a deep level of hypnosis, relive a pleasant memory or association, then rise to a light hypnosis, engage in some conversation, and then drop to a medium level of hypnosis. If you have ever listened to a sales professional, fallen in love with a product, bought it, and then not remembered why you bought it, you were probably in and out of two or more different levels of hypnosis.

There is no conflict between hypnosis and reason. That is, you or one of your customers can be both highly rational and can also be in a hypnotic state. The hypnosis may trigger the powers of the imagination, but it will not overrule logic and reason. You cannot, for example, hypnotize someone and tell them to commit murder. It won't happen. You can't and wouldn't want to hypnotize someone and tell them to buy a product they don't want or need. They won't buy it.

However, if someone does want a product and does need it, hypnosis will give you an extra edge in selling it. It is the edge that sales superstars have had for many, many years—and now you can learn how it is done.

When you communicate a message *hypnotically*, that message is more likely to bypass the listener's conscious defenses. The hypnotic message goes more directly to the prospect's subconscious mind. Communications researchers have found that there are four distinct ways of sending these messages or suggestions, and these are explained in the following section.

## Four Ways to Send Practically Irresistible Suggestions

When people use Verbal Suggestions, they use words in a very direct fashion to make suggestions. While this form of suggestion is the most commonly used, *it is not necessarily the most powerful.* Let's look at some examples from classical hypnosis, from everyday life, and from sales. From classical hypnosis:

> **"Your eyelids are getting heavy and you are beginning to feel sleepy . . . "**

From everyday life:  **"You are going to love this meal!"**

From sales hypnosis: **"You are going to be very excited about what this computer can do!"**

While the *content* of these verbal suggestions is quite different, the structure is the same. *These suggestions set up expectations.* They work because people get what they think they are going to get out of an experience. They work because thoughts can become self-fulfilling prophecies. If someone thinks they will like something, chances are they will like it. If they doubt they will like it, chances are they won't like it.

The choice of words and the ordering of words in verbal suggestions has the power to change the way people think. Napoleon said, **"We rule men with words."** In an upcoming chapter on Sales Scripting, you will learn how to script nearly irresistible sales presentations. The scripting of important presentations is now being done on a widespread basis by people in many different professions (including lawyers), and nowadays even our President is scripted before every major speech.

To be successful in sales, it is essential to understand the psychology of verbal suggestion. Verbal suggestion is what gives you the power to influence how a customer or prospect thinks. *You earn your living based on your powers of verbal suggestion.* As you will see, the suggestions that sales superstars make are planted in an elegant and nearly invisible way. Customers end up with the feeling that, "It was my idea to buy this! I wasn't sold anything—I bought it!"

If delivered with enthusiasm and sincerity, the verbal suggestion gains even more power. While the words you use in verbal suggestions are crucial, they are not the entire picture. *Presentation style is also vital.* In the coming chapters, you will learn verbal presentation techniques to add hypnotic impact to nearly all of your messages.

Why isn't direct suggestion more powerful? Because its content is easily recognizable. Direct suggestions are the kind of suggestions most salespeople make—and they are the kind of suggestions customers have the most defenses against. Prospects and customers develop a variety of sophisticated filters which screen out many forms of direct suggestion. The other forms of suggestion that you will learn about here by-pass the majority of filters that customers possess. Filters are by-passed because these other forms of suggestion seem almost "invisible" on the surface. Yet, on the subconscious or subliminal level, they have a tremendous positive impact.

The second type of suggestion is Non-Verbal. Selected gestures and facial expressions add hypnotic impact and emphasis to messages. For example, when you watch a skilled actor in a fascinating film, you can become almost completely mesmerized by the performance. You lose all perception of time. Before you know it, another half-hour has gone by. You may even lose awareness of your body, and your foot or your leg may fall asleep. You entered a hypnotic state of deeply focused attention and heightened suggestibility. Non-verbal suggestion is a tool used by both skilled actors and top salespeople.

One very powerful way of using non-verbal suggestion is to match or mirror the body language of your customer. We all trust people like ourselves, and by matching your customer's body language, you are sending a message of "I am like you are." This subconsciously increases the customer's comfort level and decreases his or her resistance. On a subliminal level, the customer feels in harmony with you. When you adopt the body language of your customer, you are telling him or her on a non-verbal level that you have something in common.

One of the classic methods of inducing hypnosis, which has been in use for at least one-hundred years, involves having a patient look into a mirror while the hypnotist counts backward and tells stories. When you match or mirror a customer's body language, you are sending back a hypnotic mirror image to that customer. Many customers look for differ-

ences in salespeople. They avoid buying by telling themselves, "The salesman is different from me. He is trying to sell me something." When the
salesperson appears to be very similar to the customer, by matching body
language and movements on a subliminal level, that salesperson is more
trusted and is harder to resist. Psychological research tells us that people
cannot resist themselves or their own actions.

Besides matching or mirroring body language, you can induce hypnosis with your smile. The smile works by sending a powerful non-verbal
message of "Let's be friends," and "Let's get closer." Sonny Salkind, one
of the top real estate salesmen in America, has a wonderful, warm smile
that melts people when they first meet him. Like Sonny, you should remind
yourself to use your smile strategically as a form of non-verbal suggestion
from the very first moment you meet a prospect or customer.

Intraverbal Suggestions, the third form of suggestion, come from
intonations and voice inflections. When a hypnotist uses the word "sleep,"
he usually pronounces it in a soft deep voice and extends it out into
"sssssssslllllllleeeeeeeeppppppppppp." These special intonations and voice
inflections give the word extra power. In the same way, sales professionals
turn certain words into action commands by changing the intonations:

**"Think of how hhhaaaapppppyyyy you wife will be when you give
her this new sports car!"**

In this example, a long resonant intonation on the word "happy,"
triggers positive feeling in the customer. He has an immediate positive
experience of his wife's happiness. If the salesman just spit the words out,
they would have little effect. It is the intraverbal suggestion that gives them
all their power. Your voice inflections can actually trigger happiness in the
listener in the instant he hears such a suggestion!

The intonations given to a word can change its impact and meaning
180 degrees. A word can send totally opposite messages strictly as a
result of intraverbal factors. "No," depending upon the intonations it is
given, can mean "Hell no! Never in a million years!" or it can mean
"Maybe." If it is spoken in a sweet, coy way, the word "No" can mean
"Yes, but please ask me again."

Even the most persuasive words in the world will have little effect if not properly delivered. In this book, you will learn not just how to craft hypnotic messages, but also how to say them.

Extraverbal Suggestions, the fourth type of suggestion, allow one to "*speak between the lines.*" Extraverbal suggestions are a synergistic combination of words, gestures and intonations. Skillfully arranged, the sum total is much more powerful than the individual units. Extraverbal suggestions can be incredibly powerful because the listener ends up thinking the action was strictly his or her own idea. This works because no one is very good at resisting his own thought processes.

Let's say you want to get someone to stand up. If you tell him, "Stand up," using simple direct suggestion, you will probably trigger a critical attitude and resistance. But, if you use the power of extraverbal suggestion and softly ask, "*Are you a little tired of sitting down?*" he may be standing up within seconds, with no idea that he was influenced! Try this yourself with a friend, and see how easily it works.

This extraverbal suggestion works because there is nothing to resist. It triggers a thought the other person probably already had in his subconscious mind. Your words simply take that subconscious thought and turn it into an action.

Extraverbal suggestion is powerful because, properly delivered, it is "invisible." It sounds natural and conversational. Extraverbal suggestion can even result in hyper-suggestibility because the listener thinks that all the ideas he is acting on are his own. He engages in action after action because "he thought of it" and because he wants to do what he thought of. In this book, we'll teach you how to use extraverbal suggestion by combining sales scripts with skillful presentation techniques on how to say those scripts.

## How to Profit from the Rich History of Hypnosis

Few people know that hypnosis has been used for thousands of years to influence, persuade and heal human beings. History shows that hypnosis has long been used as a valid tool for changing human attitudes and behaviors. The recent view of hypnosis as a carnival act or entertainment trick is just a brief historical fad, and serious practitioners of hypnosis hope these silly uses of hypnosis quickly fall out of favor.

Temples in ancient Egypt contain engravings showing people in hypnotic trances. Some of the most beautiful engravings show Isis, Nature Goddess of the Nile, using hypnosis. Other fascinating engravings record how the High Priest of Khem used mass hypnosis to calm the hysteria of thousands of citizens!

Chiron was one of the most respected physicians in ancient Greece. An engraving that dates back to almost one-thousand years before the birth of Christ shows Chiron putting his student Aesculapius under hypnosis. The famous Delphic Oracle and all other oracles of that time worked under hypnosis, which was sometimes combined with volcano fumes.

Anthropologists tell us that hypnosis has been used by cultures all over the world for thousands of years. There are numerous documents, paintings, sculptures, books, and engravings, attesting to the pervasive role hypnosis has played in human history. Given this long and distinguished history of hypnosis, it is strange that modern business and sales executives are generally so ignorant of its power and practical uses.

In the 18th century, hypnosis was "discovered" by scientists. Medical doctors found that hypnosis could cure ailments that were resistant to other treatments. In the late 1700s, Frederick Mesmer acquired fame all over Europe for his cures using "animal magnetism." It is from Mesmer that we get the word "mesmerized." He moved from the School of Medicine at the University of Vienna to Paris, where thousands of sick and ill people searched him out for cures.

The wealthy and powerful in Paris also sought Mesmer and to have been "mesmerized" was one of the great status-symbols of the day. In order to treat larger and larger numbers of people, Mesmer experimented with other ways of triggering and using "animal magnetism." He found that he could produce the same results, including outrageous laughter, tears, moans, joy, ecstasy, and medical cures, by using certain gestures of his fingers, touches, words and a steady gaze deep into the eyes of his subjects.

Unfortunately, the sensationalism that accompanied Mesmer's work led to its becoming a fad. Mesmerism had a long life as a faddish movement but eventually other fads and political events caught the public's attention. Hypnosis again returned to the scientists and the priests.

In the late 1870s, Dr. Charcot, a neurologist, re-discovered hypnosis. His scientific studies proved there are distinct levels of hypnosis. He documented how hypnosis could be used to induce many different emotional states, from extreme excitement to completely calm detachment to a light, pleasant sleep. Charcot showed how hypnosis could be used to reduce pain and to increase intellectual abilities. His findings were presented to the French Academy of Sciences and then received world-wide acclaim.

Charcot's work ushered in the new era of scientific hypnosis. Medical doctors, dentists, psychologists and other healing professionals have relied on hypnosis throughout the twentieth century. They see hypnosis as one of the most valuable and powerful tools in existence for changing human thought and behavior. Now, the business community is discovering the power and utility of hypnosis. In the next chapter, you will be introduced to some tools of classic hypnosis that have been used for over two thousand years by politicians, rulers, doctors, priests and healers. Now, for the first time, we'll show how these hypnotic tools can be used to increase sales.

# 2

## Using The Tools Of Sales Hypnosis To Build Sales

Most people  are surprised to learn that many types of hypnosis occur nearly everyday in ordinary life situations. Learning hypnotic language is therefore not a matter of learning a totally new subject, but is learning how to improve something you've been doing for a long time. Let's look at some examples:

## How Hypnotic Selling Builds Trust Quickly

**Hypnotic trust:** We have all met someone we have liked and trusted almost instantly—without any reason or justification. This is called hypnotic trust. It works because the other person does or says something that reminds you *subconsciously* of a person you have trusted or liked for many years. Thus you virtually have to like him or her. Top salespeople intuitively know how to trigger hypnotic trust.

Trust is a key element of all hypnosis because it facilitates hypnosis. Trust elicits a suggestible state of mind by minimizing resistance. We listen to people we trust. We tend to follow their suggestions. Trust gives people power. *Trust is perhaps the most powerful communication shortcut in existence.* That's why politicians, psychologists, ministers, lawyers, managers, salespeople and parents are all interested in understanding how trust works.

*Stop for a minute and picture one person who is able to persuade you.* Do you have the picture? What gives that person his or her power? We will bet that you trust that person at a very deep level. If you didn't trust that person, your defenses would be up and you'd be much more critical of his or her suggestions.

If you are an honest and reliable person, you can develop trust with almost anyone—given enough time! Think about your neighbors. You might not have liked one of them the first time you saw him. Now, after three years, you have learned he is basically honest and keeps his place looking neat and tidy. He cares about the neighborhood. He is fairly friendly. Now, three years later, you trust him.

In sales, time is limited. Few salespeople have three years to make the sale. The challenge is: **How do I build trust as quickly and deeply as possible?** Hypnotic techniques described in this book will show you how to build trust much more quickly than you ever dreamed imaginable. Of course, you still have to be honest and reliable, but these hypnotic techniques will greatly *speed up* the trust building process for you.

## Using Common Senses to Increase Sales

**Ideosensory trance** is another form of hypnosis we experience daily. It is based on our innate abilities to create in our minds visual images, feelings, voices, sounds, and even tastes and smells. When did you engage in ideosensory activities today? *When you vividly experienced something that was not going on in "real time."* Some examples: When you imagined what you might have for lunch or dinner, when you imagined what you might do at home tonight, or when you imagined a sales call, or mentally rehearsed what you might say to someone else in the office today. Did you **see** the expression on his face? Could you **hear** his words and **feel** yourself reacting? *You were in an ideosensory trance.*

Very persuasive individuals can orchestrate vivid images that influence both the perception and mood of the listener. Highly-skilled salespeople use "word magic" to bring their prospects and customers to other worlds of **sights** and **sounds** and **feelings**.

Let's give you an example now of how you can use ideosensory trance in your sales work. We'll use the example of selling cars. As a master automobile salesperson you can make your prospect **see** a vivid image of himself behind the wheel of a bright red Porsche. You can have him see his neighbors turning their heads to watch him drive down the street. You can have him **see** his wife smiling proudly as he pulls into the driveway. You can have him **smell** that new car smell and the **smell** of those new leather seats. You'll have him **feel** the steering wheel in his hands and he'll feel every little pebble and crack in the road as he races down a deserted country lane. This will all happen before your prospect even gets into the car!

Your prospect will hear the purr of the engine as it effortlessly accelerates up the steepest hill, and later he'll hear the envious compliments of his friends at the office. As a highly-skilled sales professional, you can create an ideosensory trance that is so vivid and real, your prospect will likely turn into a customer.

**One of our goals is to teach you the techniques of sales superstars.** Our experience in sales training has taught us that the best way to learn these techniques is to practice them. Throughout this book, we will share examples and case histories with you showing how you can use every technique of hypnotic selling. As you read these examples, such as the previous example of ideosensory trance, look for a way you can practice the technique. By reading about the technique, by studying the example, and then practicing the technique, you will mentally own it. You will then be able to replicate the technique any time you need it.

To master multi-sensory selling, or as we call it, *sense-sational selling*, practice using multi-sensory words to describe the benefits of your product or service. What benefits will clients **see** when they own your product? What benefits will they **hear** (compliments, etc.)? What benefits will they **feel**? Are there any benefits they will **smell** or **taste**? Now, *practice* using these persuasive descriptions with your clients and prospects and see how much more fascinating they find your presentations!

You can also use ideosensory trance to trigger negative emotions that will encourage the decision to buy. Let's say you are selling insurance to the co-owner of a multi-million dollar business. You can use ideosensory trance to have this co-owner realistically imagine what would happen to his business if his partner suddenly passed away. You can have him realistically **see** himself overwhelmed with work he doesn't know how to do; you can have him see the business struggling; he can **see** that there is no money to hire a replacement; and no time to train a replacement. You can have him **hear** other people expressing their worries, doubts and fears about him and his ability to carry on without his partner. You will have him **feel** the anxiety and nervousness of not knowing whether or not his business will survive.

This negative hypnotic ideosensory message convinces him of his need for "key man" insurance to protect himself and the business. In fact, you are likely to sell two policies, one to each executive co-owner.

Many of the things we buy are purchased because we have a negative ideosensory image in our mind. We buy not to gain the positive, but *to avoid the negative*. We buy some things not to look beautiful, but to avoid looking unattractive. We join the health spa, not to look like a model or a muscle man, but to avoid looking flabby. Sometimes, we buy a car, not because we desperately want a new car, but to prevent people from asking us, "Why are you still driving that old car?" We are sold by the negative ideosensory image.

While these are technically called "negative" images, they can have a very positive and beneficial result for all concerned. Insurance sales superstars have known for many years that policies are sold because people want to avoid negative situations. The top producers in insurance, equipment maintenance, safety, waste disposal, and many other fields have known for years the secret of using negative ideosensory images to get positive results. Negative ideosensory images can work for sales professionals in virtually any sales specialization. Chances are, very few people in your field know how to use this technique—so it could give you an extra competitive advantage.

## Controlling what Your Customer Will Forget

**Amnesia** is another hypnotic phenomenon quite common in everyday life and in sales. We are not talking about the extreme cases of amnesia in which a person forgets who he is, but rather such common forms as forgetting a friend's name or forgetting one's own phone number. When people say, "Gee, my mind just went blank," they have temporarily gone into a hypnotic state, and have temporarily left the "real world." When they come back they experience hypnotic amnesia and have no memory of where they were.

The sales super-stars we have studied have an uncanny ability to trigger this "forgetting" response in their prospects and customers, *especially about the products of a competitor*. Here is an example:

**"The other companies in this business try to overload you with so many tiny details, it is impossible to remember much of anything about their products. However, it will be *easy* for you to remember the simple and clear benefits of our products."**

In this example, the sales professional triggered amnesia for the competitor's product. Amnesia can also be triggered for a price, a name, or any other piece of data.

Who does amnesia work best with? Prospects and customers who are not detail-oriented. Detail-oriented people need facts and figures to feel comfortable about the decisions they make. Don't erase any of the details they find so helpful. Instead, find out what they are most interested in, and show them how they can get more of that with your product or service.

Some clients will come to you and report they already have amnesia. They may say they have looked at another product, but they can't remember much about it. Upon hearing this, some top salespeople will deepen the amnesia by saying, "That's only natural. It is easy to forget all those confusing figures and claims. Here is what you really need to know..." They then persuasively describe the most important features and benefits of the product using ideosensory messages.

A word of warning: hypnotic amnesia is a powerful technique. You should never use it to get a client or prospect to forget any crucial piece of data. Prospects and customers deserve to have all the facts before they make a decision. Hypnotic amnesia should only be used to erase memories of trivial details.

You can trigger hypnotic amnesia by using words such as "forget," "hard to remember," "impossible to remember," "not important to remember," or "too boring to remember." Adding extra emphasis to these words, stretching the words out, and saying them with some extra punch in your voice will give them additional impact. This is a combination of direct suggestion and intraverbal suggestion.

If another customer has ever told you that some fact or figure was "impossible to remember," or "too boring to remember," you can also quote that other customer to plant a suggestion for hypnotic amnesia. This is especially powerful if the other customer was a doctor, a lawyer, or another highly educated or high-credibility figure. People like to hear stories. Telling a customer stories about what other customers have said is a sophisticated way of giving that customer permission to do the same thing. Obviously, you should never tell a story about another customer that is not true.

What if you prefer to sell against the competition and your customer can't remember anything about the competitor's product? In that case, you may wish to use another technique of hypnotic selling: Hypernesia.

## Controlling what Your Customer Will Remember

**Hypernesia** is really the flip-side of amnesia—it refers to the enhancement of memory and recall. Many memory enhancement techniques are based on linking together related sounds and images. Were you able to remember Mr. Hammer's name because he was tough as nails to sell, or did you see a hammer every time you looked at him? You have undoubtedly already used many techniques of hypernesia on yourself to help remember important facts, dates, names and places.

The first rule of inducing hypernesia is to **tell your clients and prospects what they *will* remember**. This is especially effective if you combine the hypernesia with ideosensory hypnosis:

> **"You know, you may be lying in bed tonight and you will *see* yourself and some of your best friends sailing in this beautiful yacht."**

In the preceding example, you have told the prospect he will lie in bed and see himself in the yacht. If you hadn't said this, when he went to bed tonight, it would probably have been like any other night. It is unlikely that he would have thought of your yacht. Now, having planted this hypernesia suggestion, he is much more likely to think of the yacht when his head hits the pillow. Let's look at another example:

> **"You won't be able to forget this hot tub. You may be driving along today in traffic and all day you might visualize sitting in the hot tub with your wife giving you a wonderful massage. And, you will imagine looking up at the twinkling stars and the warm water swirling around, so comfortable and relaxing."**

Astute readers will note that this example combines hypernesia with the previously described power of ideosensory trance. If you skillfully combine these two hypnotic techniques, your prospect won't be able to get the image of your product out of his mind. This technique increases the likelihood that he will form pleasant associations when he thinks of you and your product. And, it also increases the likelihood that he will buy from you.

You can also use hypernesia to sell against the competition. If the competition's product is more expensive, your competitor might have told the prospect it "only costs $1 extra per day." That doesn't sound like very much.

You can counter that sales strategy by saying, "I don't think you will ever be able to forget that the other product costs $365 extra over the course of a year. $365. That's a lot of money. That $365 number will stay in your mind."

You can create hypernesia, or a lasting memory, of any competitive difference you want a customer to focus on. It may be price. It may be service, technical features, power, your superior warranty, or extra benefits you offer.

You can induce hypernesia by using words such as, "you won't be able to forget," "it is unforgettable," "you won't be able to get this out of your mind," "you will think of this all day," "you will think of this all week," "you will remember this for the rest of your life," or "this will leave a positive memory with you forever." You can also plant the suggestion that someone else will find this unforgettable: "your wife will always remember this," or "your children will always be grateful for this," or "your husband will remember this for the rest of his life." You can add another level of sophistication by telling a mesmerizing story about a customer who bought your product or service several years ago, whose spouse still remembers it. This is called "value-added selling" and it paints a very persuasive picture of a lasting benefit.

Negative hypernesia is a technique used by a number of top salespeople. Using this technique, you tell a story about someone who bought a competitor's product:

> **"He bought an XYZ brand of computer, some clone computers for his company. He can't even remember the name now, but he will never be able to forget what happened. The computers were almost impossible to service and they couldn't be upgraded. The hard disks had several head crashes and he lost almost a year's worth of financial data. He will remember that nightmare forever."**

Notice that the sales professional did not mention the name of the competitor's computer. This is a practice we strongly endorse. We have found that it is rarely necessary to mention a competitor by name. You can sell against them by mentioning and comparing features and benefits. You come across as much more elegant and sophisticated by not mentioning competitors by name. Under no case should you speak in a direct, derogatory manner about a competitor. This only makes you look bad, and there is no need to resort to such behavior. Hypnotic selling techniques are so powerful and so varied that you can accomplish all you wish to accomplish through ethical, friendly methods.

While negative hypemesia has the word "negative" in its name, its effects are quite positive. You are telling people a mesmerizing story about some problems some other customer encountered that the other customer will "never be able to forget." You thus, in a safe and friendly manner, warn the customer about a problem—and you show him how he can avoid it.

## Motivating Customers by Putting Them in Positive Emotional States

**Revivication**, the process of mentally reliving earlier experiences, is actually more common than most people realize. It is used by top salespeople, politicians and religious leaders to get listeners to relive previous experiences. The purpose is to tap into all of the positive emotions associated with those experiences.

By revivifying a personal experience, the listener is placed in a more emotional and suggestible state. He or she goes into the "enjoyment mode" of being. This is similar to the change of emotional state we experience upon entering a movie theater. Have you ever watched people as they enter a movie theater? Watch their expressions. You can see that some of them begin to get a glazed look in their eyes. They begin to relax. Their breathing slows down and deepens. They relive associations and memories they have had in other movie theaters. They begin entering an altered state of consciousness.

Hypnotic revivication has many uses in sales. You can use it to get a person to immediately experience any mood, emotion or affective state. You can take another person back to an almost childlike state of excitement, wonder and joy:

Sales Professional:   "**Do you remember what it was like when you got your first bike?**"
Customer:                 "**I sure do. It was the Christmas when I was 8 years old. I got a bright red Schwinn Stingray. I rode it around for hours. That night, I was**

|                     | so excited, I could barely sleep. And, when I did sleep, I had a dream about it!" |
|---------------------|---|

Sales Professional:    "That's great. That was real exciting. And, I think *you are going to have that same feeling of excitement* when you get this new ski boat. This is the ultimate toy for big kids!"

Having customers relive previous wonderful experiences is very powerful and effective for triggering buying behavior today. A person experiencing these anchored-in positive emotions finds it very difficult to be critical. In reliving these revivified experiences, they enter a strong positive altered state of awareness.

Strategically and selectively talking about "the good old days," combined with sophisticated intraverbal skills (how you say what you say), is more than just chit-chat. It is one of the most powerful sales techniques in existence. By switching from positive past experiences to what your product offers today, back to positive previous experiences then back to your product today, again and again, you effectively transfer the positive emotions of the past to your current product or service.

In a sense, hypnotic revivication is a psychological form of Pavlovian conditioning. You'll remember that Pavlov presented meat to his laboratory dogs as he rang a bell. After just a couple of days, the dogs began to associate the ringing of the bell with the food. Pavlov found that as soon as he rang the bell, the dogs began to salivate. In the same way, hypnotic revivication can psychologically link your product or service to very positive experiences or emotions your customer has had in the past. Hypnotic revivication gives you the ability to call up any emotion or state of excitement your customer has previously experienced.

### Motivating Customers by Putting Them In Negative Emotional States

THE REVIVICATION CAN BE FOR POSITIVE OR NEGATIVE EMOTIONAL STATES. Imagine you are selling expensive home security systems. You can use negative revivication to remind someone of the **peace of mind** he had *years ago* when there was little crime or burglary:

"Do you remember what it was like then, when you could leave your door unlocked all day? Do you remember when you could leave a key under the mat? Do you remember when you could sleep with the window open on a hot summer night with absolutely no fear?"

While he is reliving that wonderful feeling of security, you can let him know that *he can feel that way again*, now, through buying one of your high-quality security systems. Set up that Pavlovian link between how he felt in the past, and how he can feel today because of your product. Your product, your security system, is the Pavlovian bell that will get him to salivate. He can again sleep like a baby at night with no worries of burglary or crime.

*"Negative" revivication can lead to very positive outcomes.* One of the masters in its use is Pat Knowles, a sales superstar and consultant living in Kansas City, Missouri. For the past fifteen years, Pat has specialized in putting together and selling million-dollar real estate, insurance, oil and gas, and tax shelter programs. Pat frequently hears the objection, "I want to think about it," when selling big ticket items to his wealthy clientele. A master of sales hypnosis, Pat uses revivication to remind prospects of the price they have paid in the past for procrastinating on a decision. Pat asks:

| | |
|---|---|
| Pat: | "Tell me, did you make a lot of money in real estate during the boom years?" |
| Client: | "No." |
| Pat: | "Did you notice that real estate was soaring in value?" |
| Client: | "I sure did. I had some friends who made over a million dollars from their real estate investments." |
| Pat: | "Did you think about getting involved with real estate?" |
| Client: | "Of course. But, I never got around to it. And then the market cooled down. Now, I think the market is kind of overbuilt. I don't think it has as much profit potential." |

| | |
|---|---|
| Pat: | "So, you thought about it, but you didn't take action, and you missed the opportunity?" |
| Client: | "That right." |
| Pat: | "How about the stock market boom? You know, during the middle 1980's, the majority of stocks on the New York Exchange doubled in price." |
| Client: | "I know. I read the newspapers. I saw that the market was hitting new highs almost every week." |
| Pat: | "Did you invest? Did you double your money in the stock market?" |
| Client: | "Well, I thought about it, but I didn't take any action. I didn't take any positions." |
| Pat: | "So, you missed that opportunity as well?" |
| Client: | "I guess I did." |
| Pat: | "Let's not let that happen again. You procrastinated and you paid the price. You missed the stock market opportunity and you missed the real estate opportunity. Mr. _____, you have learned from the past that there is a price to pay from thinking about something too long and missing an opportunity. Let's not make the same mistake again. Let's not miss this opportunity. To make sure that you will be able to take advantage of this opportunity, can we take care of the paperwork today?" |

What Pat Knowles has done here is to use negative revivication to have his prospect *relive a past loss*. Using this powerful technique, he brings all the emotions associated with that loss *to the present*, to motivate the prospect to buy now, avoiding endless stalls and delays. Pat's actual presentation is somewhat longer than the example above and it is very effective. It has enabled Pat to sell million-dollar plus investments to many wealthy decision-makers.

Hypnotic revivication works in romance as well as in sales. The wide range of uses of this technique is a testament to its effectiveness. People who are very successful in the dating game intuitively know how to use hypnotic revivication. Invariably, they will ask their date a question such as, "Tell me about the best relationship you ever had. What did you like most about that person?"

Their date will then relive the most wonderful relationship he or she has ever had. In the process, they will state exactly what their current date has to do to ring all of their bells. It is truly amazing how honest and revealing most people are if you know the right questions to ask.

One of our clients was a very lonely young salesman. He was working extremely long hours and found it difficult to meet young women. When he did have dates, they didn't go well, and seldom led to a second date. Although he was earning over $200,000 a year, he felt his life was meaningless and empty without someone to share it with. At one point, his loneliness became so severe, he was contemplating suicide. When he learned the technique of hypnotic revivication, he decided to ask each woman he dated about the best relationship she had ever had.

The result was astonishing. He reported back to us that his dates were telling him exactly what he had to do to help them relive the greatest bliss they had ever experienced. One woman told him about a hot-air ballooning trip, and picnic with champagne she had with her ex-fiance. Our salesman-client duplicated that and he and his date had an exquisite time. Another date told him that her favorite musician was Jackson Browne. Our client memorized Jackson Browne songs and softly whispered the lyrics to this lady over dinner one night at a very expensive French restaurant. Talk about inducing a deep trance! She had spent dozens of hours listening to these songs in her bedroom and they triggered many deep feelings in her. She and this salesman are now engaged to be married. He traces his skill and self-confidence in building this wonderful relationship to his new understanding of hypnotic revivication. As he says, "If you know what's worked in the past, you've got a pretty good idea of what will work today."

## Increasing Sales Today by Hypnotically Placing Your Customer in the Future

**Age Progression** is the hypnotic technique which allows a person to feel as if he or she is *living in the future*. In the clinical hypnosis setting and in the sales setting, this technique can be used to assist a person in "trying out" something new. The listener may want to mentally "try out" a new behavior or a new purchase. Hypnotic age progression makes this possible.

Let's look first at an example from clinical hypnosis, and then an example from sales hypnosis. Some people go to hypnotists for help in losing weight. They think they will be totally happy if they lose twenty or thirty pounds. The hypnotist knows that the new slim figure can also bring on problems. He or she uses hypnotic age progression to warn and educate the client in advance about what might happen. Without this education, the client might lose the weight, experience an unexpected problem with the new slim figure, and decide subconsciously to regain the weight. Thus, the whole exercise will have no lasting benefit.

In hypnotic age progression, the hypnotist takes the client into the future. He or she induces relaxation and hypnotic imagery and takes the client 6 months into the future, when she will be 30 pounds lighter. Then, under hypnosis, the following may take place:

| | |
|---|---|
| Hypnotist: | "Can you see yourself?" |
| Client: | "Yes." |
| Hypnotist: | "How much weight have you lost?" |
| Client: | "About 30 pounds." |
| Hypnotist: | "What are you wearing?" |
| Client: | "Uh, a new white pants suit. I've bought some new clothes." |
| Hypnotist: | "You had to buy new clothes?" |
| Client: | "Yeah. My old clothes didn't fit. And, I was tired of all those black outfits." |
| Hypnotist: | "Now, imagine yourself at work. How are people reacting to you?" |
| Client: | "I can see Judy. She isn't very friendly. I think she's jealous. She might think I'm going to steal her boyfriend." |
| Hypnotist: | "Now, imagine the men in your life. How are they reacting to you?" |
| Client: | "I can see Tom and Bob at work. They are both hitting on me." |
| Hypnotist: | "Do you like that?" |

Client:              "No. Not really. I think when I lose the weight, they will just see me as a sex object."

By thus skillfully using age progression, the hypnotist can skillfully educate the client about what his or her life will be like once the desired changes have taken place. The client will learn that his or her life will not necessarily be a bed of roses. He or she will be able to anticipate problems and solve them, while in hypnosis. This will insure that when the changes take place in real life, they will be lasting changes. That's because there won't be any unanticipated negative side effects.

Using age progression, a person can experience his own reactions and the reactions of others to new behaviors or a new purchase. Let's look at an example of how this works in sales.

Kenny Clyde was a very successful annuity sales professional for United Resources, a major division of the huge financial services firm Integrated Resources. Kenny sold many tax-sheltered annuities to school teachers. In his sales calls, he would use age progression to take a couple into the future by saying:

Kenny:        "Where would you like your son to go to college?"

Clients:      "Stanford. We both went there, and it is a great school. But, it is very expensive."

Kenny:        "Yes, it is one of the best schools in the country. And, I have heard that it now costs over $10,000 a year to send a kid to Stanford."

Clients:      "That's a lot of money."

Kenny:        "It sure is. Now, let's go into the future. What do you think you will be doing as your son enters Stanford?"

Clients:      "Well, we'd like to be retiring. We'd like to retire early and travel around the world. But, we don't know how we can help our son go to Stanford and do all the traveling we want to do."

Kenny:        "Keep that picture. You can make it happen. Your son can go to Stanford, and you can do

> all the traveling you want to do. That is a
> wonderful dream and you can make it a real-
> ity. Let me show you how."

Kenny then goes on to describe how this couple can stash away over 15% of their income, tax-free, into a tax-sheltered annuity. While keeping them in the future in their wonderful age progression, he describes how this money will build up and grow, completely tax-free. He shows them how their deepest dreams and hopes will be realized. The only way they can resist Kenny's proposal for a tax-deferred annuity is to resist their own dreams and hopes. For most people, it is nearly impossible to resist one's own dreams and hopes.

It is no accident that Kenny was so successful in annuity sales. It is also no accident that he was rapidly promoted to Special Assistant to the President and that today he has been promoted to Vice President of Sales for United Resources. Kenny is now dedicated to teaching his intuitive techniques, and those of other sales superstars, to the 450-strong sales force of his company. The success he is enjoying is reflected in the fact that everyday United Resources is taking away business and market share from its competitors. Kenny attributes much of his success and that of his annuity sales force to their ability to skillfully use age progression to sell this exciting financial product.

## Using Hypnotic Methods to Grab and Refocus Customer Attention

**Hypnotic Dissociation** refers to the ability to separate oneself from the immediate environment— or even one's own body. It happens to all of us! *Think of a time you were in a meeting but you weren't hearing anything that was being said.* You were thinking about a subject far removed from the discussion at hand. What happened when someone asked you a question? You had no idea of what had been said. You probably needed to have the question repeated. *It is as if you weren't even at the meeting at all*—and, in a real sense, you weren't. You were hypnotically dissociated. Someone might have asked you, "Where were you?"

The answer is: You were in The State of Hypnotic Dissociation.

Hypnotic Dissociation is a very useful phenomenon in psychology, in medicine and in business. In psychotherapy, for example, a client may come in feeling devastated by a divorce. The psychologist can hypnotize the patient and dissociate him or her from the pain of the divorce. In medicine, patients can be dissociated from their physical bodies to remove the perception of pain. Patients who are allergic to anesthesia can have tonsillectomies, Caesarean sections and even amputations performed using only hypnosis as an anesthesia. In dentistry, root canals, fillings and other procedures are routinely performed by using hypnosis to dissociate the patient from sensations of pain.

Knowing how to "dis-associate" your clients from the immediate environment can be very useful in sales. By capturing and then selectively re-focusing their attention, you can get prospects to ignore or not hear honking horns, other people talking, phones ringing, critical statements, etc.

To trigger dissociation, you must first *start with honesty*. Tell your clients that they will hear horns or phones or people talking. Then, add to this truthful statement that *soon these sounds will fade into the background and almost disappear*. Say:

> **"As the horns and other noises fade into the background, you will be able to fully concentrate on what I am saying to you and you will be able to *effortlessly* remember the many ways our product will benefit you."**

Astute readers will note that we also used hypernesia in this example ("you will be able to *effortlessly remember . . .*").

Our research indicates that less successful salespeople tend to try to ignore distractions, whereas, the sales champions actually call attention to them. They then hypnotically dissociate the customer from these distractions! So-called distractions are nothing to fear if you know how to use dissociation. An example will make this more clear.

Some sections of Palos Verdes Estates, California, are full of homes as expensive as those in Beverly Hills. One million-dollar plus home was situated on a busy street and none of the agents in Palos Verdes could get a buyer to place an offer on it. Palos Verdes Estates, located on beautiful green hills along the Pacific Ocean southwest of Los Angeles, is favored by people seeking a quiet, serene natural environment. They have little tolerance for traffic. To sell this beautiful ocean-view home, realtors held open house only during low traffic hours on the weekends in an attempt to hide or get around the problem of traffic noise. Nevertheless, every potential buyer seemed very concerned about how noisy the street traffic might be during the week.

The agent who finally sold the home took the bull by the horns and decided to show the home only during rush hours on weekdays: from 7:30 to 9:00 a.m. and from 4:30 to 6:00 p.m. He directly confronted the fears of potential buyers and showed them how they would naturally "dissociate" from the slight street noise and, after a while, not even hear it.

When buyers were in this Palos Verdes home, the agent would ask, "Do you ever listen to the radio when you are home?" If they answered in the affirmative, he would ask what their favorite radio station was. He would then tune a radio in one of the bedrooms into this favorite station.

He asked if they ever watched television. If they answered in the affirmative, he turned on the television in the den. He also lit a fire in the fireplace in the living room. Prospects were surprised that just a low level of background music, the television or the crackling wood burning in the fireplace totally drowned out and dissociated the sound of cars going by. This clever real estate agent quickly sold the home and pocketed a commission of over $30,000 because he knew how to dissociate people from a distraction.

## Hypnotic Selling Techniques that Make Time Fly

**Time Distortion** is another important hypnotic technique that most people experience on a day-to-day basis. Think how long two minutes lasts when you are waiting for an elevator, or placed on "hold," or when you are waiting for your bill when you want to leave a restaurant. Now, think how long two minutes lasts during your favorite television show, or while reading a good book, or while working on a challenging work project. *We clearly have the ability to experience the same "unit" of time as rushing or dragging—depending upon our expectations and our emotional state.* Hypnosis can profoundly affect our experience of time, and you can use hypnosis to change the way your prospect or customer experiences time.

The sales superstar sometimes uses time distortion to make hour-long presentations seem brief. They can also use time distortion to slow down a short presentation so that they can pack a tremendous amount of information into just a few minutes—without rushing.

The key to using time distortion is to start with a self-confident suggestion as to how your customer will experience time. In your next sales call, say:

**"This next hour is going to be one of the most exciting and quick-paced you have experienced recently. I guarantee you will be fascinated by the benefits you will learn about, and that the time will fly by. Let's get started!"**

By doing this, you will be starting your presentation with an eager and expectant prospect. *People get what they think they will get.* Of course the time will fly.

A more subtle and even more powerful use of time distortion involves getting the client to tell you about a very pleasant experience he or she had. This could be a fascinating movie recently seen, or a favorite book just read, or a brief vacation. As the person tells you about this experience, he or she will relive it. They will relive the emotions connected with it, and the sense that time flew by.

While the other person is finishing up their story, transition over to a discussion of your product or service. *Your prospect will bring along his or her most recent emotional state.* In this case, you will be bringing along the sense and feeling that time is flying, along with all of the other pleasant emotions.

To plant additional suggestions that time is moving quickly, near the end of your presentation, glance at your watch and say, "I can't believe 45 minutes has gone by!" You will thus plant this same mindset into your customer. After saying this, look at your customer—and don't be surprised if he or she nods in agreement.

What if you are only given a few minutes to make your presentation? Don't panic. You can use time distortion to make time slow down. You can accomplish just about everything you want to accomplish without rushing the prospect, and without seeming nervous or pressured.

Direct suggestions are sometimes the most effective in slowing down time. Look directly at your client, smile slightly and in a calm self-assured voice, say:

**"Relax. We can make time slow down. In ten minutes, I will present all the highlights of this great new product to you."**

Then, with a self-confident voice, begin your presentation. Skip the small talk. Skip talking about the features. Concentrate on the benefits to the prospect. Add a couple of strong endorsements from happy customers. That's about all your prospect needs to hear. Your prospect will sense your professionalism and inner strength.

The ten-minute presentation can be very rich and satisfying. At the end of the ten-minutes, ask, "We have invested ten minutes in your learning about this new product. Are there any questions I can answer for you?"

If you have done a great job, there will be a strong level of interest and some good questions. The prospect may even ask you to go on, to tell him or her more!

The reason many prospects say, "I don't have any time," is that they don't know you and don't trust you. Let's face it: if their brother was presenting the same product, he would be given much more time because of the pre-existing level of trust. By using hypnotic trust-building techniques presented in this book, you will be able to quickly build a deeper level of trust than you ever dreamed possible. Once you have this level of trust, the prospect will lose his or her suspiciousness and will permit you—or ask you—to go into more detail.

## Posthypnotic Suggestions that Chip Away at Customer Resistance

**Posthypnotic Responses** are the actions carried out, as well as thoughts and feelings that are experienced, after the hypnotic interaction has concluded. We have all experienced posthypnotic suggestion. For example, most salespeople have attended "pep rallies" or "positive thinking" seminars. Whether or not you feel motivated after the talk will depend on the speaker's skill in using posthypnotic suggestions. The reason that these pep rallies are not more effective is that most of the speakers aren't skilled in using posthypnotic suggestions. You go home and don't use the techniques taught because the speaker did not know how to plant them deeply in your subconscious mind.

Sales managers are frequently less effective than they could be because they don't know how to use posthypnotic suggestion. Some sales managers naively think that simply lecturing someone or telling someone to do something will produce lasting behavior change. We wish it were this simple! Life and sales management would be much simpler. While a simple lecture will sometimes lead to behavior change, the change is usually of very short duration. You tend to get compliance rather than long-term cooperation. Posthypnotic suggestion can give you an extra edge by planting the suggested behaviors or thoughts much deeper in the mind, below the level of superficial thinking and psychological defenses.

We recently worked with the vice president of sales for one of the largest and best-known computer firms in America. We did a study on how people were using their sales time and found that nearly twelve hours per week were being spent reading mail and magazines. When these findings were disseminated, many sales managers tried to change behavior by lecturing to their salespeople that they should not waste so much time reading computer magazines. In general, the lectures had little lasting effect. Several months later, salespeople were still spending over ten good selling hours a week reading magazines.

We taught several managers how to use posthypnotic suggestions to change this behavior. We combined the posthypnotic suggestions with powerful metaphors and stories. Some of the stories were about sales professionals who had thrown all of their magazines and newsletters in the trash and who suddenly found they had ten extra hours of selling time each week. Other stories dealt with salespeople who had their secretaries do their magazine reading for them—and then had the secretaries type a brief summary of the 3 best articles each week. The salespeople found the stories, which were combined with many posthypnotic suggestions, to be much more fascinating than the previous lectures.

In some of the stories, a salesman in the story could "almost hear" a big trash can calling out, "Feed me, feed me, feed me with magazines." Every time they saw the big trash can, they "felt compelled" to fill the trash can with magazines and newspapers, "without knowing why." There were no lectures and no haranguing—just a "feeling" this had to be done. We re-wired the feelings and emotions with posthypnotic suggestion.

We used the image of a "big trash can" to trigger the posthypnotic behavior. Several of the sales managers we worked with then went out and bought *bigger* trash cans for their offices. One sales manager even went out and bought large oak trash cans! He later reported back to us it was the best gift he ever gave his people.

The salespeople saw the big trash cans around the office and almost automatically began filling them with magazines and newspapers. The sales managers did a follow-up deepening induction of the posthypnotic suggestion by saying something like, "That's good. You're feeding the trash can. You are making it happy." It was a light-hearted joke around the office, but it had a very serious and very beneficial side-effect. The salespeople were getting rid of a major distraction in their life: the magazines and newspapers that had been absorbing so many of their sales hours.

Within a few weeks of the planting of this posthypnotic suggestion and the installation of the large trash cans which triggered the posthypnotic behavior, sales increased. The product was the same. The price was the same. The salespeople had not received any additional training! The only thing that had changed was that the salespeople now had 8 to 10 extra hours a week to sell because the distraction of the magazines and newspapers had been nearly eliminated. The posthypnotic suggestion changed behaviors that could not be changed by lectures or threats.

Posthypnotic responses are sometimes called "waking hypnosis" because the hypnotic suggestion can be planted and acted on without eye closure or any kind of observable hypnotic trance. For example, a friend might describe to you a great Mexican dinner he had recently. He might trigger ideosensory activity with his complete descriptions of the delicious plate of tacos and enchiladas he had, and the crisp green salad that preceded the entree. You can taste the salt on the Margarita glass and feel the coolness of the icy drink. Minutes later, you seem to have forgotten most of the discussion. Then, hours later, your spouse asks, "Are you hungry?" Without consciously knowing why, you have developed a craving for a Mexican feast. The suggestion was planted earlier in the day and worked or acted itself out posthypnotically.

Posthypnotic responses are especially useful in cross-over selling. In cross-over selling, *you get a person to buy several products or services, using each one purchased as an introduction (a "cross-over") to the next.* Banks and savings and loans we have worked with are very interested in cross-over selling because they have found they cannot make money by selling you only one product or service. They must get your checking account and/or your credit card and/or your car loan and/or some other sale to make a profit. Their goal is to get most, if not all, of your banking business. We have found that posthypnotic suggestions can greatly increase the effectiveness of tellers, loan officers and new accounts representatives in cross-over selling financial products and services.

Here is an example of a posthypnotic suggestion that has helped hundreds of our trainees excel in cross-over selling additional financial products and services at banks and savings and loans:

> **"Mrs. Jordan, you've been able to buy a beautiful home with the mortgage we have provided you. Now, as you run your errands later today, *you may be able to think of* some other ways our other financial services, such as checking and savings accounts, credit cards, and certificates of deposit, can help you. And, as you think of other ways we can help you, *I want you to pick up the phone and call me.* OK?"**

What makes this posthypnotic suggestion especially effective is that it is linked with what the customer will be doing later in the day, in this case, running errands. If you know of some activity that your customer or prospect will definitely be engaging in later in the day, link your posthypnotic suggestion to that activity. Then, while he or she is engaged in that activity, the subconscious mind will bring up the subject that you have previously linked to the activity.

Also, the above example is effective because *it links thinking of buying additional products with calling the salesperson.* Highly-successful salespeople we have studied and worked with don't just get their customers to think about their products, they get the customers to take actions that lead to sales. When you plant the suggestion that someone think of your products or services, also link it to calling you on the phone.

You want to deepen the posthypnotic suggestion by asking a question at the end. Look your client in the eyes, smile slightly and say:

**"When you think of another way we can help you, do you promise me you'll call?"**

The word "promise" is especially powerful in this context. It almost guarantees that the posthypnotic suggestion will be acted on. After all, when most people "promise," their good word and reputation is on the line. Most people don't "promise" lightly. The "promise technique" is surprisingly simple and effective, yet it is known and used by very few salespeople. You can now add it to your professional tool set.

Never misuse or overuse posthypnotic suggestion. It should, of course, only be used to get customers to think about and act on buying products and services they truly need.

POSTHYPNOTIC SUGGESTIONS CAN BE MADE EVEN MORE POWERFUL BY LINKING THEM TO BENEFITS YOUR CUSTOMERS HAVE ALREADY EXPERIENCED. In the above example, Mrs. Jordan has been able to buy a beautiful home with one of your mortgage loans. This memory is *revivified* and is linked to the posthypnotic suggestion that she can think of some other ways your products and services can help her, and that she then give you a call. Since you linked the suggestion to her earlier pleasant experience, she is much more likely to follow up on the suggestion. To make it even more powerful, before using a posthypnotic suggestion, first revivify a strong benefit you have already provided to your customer. Remind them of what you have done for them, or how you have helped them in the past, then place the posthypnotic suggestion.

## The "Unfair Advantage" of Sales Hypnosis

In some of our seminars and workshops, participants have said they feel that sales hypnosis gives them an "unfair advantage." Does it?

Hypnosis is a natural state of deeply focused attention, frequently combined with relaxation and vivid imagery. As you learned earlier in this chapter, most people go in and out of hypnotic states, (such as hypnotic trust, revivication, ideosensory trance, age progression, etc.) everyday.

Since people go in and out of hypnotic states everyday, it is not necessary to induce hypnosis in anyone. Sales hypnosis is often simply a matter of *using the customer's own self-induced states of hypnosis* to guide his attention and actions. Sales hypnosis will enable you to HOLD the customer's attention, FOCUS the customer's attention, and to create positive and LASTING IMPRESSIONS in the customer's mind. It also enables you to greatly INCREASE SUGGESTIBILITY so that prospects will be much more likely to buy from you.

The hypnotic selling techniques you have learned in this chapter can be used individually or combined with one another for even greater persuasive impact. Top salespeople use posthypnotic suggestion, amnesia, hypnotic trust, ideosensory trance and hypernesia all in one sales presentation. And, they do so in a natural, conversational manner. *Since the techniques are "invisible" to the untrained ear, the listener does not consciously recognize them.*

All of these hypnotic techniques are natural and comfortable methods of communication. They are not tricky sales techniques. Every reader of this book has used these techniques at some point in his or her life. Previously, you didn't know you were using them—and you didn't know how to use them systematically. We hope to give you the power to change that. What this book offers is a proven means of increasing your powers of sales persuasion. By increasing your knowledge of hypnotic selling techniques, you will become more systematically persuasive and more successful.

Does sales hypnosis give you an unfair advantage? Yes, it does give you a real advantage, but it is not unfair. In our professional opinion, sales hypnosis is ethical *and necessary*. It is being used everyday by top salespeople, politicians, religious leaders, executives and other successful communicators. Simply ignoring it will not make it go away.

Ken Clyde, the Vice President of Sales for United Resources, says that, "Your goal in sales should be to create a win-win situation: to solve the customer's problems by offering him or her a good product at a good price, and to earn a good commission." Assuming you are offering a quality product or service at a good price, sales hypnosis will help you close more sales and earn better commissions. It will not help you sell products people neither need nor want. Remember: hypnosis will not get people to do things they do not want to do.

Would the world be a better place without sales hypnosis? No. Prospects would find non-hypnotic presentations boring and unfocused. They would not be as emotionally involved in what was being sold. Prospects would have less interest in buying products and services *that they really need*. Salespeople and marketers would be frustrated. The economy would slow down with fewer sales being made. No one would win.

Does the system presented in this book give you an "unfair advantage?" Yes. You'll have an unfair advantage over your competition—not over your customer. You and your customers will both win.

Information is power. You are holding sales power in your hands. Use it wisely.

# 3

## Profiting From The Lessons Of The World's Greatest Hypnotist

You have been introduced in the previous chapter to the major forms of direct hypnosis. A recently discovered and even more powerful form of hypnosis is indirect or conversational hypnosis. Yes, it is possible to use hypnosis conversationally—using everyday conversational words and without having anyone close their eyes.

## How Conversational Hypnosis Works

While indirect or conversational hypnosis has been used for thousands of years by religious leaders, political leaders, teachers, parents and others, only recently have researchers figured out how indirect hypnosis works. Now that the structure of indirect hypnosis has been identified, conversational hypnosis *can* be systematically taught.

The structure of indirect hypnosis was first described by Richard Bandler and John Grinder. Bandler and Grinder intensively studied Dr. Milton Erickson, who is acclaimed as the world's greatest hypnotist. Erickson was able to induce hypnotic states through conversational methods in nearly everyone he met. Patients and other doctors traveled from around the world to be treated by Dr. Erickson at his Phoenix home. Let's look at a few examples of the indirect hypnosis Erickson used.

While teaching at a medical school, Erickson was warned by the dean that one of the finest students in the school hated psychiatry. This student, who was considered a genius in pathology studies, took every opportunity he could to insult psychiatry professors. He was considered unmanageable and was feared by the entire psychiatry staff. This student was scheduled to take Erickson's psychiatry course.

When giving the first homework assignment, a book review, to the class, Erickson looked directly into the eyes of this difficult student and explained in his unique mesmerizing fashion that doing a good book review is much like studying a pathology slide. As Erickson talked about pathology, he captured this student's full attention. Erickson then overlapped pathology and psychiatry, pathology and psychiatry, showing numerous hidden links and connections between the two medical specializations until they seemed as closely related as brother and sister.

This difficult student had previously told the dean of the medical school that he would not do any of the work that any psychiatry professor assigned him. However, after listening to Erickson's hypnotic lecture intertwining pathology and psychiatry, he went home that weekend and couldn't forget what Erickson had said. His mind focused on "examining a good psychiatry book is like studying a pathology slide." On Monday, this "difficult student" handed in one of the finest and most insightful psychiatry book reviews anyone on the psychiatry faculty had ever seen.

Another medical student suffered from extremely low self-esteem. He had an artificial leg. Depressed and withdrawn, he would not socialize with other medical students. Erickson himself suffered two severe bouts with polio and was largely confined to a wheelchair. Erickson was intent on restoring this young student's self-esteem. A world-renowned researcher and clinician, Erickson knew that a physical handicap should not interfere with one's self-esteem or mental functioning. Everyone else's attempts to raise this young man's self-esteem had failed.

One day Erickson arranged to have the elevators get stuck in the classroom building he taught in. As Erickson came into the lobby, he saw a group of medical students, including the young man with the artificial leg, waiting for the elevator. After waiting with them for a few minutes, the famous Dr. Erickson turned to the student with the artificial leg and said, "Let's us cripples hobble upstairs and leave the elevator for the able-bodied."

"Us cripples," the young medical student with the artificial leg and the famous Dr. Milton Erickson (who suffered from polio) hobbled up the stairs before the able-bodied students even got into the elevator. As they entered the room before anyone else, Erickson looked into the eyes of the young medical student and smiled. A deep connection was made—Mesmer would have called it "animal magnetism." When the able-bodied students walked in, the young medical student with the artificial leg projected a new self-confidence. In a matter of an hour, the young student had made three new friends and was on his way to building a strong new identity as a strong, healthy person.

In psychology and psychiatry, it is rarely possible to say that any one individual is "the best" in dealing with complex human problems. This is not the case for modern indirect hypnosis. There is little doubt that Milton H. Erickson, M.D. was, until his death in 1981, the world's foremost practitioner of medical and psychological hypnosis. Throughout his last twenty years, researchers came non-stop from around the world to study the methods of conversational hypnosis he developed.

## The Man Behind the Miracle of Conversational Hypnosis

Dr. Erickson authored over 100 articles and several books on hypnosis, and he was the founder of the American Society of Clinical Hypnosis. When people described him, the most common statement they made was that he was the doctor who could perform miracles. His successful treatment of untreatable problems, ranging from cancer to paralysis to psychosis, was legendary. Was it magic? Was it animal magnetism? Was it medicine? Whatever it was, Dr. Erickson was consistently able to successfully treat medical and psychological conditions that had been regarded as hopeless. Some of his successes seemed to defy scientific explanation.

Do you think it is possible to hypnotize someone without their being aware that they are being hypnotized? Do you think it is possible to **deeply** hypnotize someone without having them close their eyes, or without their "going asleep"? **These forms of conversational hypnosis occur every day.** Top salespeople, politicians, religious leaders, and even parents, have been doing it for hundreds, or even thousands of years. What Dr. Erickson did was not new, but he did take these forms of indirect and conversational hypnosis to new levels of sophistication and effectiveness.

In the early years of his career, the fact that Erickson's word magic defied scientific explanation did not make him particularly popular among his peers in the medical profession. From the medical point of view, cures that cannot be readily explained are sometimes regarded with suspicion. In fact, in the early 1950s, the American Medical Association tried *unsuccessfully* to revoke his medical license. It took the passage of many years for Dr. Erickson's skills as a hypnotist to be understood and accepted. It is indeed ironic that, by the end of his career, Erickson had received almost every available high honor and accolade the American Medical Association gives in the field of psychiatry.

His home office in Arizona became an international meeting-place for psychologists, psychiatrists, linguists and communications researchers. While over two dozen books have now been published on Erickson and his methods of indirect hypnosis, none have shown how these powerful communications techniques can be applied to sales. In the succeeding chapters of this book, we will present these new applications of conversational hypnosis.

## Four Essential Steps to Master Converational Hypnosis

Until recently, Dr. Erickson was considered a "born hypnotist," not unlike the prodigies who are highly gifted in music or the arts or the sciences. His abilities seemed to be nothing less than miraculous. As a result, it was believed that many of his methods could not be taught to others.

Since Dr. Erickson's methods are conversational in nature, they do not rely on eye closure, relaxation or sleepiness. Erickson's genius was in devising a type of hypnotic induction which sounded completely **natural** and **conversational.** The subject did not perceive it as "hypnosis" and yet the subject might be placed in a very deep trance. His powerful indirect approach relies on *four essential steps*:

### Step 1: *Hold and Fixate the Client's Attention*

This step uses specific techniques (described in succeeding chapters) to attract and keep the full attention and concentration of the client. Whereas classical ("direct") hypnosis typically called for a **device or stimulus** on which the client would focus, such as the crystal ball or shiny, swinging gold watch, *indirect hypnosis frequently focuses on events, emotions or beliefs*.

### Step 2: *Present Undeniably Truthful Ideas That Are Impossible to Disagree With*

The second step of conversational hypnosis is to present ideas or perceptions which are impossible for the client or customer to disagree with. These ideas or perceptions will also show the client that you understand his or her position and needs, and will help the client recognize that you can help.

Ronald Reagan knows how to move a crowd of people with words. If you listen carefully, you will note that he usually starts his speeches by mentioning certain current events or news items that everyone is familiar with. *These are the undeniably truthful facts which start to induce the conver-*

*sational hypnosis*. He starts to talk about them in a low-key non-partisan way that cannot be disagreed with. Whether you like Reagan or not, you soon find yourself nodding your head in agreement over these "minor" points.

Because the earliest words of his speeches match or nearly match the subconscious thoughts of many listeners, Reagan rapidly builds trust. We all trust and like people like ourselves, and through strategically using these forms of conversational hypnosis, Reagan indirectly communicates "I am like you are. We are seeing eye to eye. You are safe with me. We understand one another."

### Step 3: *Increase the Client's Need and Readiness to Respond and Take Action*

To increase the client's desire to take action, it is frequently necessary to free the client from fixed mental habits. This is perhaps the one area which has been most neglected or overlooked in conventional sales training.

One powerful way to build the need to respond is to present the client with ideas that are acceptable, **but quite unexpected.** This puts the client into the position of "being between decisions." At this point, as Dr. Erickson stated, the client is in the uneasy position of "teetering." You can frequently get movement and get a decision made once you get the client teetering.

In our sales training seminars, we describe the prospect at this point as a man floating in a sea of confusion. He will grasp at anything which looks like a life preserver or the solution to his problems. The prospect becomes quite anxious to end the uncertainty. To most people, uncertainty is an unpleasant mental state. The client at this point will welcome a decision—a decision that may well have been rejected in its entirety *if made at the outset.*

Let's look at an example of how Erickson used conversational hypnosis to increase the desire to take action. Milton Erickson had a number of severely obese patients in his practice. These patients feared that their appetite and their weight were out of control. He would hypnotize them and suggest they intentionally gain weight, to learn that they could in fact control their bodies. This was, for many patients, *the first time an authority figure had ever told them to gain weight.* It was a totally new experience! *Once they gained the feeling of control* by *intentionally* making their weight go up, it was usually a relatively simple matter for Erickson to show them how to intentionally make their weight go down, permanently.

The careful use of a surprising statement can get your customers to take a fresh look at your products or services. If you have a "know-it-all" customer, you need to use mildly surprising statements to re-educate that customer so that he or she will take action.

### Step 4: *Provide the Client or Prospect with Clear and Direct Actions to Take During and After the Session*

You have your customer's attention. You have used undeniably truthful statements to build a climate of agreement. You have increased your customer's readiness to take action. Now, you need to guide your client down the desired action pathway.

Use age progression to take your client into the future. Have your client imagine every possible negative situation that could impact on his making the purchase decision. Then, while the client is still *"living in the future,"* solve every one of these problems. This will remove any remaining anxiety about the purchase and will also insure against buyer's remorse later.

If you cannot solve every problem surrounding the purchase, this may not be the right product for that customer. Do another needs assessment to make sure you are selling the customer something he needs and something he can afford. If not, then sell him a more appropriate product, following the steps outlined above.

## Understanding the Verbal Power of Conversational Hypnosis

The field of linguistics provides further insight into the persuasive techniques used by Dr. Erickson. It is well recognized by scientific researchers that **every** word we hear is processed in some way by our brains. The listener or prospect processes language by relating what is heard to memories, previous experiences, and expectations. This processing occurs instantaneously on both a conscious and unconscious level.

Human speech is nothing more than carefully formed sounds. We, as salespeople, are just "making noises" in the air. *Depending upon our skill in making these noises, some of us will become multi-millionaires* (such as the great insurance salesman Ben Feldman), *and others will starve*. There is an old saying in sales that, "Shy salesmen have skinny kids." This should perhaps now be updated to say, "Unskillful salespeople have skinny kids."

## Influencing Others by Using Hynotic "Instant Replay"

One of the most innovative techniques Dr. Erickson developed has become known as "Instant Replay." Erickson believed that if a person had done something once, they could do it again. Let's say that you are overweight, but that you had once lost 50 pounds. Erickson would find out everything that went into your losing that 50 pounds, and he would replay it and re-wire it into your mind— thus, the "instant replay." He found this virtually always worked in helping people to lose the weight again. If you had once stopped smoking, Erickson could get you to stop smoking again almost immediately. He did this by finding out all of the conditions that led you to quit previously. He would then use indirect hypnosis to *mentally recreate* those conditions today.

The use of Hypnotic Instant Replay underscores a fascinating research finding regarding Dr. Erickson's work: much of his effectiveness centered on his ability to have clients re-access *actions they had taken in the past.* Erickson believed that if a person had ever done something, odds were good they could do it again. In addition to using this Hypnotic Instant Replay to help solve problems, Erickson would use it to help clients achieve new levels of success. Erickson would have patients relive their own greatest moments of success and he would anchor these moments of excellence in the present so that patients could access this personal power whenever they needed it.

## A Frame-by-Frame Look at the Hypnotic "Instant Replay"

The Hypnotic Instant Replay, based on re-accessing, is a powerful technique in sales. Here is how to use it. Ask your next customer how he made a decision to buy in the past. Find out the mental steps he went through. Ask him which buying criteria are most important to him. Then order the criteria *by level of importance*. Now, when you sell your product, sell it by starting with his #1 criterion. Start with this criterion, even if it is not your

#1 criterion. When you have satisfied your customer on this #1 criterion, go on to the #2 criterion, and so on.

By re-accessing and replaying the way he made a decision in the past, you are increasing your odds he will make the same decision to buy again today. This "Instant Replay" technique works in virtually every kind of selling.

We know the Instant Replay Technique works because we use it ourselves and we have seen hundreds of times how effective it is. Whenever we are selling training programs to Fortune 500 companies, we always ask, **"How did you decide to buy your last training program?"**

Most people are incredibly honest and they will reveal their buying strategy if you know how to ask for it. If a sales manager tells us that the last sales training program he or she bought was: one of proven effectiveness, was based on scientific research and was customized for his company—that's what we sell him. We will start with his number one criterion by showing the proven effectiveness of our program and the results we have been able to achieve in Fortune 500 companies. Then, we will move into a discussion of the scientific studies (his #2 criterion) that support our work, including doctoral dissertations which analyze its effectiveness. Then, we will show him how we will customize a program for his company (his #3 criterion), teaching his people how they can sell more of that company's products and services with less effort. By hypnotically matching his buying criteria, it is almost impossible for him to ignore our presentation. The only way he can resist our presentation is to resist his own thinking and value system—which for most people is nearly impossible.

If a sales manager tells us that he bought his last training program because the speaker was entertaining, fascinating and fun to listen to, we produce letters from major corporations showing how our programs are entertaining, fascinating and fun. We then go on to sequentially sell to each of his buying criteria—*in exactly the same way he has bought in the past.* Past behavior does predict future behavior. And, when you sell someone by exactly matching the thought processes and criteria they have used in the past, the effect is positively hypnotic. Our own sales presentations are all based on getting an "instant replay" of a sales manager's previous decision to buy—and our success in working with major corporations is a testament to the effectiveness of this approach.

This hypnotic technique is so effective that some sales executives have hired us to give speeches on it alone. We will spend the entire 3 hours of presentation time on Hypnotic Instant Replay. After hearing about it, seeing it demonstrated and after practicing it for 3 hours, salespeople can do it intuitively. We have collected hundreds of sales stories from around the country showing how the Hypnotic Instant Replay can be used to sell anything from photocopier machines to real estate to corporate jets.

Top automobile salespeople use the Hypnotic Instant Replay by asking, **"How did you decide to buy the last car you were truly happy with?"** In obtaining this information, they have a very good idea of how to sell you a car today. They simply replay the mental steps and behaviors you engaged in when you bought the last car you truly loved. Tough to resist this approach.

Highly successful realtors ask, **"How did you decide to buy your last home?"** Human beings are creatures of habit. When you know the mental habits of someone making a purchase decision, your chances of success go up dramatically. The beauty of the Hypnotic Instant Replay technique is that it works even if you recognize it. Dr. Moine's realtor used the Hypnotic Instant Replay on him. He says, "I knew what she was doing every step of the way, and in utter amazement, I watched myself buy another house (even though I thought I was not in the market for a house!).

"I had bought a house about ten months earlier in Hermosa Beach, California. My realtor learned that I was a visual thinker and that having a home with a spectacular view was my #1 criterion. She learned that my second criterion was to have a home with a lot of land, because I like to plant flowers, ferns and decorative trees in the old English country garden style. She discovered that my third criterion is to live close to the ocean because I love the cool ocean breezes and the clean air. She uncovered my fourth criterion which is a spacious floor plan and very high ceilings. It is difficult to meet all of these criteria in Southern California unless you have an unlimited budget—which I don't.

"When she found me the house in Hermosa Beach, I bought it the first day I saw it. When she showed me the house, she hit all of my criteria in exactly the right order. I even offered full price for the home (which I had never done in the past for any house) because I wanted to make sure that no one else could get it by outbidding me.

"Ten months later, I had barely unpacked all of my books and had only started to re-landscape the yard when my realtor called. She had found another home she thought I would be interested in, and she wanted me to take a look at it. When she told me it was in Palos Verdes, California, I told her to forget it. There is no way I could afford a home in Palos Verdes.

"However, I did allow her to tell me about this new house. It had an even more spectacular view and a huge terraced hillside garden. She then told me that the property had a view of all of Los Angeles County and of the coastline and Pacific Ocean all the way up to Malibu. Next, I heard about the spacious floor plan, the hardwood floors, the fireplaces and the bedrooms. As she described the house, I realized she was using the Hypnotic Instant Replay on me! She presented all of the features and benefits in exactly the order I think of them myself. Even though I knew exactly what she was doing, I couldn't resist it! I had to see the house.

"She continued to use the Hypnotic Replay in showing me through the new home. She sold me in exactly the same way she knew I had bought in the past. Although I had just bought a home from her a few months earlier, I ended up making an offer (which was later accepted) on the home in Palos Verdes. Besides buying a beautiful home that day, I learned a valuable lesson: the Hypnotic Instant Replay is one of the only sales techniques in the world that works even when the customer realizes it is being used! Used properly, it is almost impossible to resist."

In your next sales presentation, be certain to ask, **"How did you decide to buy your last _____ (product)?"** As they describe their buying habits, take careful notes. Then do an "instant replay" of the criteria that led them to buy in the past. With just a little practice, you should become very skilled at this technique and you will find it helps you close many sales.

## How to Win with the Five Key Elements of Vocal Flexibility

Researchers studying Erickson found that another key to his success was his **vocal flexibility.** Erickson had the uncanny ability to talk to you in a way that nearly matched your own speech rate, volume, rhythm and tonality. **It was as if you were talking to your own unconscious mind!** This is one of the keys to indirect hypnosis. When you talk with customers, match their:

1. Speech Rate,
2. Speech Volume,
3. Vocabulary,
4. Sentence Length, and
5. Speech Rhythm.

The matching doesn't have to be exact and you don't have to match or mirror all of these speech characteristics with every prospect. Any closeness or similarity will help to subliminally convey, "I am like you are." In addition, customers will feel safer and more comfortable with you, almost instantly. Remember that we trust and like people like ourselves. When you speak the way your customer speaks, he or she will instinctively perceive you as being "normal" and therefore more likeable.

## How to Tell Hypnotic Stories that Sell

Another key to Erickson's effectiveness was his use of metaphors, parables, and anecdotes. These hypnotic stories were designed to pace or match the listener's view of reality, and then to take them one step beyond. Erickson gradually led the listener into new territory by skillfully sequencing from one "word picture" to another. We have devoted an entire succeeding chapter to mastering the art and science of stories and metaphors in selling.

## Hypnotic Techniques for Turning Customer Resistance Into Enthusiasm

Erickson developed some unique and powerful ways of handling **resistant clients**. If he knew a client planned to resist him, Erickson would order that client **not** to go into hypnosis. The only way the client could resist Erickson was to go into hypnosis!

This same principle for handling resistant people works very effectively in sales. For example, you may suspect your customer wants to "check out the competition." *You can actually tell your client to check out the competition.* Tell your client to spend several hours or several days checking them out. Tell your customer that *the more hours or days of investigation he or she does, the greater the likelihood he or she will buy from you.* This shows a tremendous amount of self-confidence. The only way your resistant customer can resist you is to not check out the competition!

The upcoming chapters of this book present Erickson's powerful methods of conversational hypnosis in even greater detail. *Each method is translated into a technique you can use everyday in sales.* With just a little practice in using Erickson's methods of hypnotic matching and mirroring techniques, you'll find you'll be able to sell more with less effort. Let's now take a closer look at how to *rapidly* build a deep level of trust using conversational hypnosis.

# 4

Building Trust
And Rapport
Through The Power Of
Hypnotic Pacing

Think of someone you trusted the moment you met him or her. *What made this person so special?* How did he or she win you over so quickly? What did he or she do or say or represent to earn your trust instantly?

There have been people who have trusted **you** the moment you met. *What did you do?* How can you do that again?

This chapter is about the psychology of trust and rapport. Trust is a cornerstone for hypnotists and super salespeople alike. It is very difficult to hypnotize a client who does not trust the hypnotist, and it is very hard for a salesperson to sell a product to a customer who is wary and distrustful.

*Trust-building is the first, and perhaps the most important step, in the persuasion process.* As important as the trust-building step is, many salespeople ignore it or give it short shrift, and immediately jump into their sales presentation. This undermines the sales process before it has started!

How do the sales superstars almost instantly trigger the perception, "I feel like I've known you all my life"? Through a hypnotic process called "pacing."

## How to Send Important Sales Messages through Pacing

The best way to understand pacing is to picture a long distance runner gliding along a country road. Now picture a faster runner pulling up next to the first runner and slowing down to run next to him. Soon you see that each runner is breathing at the same rate, matching one another stride for stride, and really moving as one. The faster runner is now pacing the slower runner.

Pacing is *matching or mirroring the prospect or customer.* Pacing or mirroring can be done on many different verbal and nonverbal levels. It is one of the most powerful means of communicating, "I am like you are."

Hypnotists and master salespeople pace their clients in much the same way. They pace or mirror dozens of subtle behaviors of the other person. And by doing so, several clear, yet unconscious, messages are sent: "You and I have a lot in common. I think like you. I have needs like yours. I am like you in many important ways. I understand you. You are safe with me. You can trust me."

Pacing is the most effective means of getting two people into synchrony. *In sales, you are either in harmony with someone else or you are not.* Pacing shows you how to get in harmony, on one or more levels, with everyone you meet. In conducting their studies of Milton Erickson, M.D., Richard Bandler and John Grinder found that Erickson used pacing as an all-purpose tool for inducing conversational hypnosis.

## Proven Steps to Pace Like a Sales Superstar

There are many different ways you can pace your customers to build rapport. Sales champions use these methods *intuitively* throughout the sales interaction. They know that it is essential to start pacing, or trust-building, from the very first moment of contact with a prospect. Here are the key types of pacing and some examples of how the sales pro uses them:

## Pacing what You See and Hear to Build Customer Trust

Highly skilled Ericksonian hypnotists can put clients into deep trances by pacing all of the observables in the client's environment. As the client is sitting in the hypnosis chair, the hypnotist will say:

**"You can feel yourself sitting deeply in the chair,
and you can feel your arms moving across the armrests,
and you can feel your feet resting firmly on the floor,
and you can feel yourself breathing ... in ... and ... out ... and
you can feel your eyelids beginning to drop down just a little bit .
.. and ..."**

In this example, the hypnotist has already paced five observables in the environment. He has talked about the undeniably truthful sensation of sitting deeply in the chair, of the arms moving over the armrests, of the feet being firmly on the floor, of breathing in and out (these words are said precisely as the client breathes in and out) and of the eyelids beginning to drop.

As the hypnotist continues to talk about undeniably truthful events in the environment, the prospect no longer has to worry about these things. The hypnotist takes over all the worries, concerns and conscious functions of the client. The client finds this very relaxing and drops deeper and deeper into the subconscious mind. The Ericksonian hypnotist talks about and paces everything the clients is doing exactly as the client does it. The hypnotist thus becomes a mirror image of the client. It is almost as if there are two clients in the room, and no hypnotist! In this comfortable, relaxed trusting state, the client drifts into a deep, healthy hypnotic state.

A very similar process takes place when top salespeople interact with clients. The sales professional mirrors all of the client's concerns, worries, fears, needs, and dreams. It is almost as if there are two customers, and no salesperson. Top salespeople induce this very comfortable state by consistently pacing and talking about what they observe and hear *in the immediate environment*. They talk about the undeniably truthful events going on around them. The customer can't help but agree with what the salesperson is saying when he or she talks about obviously truthful events!

You can see the power of using this type of pacing statement in the sales work of Neil Campbell, one of the top Porsche-Audi salesmen in the country. A prospect had been looking at several cars at the dealership Neil works at when Neil walked up to him and said, *"I noticed you were standing here looking at this car on this beautiful afternoon."* All that the prospect could do was smile and agree. It was a beautiful afternoon and the prospect had been looking at the car.

Neil then said, "And I noticed that a few minutes ago, you were looking at that car." Neil gestured to another nearby car. The prospect nodded his head in agreement. Neil was talking about undeniably truthful events.

"We've had a lot of people in here today," Neil said. The prospect looked around the crowded showroom and said in agreement, "Yes, I can see there are a lot of folks here."

The conversation continued with some additional pacing statements which built a mind-set of agreement in the prospect. Neil then began to ask the prospect what features and benefits he was most interested in having in his next car. Their relationship started on a note of friendship and continued to deepen. The prospect perceived Neil as being genuinely interested in his needs, and in fulfilling those needs.

Neil asked the prospect how he had decided to buy his last car. The prospect described how he had bought that car, and Neil learned the prospect's thinking patterns and buying criteria. They went inside the showroom to have a soft drink and look at a new Audi catalog of options.

Inside the showroom, Neil continued to pace observables. "You will see a Porsche on the north side of the showroom that has the new fire-engine red paint," Neil said. Sure enough, when the prospect looked in that direction, he saw the Porsche in that bright red paint.

Neil continued to talk about undeniably truthful things in the environment, including the cars, furniture and a few other salespeople. He also continued to probe about the prospect's needs and what he could afford to buy. That afternoon Neil used the instant replay technique (described in the previous chapter) to sell this prospect a fully-equipped $35,000 car. Total time invested: about 90 minutes. And the prospect didn't say, "I want to think about it." He trusted Neil, felt comfortable with Neil and was convinced Neil could give him as good a deal as any other salesperson. Plus, the prospect just wanted to deal with Neil. It was like he had known Neil all his life.

This type of pacing statement does not have to be clever or analytical to be effective. Just concentrate on starting your presentation with some undeniably truthful statements. *This gets the prospect into an agreeable frame of mind.* Some other examples of pacing what you see and hear include: "I can see that you are well-dressed for this cold weather." Or, if the prospect is acting fidgety or is glancing at his watch, "I can see that you are pressed for time." By getting the prospect's agreement *from the outset*, you communicate, "I am someone who understands you." This establishes a firm foundation for building a relationship.

## How to Pace Customer Opinions and Beliefs to Build Credibility

Opinions and beliefs are a person's reality. *What a person believes is his or her TRUTH.* People will march off to war and risk life and limb to protect their opinions and beliefs. To tamper with a prospect's opinions or beliefs in the sales context is very dangerous!

Patients with extreme belief systems were often referred to Dr. Erickson because other psychiatrists and psychologists could not figure out a way to help them. One young obese woman came in to see Erickson and explained that she felt very very ugly. The daughter of alcoholics, she was slapped and kicked as a child. When her only sister died, she was not allowed to go to the funeral. After her mother died of kidney

father married another alcoholic who was even worse than her
stepmother wouldn't let Erickson's patient enter the house.
Erickson's patient was kept in the garage and was fed corn meal mush, potatoes and slop. When this stepmother died, the social worker told the young woman she had to get a job. The only job she could obtain was washing floors. The men at work would offer to pay one another if anyone would have sex with the young woman, but no one wanted to.

This young woman came to Erickson with a belief system that she was quite ugly and unappealing. Other people had told her she was not ugly, but she would not believe them. Their thoughts did not match her belief systems. Their comments of "you are not ugly," did not help the girl and did not raise her self-esteem.

Erickson started his therapy by hypnotizing the young woman and by matching or pacing her belief systems. She trusted Erickson because he said what she already believed—that she was ugly. However, when she was in the hypnotic trance, Erickson gave her a posthypnotic suggestion that she would go to the library and study books on anthropology. He directed her to study photographs of "all the hideous kinds of women men will marry. . . . Look through book after book and be curious. Then read books that tell about how women and men disfigure themselves, tattoo themselves, mutilate themselves to look even more horrible."

The young woman spent many hours at the library studying these books. She saw that men would marry women who seemed to look much worse than she looked. Erickson then hypnotized her and gave her a posthypnotic suggestion to read books on fashions throughout the ages to see all the bizarre and unusual clothing styles people have worn. She followed this posthypnotic suggestion and spent many hours reading such books on the history of fashion. In the process, she obtained a fine education on clothing, styles, and what fashions flatter a person. She began to change her self-perspective, and her self-esteem increased. She soon began to dress better and lost a great deal of weight. She had her teeth straightened. Erickson matched her belief systems as they evolved—and he took her to the next higher level. She actually became quite attractive and got a job as a fashion artist! She ended up studying and graduating from a university, marrying and having three children.

Looking back on the hypnotic therapy Erickson had provided her many years ago, she told him, "When you said those awful things about me, you were so truthful. I knew that you were telling me the truth. But, if you hadn't put me in a trance, I wouldn't have done any of those things you made me do." Since he started by pacing her existing belief systems, Erickson was perceived as being truthful. She trusted him and his suggestions, both on the hypnotic level and the unconscious level, were followed, leading her to new levels of self-confidence and personal growth.

Sales superstars use a very similar process to selectively pace the opinions and beliefs of their prospects and customers. However, you don't have to agree with every idea and belief of your prospect! Never say something you don't fully believe in. You don't have to be dishonest to be a sales champion. In fact, if you did agree with everything a prospect said, you would quickly be perceived as a phony.

## How to Handle Differences in Opinions and Beliefs Skillfully

How can you handle prospects with very strong beliefs you don't agree with? Start by simply repeating back what the prospect has said. Show him or her that you have listened. If your prospect says, "The last salesperson I dealt with didn't tell me about all the different prices and options that were available to me," you can pace back, "You believe that the last salesperson treated you unfairly." Notice that you are not saying that the last salesman was a crook or that he was dishonest. You prefaced your statement with, *"You believe that . . .."* Use this language to avoid calling another salesperson names. You don't want to criticize the competition because that only makes you look bad.

If your prospect says, "I can get a lower price somewhere else," you can pace that opinion by saying, "You think that you can get a better price from someone else." Your prospect will probably nod his head. You have just taken what could have been an adversarial confrontation or an argument over price and you have turned it into a form of minor agreement.

Why does pacing or matching opinions work so well? Many salespeople are more interested in talking than in listening, and this turns off customers. The most common complaint people have in marriage is, "My spouse doesn't listen to me." The most common complaint employees have in business is, "My boss doesn't listen to me." The most common complaint teenagers have is, "My parents don't listen to me." One of the most common complaints customers have is, "The salesperson didn't listen to me. He didn't hear me when I told him my needs and wants and my concerns." When you pace opinions and beliefs, you communicate that you are truly hearing the customer.

When you communicate that you have listened to someone else, that person knows you care about him or her. By pacing opinions and beliefs, you distinguish yourself from the mass of ordinary salespeople who are more interested in "telling" than in listening. There is some truth in the old joke about the salesman who said, "You can't buy yet! I haven't finished my presentation!" There are many salespeople who have talked their way out of a sale. However, we've never seen a salesperson who has listened his way out of a sale.

This technique of pacing or reflecting back opinions shows empathy and understanding for the customer. And, more importantly, *such pacing calls for a nod of agreement or statement of agreement from the client.* There are few things more valuable in sales than to get the prospect into an agreeable frame of mind with you. Pacing opinions accomplishes this.

How do you know when your pacing is working? Indicators of effective pacing include the client demonstrating verbal and nonverbal signs of agreement such as nodding, saying "yes," "uh huh," "I agree," and so on. The customer engaging in these behaviors is telling you he feels comfortable with you. This shows you that you have planted the seeds of trust.

## Secrets of Turning Objections into Advantages

Psychologists, psychiatrists and hypnotists have to deal with objections almost as much as do salespeople. Other psychologists and psychiatrists would often send their most difficult patients to Dr. Erickson, the master of indirect hypnosis. These obstinate patients might say, "No one can hypnotize me!" upon meeting Dr. Erickson. Some would pridefully recount how they had been to numerous psychologists and psychiatrists— and that none were any good. These impossible patients put notches on their gun for every mental health worker they could frustrate or get to quit their case.

When such an "impossible client" was referred to Dr. Erickson, he would ask them to describe why they could not be helped. He would ask them to describe why they could not ever be hypnotized. He never argued with the patient, he simply listened with rapt attention. Difficult patients were surprised by this because they expected a psychiatrist to tell them that they could and should "get better." They expected a psychiatrist to say that he could hypnotize them.

After hearing their story, Erickson would pace the opinions and beliefs. With utter sincerity, he might say something like, "You are right. Your problems may not have a solution. And you may not ever be able to experience the comfort and pleasure of hypnosis." Notice that Erickson did not say that the problem did not have a solution. He said it might not have a solution. Erickson always left the door open for hope.

Erickson did not resist the difficult patient. In fact, he sometimes took the resistant patient's beliefs one step further. Erickson might say, "You're right. You may never, ever be capable of experiencing hypnosis." The only way the resistant patient could resist Erickson would be to go into hypnosis!

Objections can be handled in one of two ways: (1) You can wait for the customer to bring up an objection, and then try to talk them out of it or un-do it. (2) You can bring up the objection first and disarm it. We call this second method "Mental Judo," and it is the method preferred by sales champions.

We have had the privilege of studying one of the top life insurance salesmen in the world—a fellow who should be granted a black belt in Mental Judo. If he knows his prospect thinks that insurance is a bad investment, he will sometimes start his presentation by saying, "Insurance is a terrible investment. It is a very poor investment." The prospect hears his own thoughts coming out of this salesman's mouth. He has no alternative but to agree with the salesman, and nods his head.

Then, this sales professional says, "While it is a bad investment, it does have a few important uses. Would you like to know why many of your friends have bought hundreds of thousands of dollars worth of life insurance for their families?" His curiosity piqued, the prospect now listens with rapt attention as this sales pro describes the many important uses of life insurance.

If the prospect ever again says, "Insurance is a terrible investment," the salesman will agree with the objection and pace it on some level. He shows no fear of the objection. The fact that he can agree with the objection shows great maturity and self-confidence. Once he has paced the objection, he goes on to unravel it and to show the prospect the many wonderful non-investment uses of insurance.

Virtually any objection can be paced. For example, an objection related to price can be countered with a statement like "You are concerned with the price." The prospect will say, "yes," and will feel that you have heard him and that you understand him. Now, be quiet. Let the client elaborate on what is bothering him or her. *Experience shows that once a client has ventilated his or her feelings, he or she is much more likely to buy.*

When you encounter an objection or stall, rather than immediately jumping in to fight it, reflect it back. Let the prospect hear his own words. Sometimes, the prospect will say, upon hearing the objection back, that it really isn't that important. *Sometimes the prospect will elaborate and will tell you what his exact concern is.* And, sometimes you will see that the price issue is really just a smoke screen hiding the real concerns.

## How to Pace with Action Words that Induce a Customer to Act

Salespeople have always wondered, "How can I motivate my prospect to take action?" The answer given by top salespeople is: pace with action words. You can pace whatever your prospect or customer is talking about, but replace their passive words with power-packed action words. Top salespeople know the effectiveness of using words such as "grab," "run with it," "take advantage of," "attack," "wrestle," and hundreds of other action words. The use of these action words puts your customer into an active frame of mind.

By using action words, the prospect does not remain a passive observer in the sales process, but rather becomes more deeply involved in it. When you use action words, you will soon find your prospect using them. And, *when someone is talking the language of action, they are much more likely to take action!*

There are literally thousands of action words in the English language. *If you analyze the speeches of powerful orators such as Ronald Reagan or Reverend Robert Schuller, you will see that they use these action-based words much more frequently than less-successful politicians and less-successful religious leaders.* To acquire the power of great speakers, use the same verbal techniques they utilize. Here are some power-packed action sentences you can start using today:

**"Do you grasp the many benefits of our product?"**
**"Do you have a handle on how this works?"**
**"Let's take the bull by the horns and make a decision on this today."**
**"Let's run with it."**
**"Don't stick your neck out with that other company."**
**"Are you stuck in a rut with that old technology?"**

Notice the difference between the first sentence and this passive equivalent: "Does this make sense to you?" This passive sentence fails to deeply involve the client. Compare the third sentence with its more passive equivalent: "Can you make a decision today?" When you use passively-worded sentences, you get minimal customer involvement and you risk boring your prospect. Pace the customer with action words to call him or her into action!

## How to Pace the Future to Get Sales *Now*

By talking about undeniably truthful events that will take place in the future, you can build expectations and excitement. Skilled hypnotists use future-pacing by making statements such as, "In a few minutes, you will begin to feel a heaviness in your arms and hands and a deep feeling of relaxation in your neck and shoulders."

In sales, you can use future-pacing statements such as, "You are going to be paying more taxes in a few years and you might be interested in knowing some methods we have developed to avoid that." For many people, the prospect of higher taxes is undeniably truthful. Bringing this subject up triggers a *"Yes, that's right"* response. While they are in a frame of agreement with you, you mention your methods for solving this problem.

If you are leasing or selling office space, you can use a future-pacing statement such as: "Soon, your company will need extra office space." If you are selling computers or data processing systems, you can future-pace by saying something undeniably truthful such as, "With your rapid growth, your information processing needs will be increasing." If you are selling financial investments, you can future-pace by saying, "In the uncertain times ahead, it makes sense to have certain investments which are *guaranteed* to appreciate." What are some future-pacing statements you can design for use in *your* industry or area of sales specialization? Write these down for use in your next sales call.

Each of these pacing statements demonstrates to the customer that the salesperson understands the customer's view of the world. Customers like to do business with salespeople who understand and respect them. Pacing or mirroring communicates your understanding and respect of the customer better than perhaps any other sales technique.

## How to Pick Up the Pace to Lead the Customer

By thoroughly pacing a client, Dr. Milton Erickson entered that client's world. When he adopted a similar speech pattern, similar body language (only limited by the damage polio had done to his body) and similar beliefs, Erickson almost became the client. He would so thoroughly pace clients that he could enter their minds and predict what they would say next.

We have been hired by a number of companies to travel with their top salespeople to figure out "how they can outsell everyone else." We have found that the top performers in the sales world thoroughly pace and match many aspects of their customer's behavior and their customer's thought patterns. In some ways, they become mirror images of customers. This also gives them the ability to predict what customers will think, what they will say, and what they will do.

From prediction comes power. When you can predict what another person does, you have more power. When Erickson had thoroughly paced and synchronized with the client, he then started to lead him or her. The hypnotic techniques he used to lead the client can also be used very effectively in professional selling. In our seminars and training programs, we call the process of influencing "picking up the pace."

For example, an Ericksonian hypnotist might pace a client by talking about undeniably truthful things the patient was experiencing:

**"You can feel yourself sitting deeply in the chair,**
**and you can feel your arms moving across the armrests,**
**and you can feel your feet resting firmly on the floor,**
**and you can feel yourself breathing ... in ... and ... out ...**
**and you can feel your eyelids beginning to drop down just a little**
**bit ... and ..."**

Each of these statements is a pacing statement except the last one. When the hypnotist says, "You can feel your eyelids beginning to drop down just a little bit," he is picking up the pace. He is leading the patient.

In old-fashioned hypnosis, the hypnotist would start by picking up the pace. He or she would tell you that your eyelids were getting heavy, your arms were getting heavy and that you were feeling sleepy. The reason this didn't always work is that the hypnotist had not paced you first.

It is much more effective to pace someone by using subtle matching and mirroring techniques before you begin trying to influence them. "Picking up the pace" too early, before trust is established, can be disastrous. It is usually safest and wisest to pace, and pace, and pace and then pick up the pace rather than to start by rushing the pace. People resist when you pick up the pace too quickly.

Pacing builds trust and it minimizes resistance by communicating, "*I am like you are.*" Once the person has been well-paced, he or she is much more easily influenced or led. If the person has not been paced, he or she will be almost impossible to lead. This is as true in politics or in marriage as it is in sales.

## Three Types of Hypnotic Leading Statements that Lead to Sales

In doing their research on Milton Erickson, Bandler and Grinder found that you can lead another person or "pick up the pace" by using **three**

**different types of hypnotic leading statements.** The simplest way of picking up the pace is to use conjunctions such as "and," "or," and "but " to combine the pacing statement and the leading statement.

You have known for a long time that there are many differences between top salespeople and less successful salespeople. However, you probably didn't know that they differ even in the ways they use seemingly simple little words such as "and," "or," and "but." Less successful salespeople more frequently use the word "but," while top salespeople use the word "and." Compare the following two sales sentences:

**"That's a good idea, but . . ."**

**"That's a good idea, and . . ."**

A prospect who hears the first sentence will feel that cold water has been splashed in his face when he encounters the word "but." He'll be unlikely to hear anything that comes after the "but."

A prospect who hears the second sentence will feel complimented that you like his idea, and he will be much more likely to pay attention to whatever you say after the word "and."

We have tape recorded and compared the presentations of many average salespeople and top sales producers. We have found that average salespeople speak in short, choppy sentences while top salespeople speak in longer, more fluid sentences which are linked to one another with the word "and."

When you pace a customer, you are telling him something he already knows or does. You are presenting back "old" information he already believes. Therefore, you never encounter resistance. When you lead a customer or "pick up the pace," you are presenting new information. *Any time you present new information, you may encounter resistance.*

To minimize resistance, start your sales calls with undeniably truthful pacing statements. You can connect these pacing statements to leading statements with the simple word "and." Our research indicates that many top salespeople use a ratio of approximately three or four pacing statements for every "picking up the pace" statement. In other words, they pace and pace and pace and then they "pick up the pace." Let's look at an example from hypnosis and then an example from sales:

**"You are sitting here now, and you are listening to the sound of my voice, and you are staring at the wall, and you are beginning to relax deeply."**

This example includes three undeniably truthful pacing statements and then one picking up the pace statement ("you are beginning to relax deeply."). All of the pacing statements and the picking up the pace statement are connected by using the sales conjunction "and." Here's a sales example:

**"We are talking about the performance of our new mainframe computer, and you can remember what you have read about in all the magazines about this computer, and you can get very excited about what it can do for your company."**

This sales example of pacing and picking up the pace has two pacing statements and one picking up the pace statement ("you can get very excited about"). The sales conjunction "and" elegantly connects the pacing statements to the picking up the pace statement.

Interestingly, there does not have to be any logical connection between the pacing statements and the picking up the pace statement for persuasion to take place. Start with several pacing statements that are undeniably truthful and then connect them to a picking up the pace statement about your product or service. Here is an example of how you can connect undeniably truthful pacing statements to a seemingly unrelated picking up the pace statement.

One of our assignments involved studying top salespeople working for Automatic Data Processing. A sales champion within that organization, who has since been promoted into sales management, would say to prospects, "You are sitting comfortably in your office, and you can feel the peace of mind that you will have when ADP is doing your payroll every week." There is no logical connection between the undeniably truthful pacing statement ("sitting in your office"), and the picking up the pace statements ("ADP is doing your payroll every week.") However, prospects respond to this sentence. It paces them and then leads them. The pacing statement and the picking up the pace statement work well together. Why? The prospect develops a "yes set" or an agreeable frame of mind to the undeniably truthful pacing statement. This agreeable frame of mind *warms him up to accept the picking up the pace statement which comes next.*

Another very effective means of "picking up the pace" is with what we call "sales adverbs." The concept of combining pacing and picking up the pace statements is the same, but this time the two statements are linked together with an adverb, such as "while," "since," "when," "before," or "until."

Ericksonian hypnotists use adverbs to connect pacing statements with leading statements in the following way:

**"As you sit deeply in the chair, and as you feel your arms resting at your side, and as you listen to my voice, you can begin to feel your conscious mind going to sleep and you can feel you subconscious mind taking over."**

In this example, the pacing statements involve the actions that are undeniably taking place (sitting in the chair, feeling your arms resting at your side, listening to the hypnotist's voice). These are connected to the leading statements of feeling your conscious mind go to sleep and feeling your subconscious mind taking over. By thus adverbially linking the pacing statements and the leading statements, a deep trance can be induced conversationally.

A top automobile salesman we have worked with uses sales adverbs in the following way: **"As you look at this car, and as you sit in it, and as you feel its power while you drive down the road, you will be able to imagine how proud you will be to own it."** In this example, three pacing statements (looking at the car, sitting in the car, and feeling its power as you drive down the road) are connected to the picking up the pace statement ("you will be able to imagine how proud you will be to own it"). This linkage is accomplished through use of the adverb "as."

As you know, we believe in giving homework to the trainees in our corporate sales seminars. We have found that homework and skill-building exercises guarantee that our seminar attendees will master the sales skills we teach. To improve your sales skills in the area of hypnotic

pacing and picking up the pace, write down some sales
these adverbs to connect your sales pacing and pick
statements. Construct examples using the products or s
With just a little practice, you will soon become quite sk
up the sales pace in your own selling to more quicl
customers to the close.

Perhaps the most powerful form of picking up the pace is **cause-effect
leading**. Clinical hypnotists use it in the following way:

> **"Just sitting deeply in this soft leather hypnosis chair will make
> you begin to drift off into a pleasant hypnotic trance."**

This technique combines an undeniably truthful pacing statement (".
. . sitting deeply in this soft leather chair")  with a picking up the pace
statement (". . . . drift off into a pleasant hypnotic trance") by using the
cause-effect word "make."

Cause-effect words include "make," "require," "must," "have to,"
"cause," and "force." A few years ago, Bill Kirk was Sales Manager of the
Year for Control Data Corporation. Bill is a master at using cause-effect
leading to pick up the pace. In introducing a new Control Data product, he
would say to the  customer, "I don't know if I should show you this new
disk drive, because just looking at it will make you want to buy it." His
customers couldn't wait to see the new disk drive!

Bill Kirk first concentrates on building trust and rapport with his
customers. Without the trust and rapport, which he builds through pacing,
Bill's leading statements (picking up the pace statements) about the new
products would not be as persuasive as they are. Bill is a sales professional
who really knows his clients and their needs. When he says that the client
cannot be shown something because the client will absolutely have to have
it, the message to the client is clear: *you may have to stretch in order to buy
it, but this is THE disk drive for you!*

As part of your skill-building homework, take out a piece of paper and
write down 10 or more cause-effect hypnotic statements you can use in your
own selling. Be sure to mention your own product or service. Use words
such as "make," "require," "must," "have to," "cause," and "force" to
connect the undeniably truthful pacing statements with the picking up the

pace statements. Then, try these persuasive statements out in your sales presentations and see how irresistible they are.

Cause-effect hypnotic statements will also work beautifully in your personal life. The next time you want someone to agree to go to a new restaurant, say something like, "I don't know if I should show you the menu or not, because just looking at it will tempt you to order about a dozen different delicious things!!!"

## How to Use the "Yes Set" to Make It Easier
## for a Customer to Say "Yes"

Many of the techniques of conversational hypnosis are designed to garner agreement, whether on a conscious or unconscious level. To induce conversational hypnosis, the hypnotist may use statements such as:

**"It is nice to relax deeply, isn't it?"**

**"You'd like to be free of stress, wouldn't you?"**

**"You'd like all your problems to float away, wouldn't you?"**

**"It feels comfortable to melt away, like melting chocolate, doesn't it?"**

As the patient agrees with these yes-set questions, he or she begins to experience the comfort and relaxation that are being discussed. The earliest yes-set questions you use should be the ones that are easiest to agree with. As a "climate of agreement" is built, bigger requests can be made. The patient, who is now in a "habit of agreement" is much more likely to follow these suggestions.

As people agree with a salesperson or hypnotist, they tend to fall into a habit that increases the likelihood of continued agreement. *The more people agree, the more they are likely to continue agreeing.* Many highly skilled persuaders seek some form of minor or major agreement at least once each minute during their presentations.

*How can you continually build agreement?* You can do it from the very first moment of contact up through the close, as you use "yes set" questions at each point along the way. You can start with introductory "yes set" questions, such as **"This is October 1st, isn't it?"** and **"You are Joe Smith, aren't you? I"**'m glad to meet you."

You can then transition into need-building "yes set" questions such as **"People like to buy products with good warranties, don't they?"** or **"You are interested in saving on your taxes, aren't you?"** In addition to garnering a yes-response and building the climate of agreement, these questions gently remind the prospect of his or her needs (which you can then fulfill).

Top salespeople continue using yes-set questions throughout their presentations, all the way to the close. At the close, you can use a yes-set closing question such as **"People like to make many purchases today with credit cards, don't they?"** Since this is undeniably truthful, your customer will say, "yes," but may then inform you that he would like to pay by check or with cash. In either case, you have gotten some additional agreement and you have closed the sale. If you are selling life insurance, a yes-set closing question you can use is, **"Many people prefer to make their spouse the beneficiary of their life insurance policy, don't they?"** This will trigger a "yes" response and usually gets your client to tell you if he or she would like to make the spouse the beneficiary. As they talk, you can begin writing on your applications and you are well on your way to closing the sale.

As a skill-building exercise, take out a piece of paper now and write down ten "yes-set" questions you can use in your next sales call. Be sure to include questions you can use to: (1) open the call, (2) build need and (3) close the sale. With practice, you will be able to skillfully use yes-set questions in every step of your sales presentation, *won't you?*

Through the process of using yes-set questions, people get into a mental habit of saying "yes" to persuasive people, whether they are politicians, religious leaders or salespeople. *When a customer has said "yes" throughout the presentation, it is very hard for him to say "no" at the close.*

## Key Steps to Transform Ordinary Statements Into Yes-Getters

To increase your closing ratio, work more "yes-set" questions into your sales presentation. Instead of making ordinary statements, such as, "People like to save money," *transform it into a "yes set" question such as,*

"**People like to save money, don't they?**" Transform "Having the most advanced office automation is important," into "**Having the most advanced office automation is important, isn't it?**" Prospects find presentations much more interesting when they are involved and when you ask their opinions, don't they?

Add tag questions to the end of any factual statement to turn it into a "yes set question." Here are some sample tag phrases you can use to transform ordinary sentences into yes-getters:

| | | |
|---|---|---|
| "**didn't they?**" | "**won't they?**" | "**isn't she?**" |
| "**don't they?**" | "**isn't it?**" | "**wasn't it?**" |
| "**wouldn't they?**" | "**aren't you?**" | "**couldn't they?**" |

You can easily close a few extra sales this week by using these phrases, *can't you?* Notice the flexibility of these tag statements. They can be used for the **present tense** ("This **is** a beautiful home, **isn't** it?") or the **past tense** ("That **was** an exciting and profitable week in the stock market, **wasn't** it?"). They can get agreement by referring to the **customer** ("**You** do like to save money, don't **you?**") or by referring to **other people** ("Classic car collectors really like this model, don't **they?**") or even by referring to **inanimate objects** ("The **trade magazines** have certainly given this computer a lot of great publicity, haven't **they?**"). You can even use yes-set questions in reference to **animals:** "**Dogs** like to eat a dog food that has a lot of meat and a lot of texture, don't **they?**"

Use your creativity to come up with dozens of new yes-set questions to sell more of your products or services. If you are not getting enough agreement from customers, you are probably not using enough yes-set questions throughout your sales presentations. Persuasive sales presentations are built upon agreement, and yes-set questions are one of the most powerful and flexible tools for building agreement.

## Repetition Techniques to Plant Messages Deep in Your Customer's Mind

For thousands of years, people have known that repetition is hypnotic. Hypnotic devices such as swinging pendulums and rotating wheels have been used since the time of the ancient Egyptian sleep temples to induce hypnosis. The repetitive quality of ocean waves cresting against the shore is hypnotic to many people. Long-distance driving can be hypnotic due to the repetition of the dotted lines on the road and the repetition of fences and walls and trees.

Skilled hypnotists do not have to use shiny pendulums, swinging watches or other physical objects to induce hypnosis. They can use relaxing words in a repetitive fashion to get the same effect:

**"You are dropping deeper and deeper and deeper into hypnosis."**

**"Your body is melting, melting, melting away."**

**"Your eyelids are getting heavier, heavier, heavier."**

Top salespeople know that words can also be used repetitively to induce a relaxed, yet focused hypnotic state. While average salespeople speak in short, choppy sentences, sales pros speak in longer, flowing, rhythmic streams. **Sales pros are not afraid to repeat key words or benefits to arouse desire and build even more interest.**

When used by sales professionals, repetition of key words can have the same relaxing effect as the gentle sound of ocean waves as they roll to and from the shore. The repetition tends to hypnotically focus the customer's attention on whatever is being communicated.

The skillful use of repetition prevents the customer from being distracted by other events in his or her environment, or by other thoughts. A glowing example of this technique is illustrated by Tom Olds, the sales champion described in the preface to this book. In his presentation on a tax-shelter program, Olds states "Your taxes are going to be going up and up and up and up, year after year after year. Uncle Sam has a very, very, very sophisticated strategy to take your money away from you and your family. *What is your counter-strategy*?" It is no accident that wealthy clients listen when Tom Olds speaks. Tom knows the secrets, including hypnotic repetition, of mesmerizing sales presentations, and he uses them skillfully.

We do a lot of work in recruiting and hiring salespeople to help companies build powerful sales teams. We have found that hypnotic repetition is a wonderful way of making a strong positive impression on people who are considering working for your company. The power of hypnotic repetition is illustrated by Jim Sweeney, who has earned over $1 million a year by recruiting salespeople.

Jim has specialized in doing group presentations and seminar presentations to recruit salespeople. He has found it is much more effective and efficient to do a presentation to 50 people at one time than to do 50 separate presentations. When he is describing the rapidly-growing company he works for and the opportunity the company offers, Jim says:

**"Our company is getting bigger and bigger and bigger and bigger and better and better and better and better all the time . . . and why don't you join us NOW?"**

Many job-hunters have never heard anyone talk so self-confidently and so positively about the company they work for. Jim Sweeney's presentation is positively mesmerizing. Although Jim is doing a very difficult type of sales recruiting (for commission-only positions), his verbal skill is so great that he is able to recruit people no one else can recruit.

Chances are, none of your competitors are using hypnotic repetition. Your presentations will have extra verbal sparkle when you use this hypnotic tool. Your prospects and customers will really enjoy listening to you speak.

To build your sales presentations skills, take out a piece of paper and write down five key phrases you can hypnotically repeat in your sales presentations. Here are some tips. You can say:

**"Our prices are low, low, low!"**

**"Our engineering design is advanced, advanced, advanced!"**

**"This home has an incredible, incredible, incredible view!"**

**"The power this new car has is awesome, awesome, awesome!"**

Now, write down your own creative uses of hypnotic repetition.

## How to Use "Must-Do" Statements to Propel Customers to Act

Once he has built a deep level of trust, the hypnotist may say:

**"You must go into a trance now,"**

**"You need to go into hypnosis now."**

**"You have to go into a relaxing trance now."**

The key is to first build the deep level of trust. When you have built the deep level of trust, the other person is much more likely to follow your suggestion. The trust is best-built through hypnotic pacing techniques previously described.

Hypnotic must-do statements are used by top salespeople to propel prospects to take action. This is accomplished through the use of "Must Do" words such as: "must," "have to," and "need to," as the following example illustrates.

We are currently working with one of the top mortgage software companies in the country. The company not only sells software but will also sell computer hardware to go along with it and together the hardware and software make up a "bundled system." The president of the company first builds a deep level of trust with the prospect and then uses a series of must-do statements to propel the prospect to take action. Here is just one of the Must Do statements he uses to motivate his customers:

**"Most people in a position like yours feel that they MUST have a powerful computer and software program to do accurate comparisons between loans."**

Let's examine what is happening in this statement. The president is pacing the prospect by recognizing his "position." Inferred is that the position has a great deal of responsibility. This statement also gains power by implying that other intelligent people in his position feel they must have this computer hardware and software solution.

This must-do statement could be made even more powerful by turning it into a must-do "yes-set" question. This can be accomplished through using the yes-set hypnotic tags you previously learned about in this chapter:

| | |
|---|---|
| Sales pro: | **"Most people in a position like yours feel that they MUST be able to do accurate comparisons between loans, don't they?"** |
| Customer: | **"Yes."** |
| Sales pro: | **"And, most people in this field think the best way to do these complicated loan comparisons is with a customized loan comparison software package, don't they?"** |

You have now gotten two nods of agreement before you have even started your presentation. You have started to build the climate of agreement that is so crucial for closing a sale. And, you have started to build the need for your solution.

As a skill-building exercise, write down 5 must-do statements you can use in selling your products or services. Use words such as "must," "have to," and and "need to."

Be careful about how some customers will use "Must Do" statements on you. If you don't recognize and effectively handle these "Must Do" statements that customers use, much of your sales energy and sales time can be wasted. "Must Do" statements used by prospects can block a potentially successful sales interaction.

Here is just one way a prospect may use a "Must Do" statement on you. The prospect may say, **"I really have to compare products before I decide what to buy."** This is a legitimate concern for many clients, but it can degenerate into an endless stall if not properly dealt with. The customer feels he has to compare products, compare products and compare products—and he may end up becoming an unpaid product comparison expert. He may never buy the product; he may buy it from someone else; and he may even end up with an inferior product or an over-priced product.

Who could sell to the customer who says, "I really MUST compare products"? The sales professional who knows how to un-do the must-do statement. One way of undoing this "Must Do" statement is to start by saying, **"You feel that you need more information before you make a decision, don't you?"** This is an undeniably truthful pacing statement. You are showing the customer you heard his concern. Then, you turn it into a "yes-set" question by using the tag, "don't you?" He almost has to say "yes." If he says "no," you have already won and can proceed toward the close.

If the client says he has to compare products, you can start undoing the must-do by saying, "That's fine. I understand." This reassurance statement puts the client in a comfort zone. He feels you understand him. He will thus be much more likely to listen to what you have to say next.

After you have reassured your client, say, "I compare products in this field everyday. We have brochures on almost every product out there." This shows the client that you are very well-informed. It also implies that you have little or no fear of the competition.

Continue to un-do their must-do statement by saying, **"I'll be happy to answer any questions you have or to show you the brochures."** You have already built a yes-set of agreement. You have paced the client's concerns. You have reassured the client and put him or her in a comfort zone. Now, you tell the client you will show him or her the brochures of competitors and answer any additional questions.

Continue by saying, **"This will save you a lot of time and energy. I think you will be able to make up your mind after you see this."** By mentioning the time you will save the client, you have added another benefit the client will experience by doing business with you.

Following the same sequence of steps provided above will enable you to un-do almost any "must-do" statement that a prospect uses on you (or on himself). Knowing how to un-do must-do statements will enable you to free up the prospect's selling energy. You will almost never "get stuck" if you know how to un-do the must-do statements that prospects use.

## How to Use "Can-Do" Statements to Show the Widest Range of Product Benefits

"Can-Do" statements focus on possibilities and make use of words such as **"can,"** and **"can't"**; **"possible,"** and **"impossible"**; **"able"** and **"unable."** In hypnosis, the skilled hypnotist says:

"As you go deeper and deeper into trance, you will find it
impossible to open your eyes. You can't open your eyes, no
matter how hard you try. You are so relaxed, so relaxed, so
relaxed, you can't raise your arms. They feel like they are made
of lead. It is impossible to worry about anything. Your conscious
mind has gone to sleep and your unconscious mind will take
care of you. It is impossible for you to do anything except fall
deeper into a healthy hypnotic trance."

Just reading this induction, you may begin to feel some of the relaxation yourself. Also, notice that hypnotic repetition was also used in this
example.

"Can do" statements are frequently used by top salespeople as a
powerful form of suggestion:

**"You can see yourself driving home this beautiful Lincoln."**

**"You can see your boss smiling when you tell him you bought the
IBM system!"**

**"You can imagine all the enjoyment this fishing boat will bring
you."**

**"It would be impossible for you to get a higher quality product at
a lower cost."**

As a skill-building exercise, write down ten can-do statements you can
use in selling your company's products or services. Use can-do statements
to help your prospects and customers focus on the vast array of possible
benefits they can experience from using your products or services. Use
words such as "can," "can't," "possible," "impossible," "able," and "unable" in your can-do statements. Refer to the sales and hypnosis examples
above for additional inspiration and guidance.

While the vast array of "Can Do" statements will serve you well in
increasing your sales effectiveness, you'll want to be wary of customers
who use them with you. Let's look at a situation from real life where a
prospect used a "Can-Do" statement that almost prevented a sale. We'll
also look at how a top sales professional countered it. This example is

from Leo Castillo, one of the most successful jewelry salesmen on Rodeo Drive in Beverly Hills.

A customer told Leo, "I just **can't** justify spending that kind of money for a necklace." Upon hearing this, Leo knew that he had to expand the customer's thinking as to what was possible. He knew that the customer had the money. That wasn't the problem.

Leo decided to focus on the "can't" word that blocked the sale. Here's what happened:

| | |
|---|---|
| Leo: | **"Why can't you? What stops you?"** |
| Client: | **"I just can't justify it."** |
| Leo: | **"Who said you have to justify this?"** |
| Client: | **"I don't know. I like to justify whatever I buy, whether I buy a computer or something for the house."** |
| Leo: | **"This isn't like buying a computer. This isn't like buying a can opener. This is a true luxury! You don't have to justify buying your wife a luxury. She either deserves it or she doesn't. What do you think? Can you imagine the expression on your wife's face when you present her with this beautiful rare necklace?"** |
| Client: | **"Yes, I can."** |

Leo made the sale because he had the ability to un-do a "can't do" statement.

Think of the can-do and can't-do statements that clients and prospects use on you. Remember, when a prospect says he "can't do" something, sometimes it is true, and sometimes the barrier or the limitation is only in his or her mind. Your job as a true sales professional is to distinguish the real "can't do" from the imaginary "can't do."

Don't accept "can't do" statements at face value. Too many salespeople accept almost every "can't do" statement as the absolute truth. They end up losing sales they should be making because they accept the prospect's limited thinking as an absolutely truthful statement about reality.

If you gently challenge "can't do" statements, as Leo did above, you will find that many of them fall apart. There is no logic or reason to justify why something "can't" be done. If you gently challenge these "can't do" statements, you will make many sales that other salespeople "can't" make.

   You are now familiar with all of the basic structures and tools of hypnotic selling. You know that we trust and like people like ourselves. You know that pacing through matching and mirroring is the most effective way of creating the experience of, "*I feel like I've known you all my life!*" You know that pacing and mirroring give you the ability to become like the other person. Now that you are familiar with pacing and now that you know several methods for "picking up the sales pace," you are ready to learn some more advanced techniques for giving mesmerizing sales presentations. Just turn the page, and this new world will open up to you.

# 5

## Creating Sales Presentations That Mesmerize

Having gained your customer's trust through pacing and mirroring speech patterns and thoughts, the next step is to learn more about his or her needs, and to help him or her make a wise purchase decision. In this chapter, you will learn how to use special combinations of hypnotic words that will produce more and more sales with less effort. These are the verbal techniques of persuasion employed by both sales superstars and highly skilled psychologists and psychiatrists trained in hypnosis.

## How to Select and Express "Hot Words" that Have Special Persuasive Powers

Our language is full of emotion, *but some words clearly fire off stronger emotional responses than others*. Words that trigger our emotions are known as "hot words." Words like "pain," "money" "baby," "mother," "loss," and "gain" have a strong emotional charge. When such words are heard, there is more than passive recognition of the words themselves. *There tends to be a deeper emotional reaction as well.* Maybe the reaction is in the pit of the stomach, maybe it is just a "tingle", but the word sends off a number of unconscious messages and feelings, which can be quite effective in sales or any kind of persuasion.

Think about your own reaction to the word "baby" as opposed to words such as "kid," "child," "offspring," or "progeny." They may all refer to the same little person, but which word has the greatest emotional charge?

Hot words can have a dramatic effect on the emotional state of the listener. Richard Bandler and John Grinder, creators of the field known as "neuro-linguistic programming," call these words "anchors." In a real sense, our feelings and emotions are anchored to these words and then our feelings are "fired off" when we hear these words.

Hot words can be positive, such as "love," "free," and "new," or they can be negative, such as "Nazi," "pain," or "death." The name of a loved-one can be a very positive hot word. Just mentioning the name of a loved one can cause someone to smile and feel good. Mentioning the words "freedom," "America" or "the flag," to a patriotic American can fire off many positive emotions. Mentioning the words "abortion" or "freedom of choice" to someone who is against abortion can fire off many negative emotions.

By skillfully combining emotionally-laden hot word combinations, a salesperson can guide and control the emotional climate of the sales call. There are words to produce any emotional state you desire in your prospect and customer. If you are not producing the emotional states you want your customer to experience, it's because you are not using the right combinations of hot words.

*An important note:* Emotional words tend to have an even greater impact on the listener when spoken with a shift in tone or vocal emphasis which makes them stand out from the rest of the sentence. You can change your vocal emphasis by speaking the words softly or more loudly; slowly or more rapidly. The purpose of such "verbal marking" is to further distinguish the emotional words from all the other words in the sentence.

How do top salespeople and hypnotists know which emotional words to use? They look very closely at their clients and the clients' surroundings. They ask themselves: What is important and meaningful to this person? They listen equally carefully. They ask themselves: *What turns this person on? What turns him off? What are his pet interests and hobbies?* What are the significant events in his life?

They skillfully use probing techniques (see Chapter 7) to find where some of these words may be buried. As they unearth meaningful emotional words, they incorporate these hot words into their presentations. Skilled hypnotists can string together dozens of emotional hot words about childhood, achieving one's potential, relaxing deeply, being free from stress, and having radiant health, into a single hypnotic induction.

Skilled salespeople can string together dozens of hot words about: saving money, decreasing expense, getting a good return on investment, and pride of ownership into one mesmerizing sales presentation.

Hot words can be used in each step of the sales presentation, from the opening remarks through the close. Which opening statement by the life insurance agent makes the best use of hot words:

**"Congratulations! I understand that there is a new baby in your home!"**

or

**"I understand there is a new child in the house."**

The first sentence has much more emotional impact than the second. The word "congratulations" triggers feelings of pride and accomplishment. The word "baby" is more emotionally charged than "child". But there is more. Think of the emotional difference between referring to "the house" as opposed to "your home," particularly when the speaker uses a warm tone of voice and a smile when saying "your home."

The skillful use of such subtle emotional language throughout the sales presentation can mean extra closeness between the sales professional and his or her customer—and it can mean extra sales.

Opportunities to use emotionally charged words are abundant in the sales process. Top salespeople discover these opportunities by being super-sensitive to their clients. Pat Knowles of Kansas City is one of the most successful sellers of tax-favored investments in America. He is a master at using words related to taxation and the Internal Revenue Service to strategically fire off emotions in his customers' thinking:

**"How do you feel every April 15?"** Pat inquires.

"Terrible," the prospect says. "I pay a fortune to the government every April 15."

**"Well, why not join our group of investors?  We celebrate every April 15!"**

The hot word "April 15" predictably fires off negative feelings in the prospect. Pat then juxtaposes this hot word with the positive emotions fired off by the word "celebrate." It is a surprising and fresh perspective for the listener. Potential clients *invariably* ask for more information as to why Pat's investors can celebrate. This is just one of several hundred emotionally charged sentences which Pat Knowles uses. It is no accident that his personal income from sales exceeds one-half million dollars a year.

By skillfully using emotional language, the sales professional is able to cut through intellectual defenses a customer may have erected. Most people buy emotionally and then later justify their purchase decision with logic. That is why it is so important that you first reach them emotionally. Hot words enable you to do that.

Emotional language helps the customer see a new way of solving his or her problems. The salesperson is now even more likely to be perceived as an insightful individual who understands the customer and his or her needs. This contributes to better communication and deeper trust between salesperson and customer.

## Using Attention-Focusing Statements to Grab and Direct Customer Attention

Whether during hypnosis or a sales presentation, there are limits to the client's attention span. As a consequence, there is a need to give the client a verbal nudge periodically in order to regain attention and concentration. Without such words, the client can drift into an unfocused mental state or become preoccupied, and will miss keys points that are being made. This undermines the entire sales process.

Words such as **"now," "here"** and **"again,"** *bring attention and emphasis to the statements that follow them*. If interspersed throughout the sales presentation, these words can help you sustain the customer's interest longer. They can also cause the client to pay more attention to the **exact** points that the sales professional wishes to emphasize.

Successful hypnotists make frequent use of the word "now." Once a deep level of trust and rapport has been established through the use of pacing statements and voice-matching, the hypnotist will begin the hypnotic induction:

**"You can begin going into hypnosis NOW."**

Throughout the hypnosis session, the hypnotic trance is deepened with focusing statements such as:

**"You can go deeper and deeper into hypnosis NOW."**

The word "now" acts as a hidden action command for the client to stay at a deeper level of hypnosis.

The effectiveness of these attention-focusing statements is apparent in the following example from a sales presentation for an oil and gas limited partnership. Which one will command more client attention?

**"There are 5 advantages of our program,"**

or

**"NOW, let's look HERE at the 5 advantages of our program."**

Clearly the second sentence grabs the client's attention more powerfully than does the first one.

*An Important Note:* The impact of these attention-grabbers is even greater if they are **pronounced in a sustained voice that is deep and soft.** Try to stretch the word out for several seconds. Turn "now," into "N-N-N-O-O-O-W-W-W". To the listener, this sounds beautifully resonant and it also grabs his attention.

Listen to the way professional television announcers use attention-grabbers such as "now." Their challenge is to grab and focus your attention in 30 seconds or less. Advertisers and those who design advertising want their ads to be as effective as possible. That's why many people in the advertising field are now studying hypnotic techniques and hypnotic language patterns. Both scientific research and hard-earned experience show that conversational hypnosis works in advertising. *In our sales training seminars, we have found it great fun, and also very effective, to have the group practice d-r-a-w-i-n-g out words such as n-n-n-o-o-o-w-w-w and h-h-h-e-e-e-r-r-r-e-e-e.*

Most of the prospects you call on are already preoccupied. Their attention is focused—but it is focused on something other than what you are selling. They are preoccupied with the problems of the day, with thinking about people and events in their work lives and personal lives. They are talking to themselves about their problems and responsibilities. *Unless you have the ability to attract and maintain their attention, you will be unable to counter their existing preoccupations.* Attention-focusing statements give you this power. Our research shows that these special words are used with much greater frequency by top salespeople than by less successful salespeople. Join the ranks of the top salespeople and make them a part of your vocabulary.

## How to Make the Sale by Taking the Sale Away

One of the reasons average salespeople are not more successful is that they push too hard. No one likes to be forced into something. *"Taking the sale away" techniques are effective because they get the customer to sell himself or herself.*

"Taking the Sale Away" is best used to advise a prospect that he or she cannot make a purchase that he or she has little interest in making anyway. You have almost nothing to lose and a lot to gain by using this technique in this circumstance. "Taking the Sale Away" works especially well with highly resistant prospects who have a strong interest in resisting the salesperson!

To illustrate "Taking the Sale Away," let's first look at an example from clinical hypnosis. How would you try to hypnotize someone who claims, "NO ONE CAN HYPNOTIZE ME!"? Psychologists and psychiatrists are commonly faced with this problem. The solution they have developed is a psychological version of "Taking the Sale Away."

The therapist has the patient sit in a big soft chair and then starts speaking in a soft, low tone of voice:

"Maybe you are right, maybe you can't be hypnotized. Maybe you will never know the **comfort** and **pleasure** of hypnosis. Maybe you will always deny yourself the **benefits** of hypnotic relaxation. *I don't know.* It's up to you. *Maybe you are too frightened to allow yourself to experience hypnosis.* Maybe you are not interested in the **improved health** hypnosis can bring you, as you begin to **relax** just a little more, **NOW**. And you can **relax** just a little at a time, as you do every night as you begin to go to sleep..."

The highly resistant patient wants to push against the hypnotist. When the hypnotist tells him he **cannot** go into trance, the only way the patient can resist is to go into hypnosis!

To make "Taking the Sales Away" even more effective, you should state the many benefits of the product or service (which the customer will not enjoy unless he makes the purchase). In the hypnosis example above, you will note that many of the healthful and relaxing benefits of hypnosis were emphasized.

Now, let's examine how a computer sales professional used "Taking the Sale Away:"

| | |
|---|---|
| Salesperson: | **"I really can't recommend that minicomputer because I suspect it is more computer than you need. It has more power, faster processing times, and more storage than you need. Plus, it is built to take much more use than you are going to give it. This is really a computer for bigger businesses."** |
| Client: | **"Well, I can afford the minicomputer, and I've got some growth plans for my business. I think my business needs the features and benefits of this minicomputer."** |

This salesperson comes across as very honest. He is not a product pusher. It seems that the salesperson knows the client and knows what the client needs. The salesperson knows what will make the client happy.

Since the salesperson was not a product pusher, there was nothing for the client to resist. The salesperson was not pushing against the client, so the client did not need to push back. In preventing the salesperson from "taking the sale away," the customer bought the computer. He sold himself on his need for the machine.

If the sales professional had tried to push the minicomputer from the outset, he might not have succeeded. The seemingly gentle method of "taking the sale away" was actually much more effective than a direct sales approach, just as indirect hypnosis can be much more powerful than direct hypnosis.

*What if the prospect had agreed with the salesperson?* What if the prospect had said, "I agree with you, this is too much computer for my business"? The sales professional would still win. He could use a probing sequence to find out exactly what kind of computer the client thought he needed. With the trust he had just built, he would have a very good chance of selling that computer to the client. So, no matter what happens after you use "Taking the Sale Away," you are likely to make a sale.

*We believe it is extremely important to be truthful in all your sales work.* Never say that a product will not meet a customer's needs—unless you sincerely believe what you are saying. Do not use these powerful language patterns just to pull a reversal to get a customer to buy. Our research shows that the only way to sustain high-level sales success over many years is to be truthful with your customers. There are an unlimited number of truthful statements you can use to get sales, and thus there is never any need or justification to use any form of deceit.

**Missing Words:** Most salespeople concentrate on what to say. Top salespeople understand that it is just as important to know what **not** to say.

If you know how to paint word pictures, the words you leave out will be automatically "filled in" by customers. The "Missing Words" technique is engineered to trigger the customer to effortlessly use his or her imagination to "fill in the gaps."

"Missing Words" are also designed to prevent the boredom which can result when a salesperson "tells you too much." One of the most successful car salesmen in the world says, "I've seen many salesmen sell a car. The customer is all excited and ready to buy. But then, sometimes, the salesman talks them out of the deal. He talks too much, and the prospect changes his mind. The salesman ends up taking the car back."

Salespeople who know how to use "missing words" never say too much. The hypnotic pattern of "Missing Words" allows them to leave out unnecessary details. Here is how it is used in hypnosis. Once you are in hypnosis, the hypnotist might take you to another time and place by saying:

"You are walking along a beach and you can hear the surf roll in as you relax a little more deeply and you can smell the salt in the air and you can see sea-gulls flying around. Off in the distance, you see a stranger and you walk towards the stranger, feeling excited about who this person might be. As you get closer, you can see how the stranger is dressed and you recognize the stranger. This person has a very special message for you. This person has

> an answer to a question you have been
> thinking about. And, as you stand next to
> this person, you hear the answer."

Notice that the hypnotist did not specify what the beach would look like or where it was. The hypnotist did not specify what time of year it was or what time of day it was. The hypnotist did not specify whether the stranger was male or female. The hypnotist did not specify what the message was. *Your subconscious mind effortlessly and instantaneously fills in this missing information.* As you read the above passage, you might have seen a specific beach and a specific stranger. In hypnosis, the imagery is much, much more vivid and powerful.

The **specific beach** you would see, the **specific stranger** that approaches you, and the **specific message** he/she delivers would not be random. Rather, it would be based upon your own experiences, expectations, and needs. You might see a beach at Maui, because your honeymoon was on that beach. Or, you might see a beach in Florida, because you once lived in that Florida coastal community. It might be early morning or it might be sunset. Your subconscious mind would effortlessly fill in your favorite time of day to walk along the beach. The stranger might be your last boss, because you have been thinking about him recently. Or, it might be your father or your mother, because you have been thinking about one of them recently. You would not see a random generic non-person.

*The message the stranger gives you would not be random either.* You might hear him or her say, "You are going to make it," because that is exactly what you need to hear him say. Or, you might hear the stranger say, "Take life a little easier," because that is what you need to hear.

In a real sense, "Missing Words" allow the hypnosis client to tailor-make the hypnosis to best-fit to his or her own needs. There is no way that even the most skilled hypnotist in the world could come up with anything more meaningful than what the patient's own subconscious mind will come up with! This is why highly trained hypnotists don't even try to specify all the details in hypnotic visualization. Instead, they use "Missing Words" to trigger the client's imagination. As a result, **the hypnotic vision becomes far more vivid, desirable, persuasive and real.**

Exactly the same process can be put to work in sales. You don't have to give the prospect all the details. To try to do so will actually **lessen** your effectiveness, and it might bore the prospect! Another benefit of using "Missing Words" is that you will have much more selling energy, as you won't have to try to think of "everything" to say on each sales call.

Let's examine two brief sales presentations, one with detailed information and the other using "Missing Words." A word about the prospect and product: The prospect is an individual who is not technically oriented, but is interested in buying a home computer *to write letters and do simple word processing.* Which presentation do you think might be more effec:ive with this individual:

**"This computer, which runs on MS DOS, has serial and parallel ports, a Winchester hard disk and a 9600 baud modem, seems like something that would fit your needs."**

or

**"I think you'll be really happy with this computer because it will help you write wonderful letters and reports and it will check the spelling too!"**

In the first statement, the salesperson is showing off his technical knowledge—and is wasting energy with his long-winded technical statements. The prospect is probably thinking, "What is this person talking about? I don't even understand the words he is using, let alone what those gizmos are supposed to do."

In the second sales presentation, which uses "Missing Words," the prospect is communicated with on a more humanistic and respectful level. The prospect can fill in whatever details he needs—or ask for additional information. In the second example, the client is being addressed using his own words, which is much more effective than talking to him in a highly detailed technical language.

When a sales pro uses "Missing Words," the customer actually conducts an automatic mental search to fill in the missing information. Because the information the customer provides comes from his or her own personal experience, from his or her **"view of the world"**, it will be maximally relevant....a perfect fit. And, "Missing Words" give the listener the experience that he and the salesperson are on exactly the same wavelength. *That's a good feeling.*

## Profiting from "-ly" Hypnotic Words

"-ly" hypnotic words can be recognized by their "ly" endings. These include "obviously," "apparently," "certainly," and "clearly." Let's look at how these "-ly words" are used in hypnosis:

> "You **obviously** know how to relax, and it is **clearly** your right and privilege to enjoy relaxation. **Apparently**, you have been having some stress in your life, and now it is time to let all of that go. **Certainly**,you know how to day-dream and how to go to sleep at night. Hypnosis is as easy as that and **obviously** it takes no effort...at all...and now you can **gently** let your eyes begin to close...as you **softly** drift off..."

The patient begins to drift off into a pleasant hypnotic state as his mind fills in the blanks in the hypnotist's beautifully mysterious delivery. "-ly words" are a specialized form of "Missing Words." *What is missing?* The reference points. Let's look more carefully at the example above. "Obviously" is an "-ly word" that leaves out what makes it obvious. In "clearly," the missing information is "clear" compared to what? The customer also fills in the details on "apparent" compared to what? "Certain" compared to what? The customer's mind will automatically fill in these details. There is no need for you to provide all of these details.

Look carefully at this sales presentation made by Larry Halpern, a star salesperson in the insurance industry:

> **"Obviously, I wouldn't be telling you this if it wasn't important. Clearly, the cash buildup in this policy cannot match what you could earn in a money-market fund. But—just as obviously, insurance can do things for you and your family that no money market fund could ever do."**

Notice that Larry never clarifies what makes these statements "obvious" or "clear." *But, the customer feels what is being said is important and he pays more attention.* The client supplies the missing, or deleted, information from his or her own experiences, from his or her own "view of the world." The information the customer supplied to himself fit perfectly. *Larry made the sale.* We know, because he sold the insurance policy to one of the authors of this book!

## Using "Frozen Words" to Motivate Your Customers to Buy

If used properly, some words can actually "freeze" a customer's thinking.

In using "Frozen Words," you can take processes (such as thinking or emotions) and turn them into fixed events (such as "decisions"):

| | |
|---|---|
| Customer: | **My thinking is that I am not ready to buy that equipment today.** |
| Salesperson: | **What is your thought *as to when you will be ready to make a decision to buy?*** |

Now, notice what the sales pro has done here. The customer is in the process of thinking about buying the product. *Such thinking can go on for a long time.* The salesperson moves the customer from thinking about the purchase to the final thought to buy it. The customer's "thinking" is being frozen into a decision. Knowing how to use "Frozen Words" can save a great deal of time and energy in selling.

Hypnotists will sometimes "freeze" words so that patients can own feelings of comfort and self-confidence. For many people, including salespeople, self-confidence is a fleeting thing. It is here one moment and gone the next. The hypnotist can freeze self-confidence by turning it from a constantly changing feeling into a concrete thing:

| | |
|---|---|
| Patient: | **"I was feeling nervous and insecure."** |
| Therapist: | **"What would enable you to have lots and lots of self-confidence?"** |

When the patient talks about feelings (which are constantly changing), the therapist freezes this as a quantity (lots and lots) of a thing (self-confidence). The thing (self-confidence) is something the patient can possess and own. It is much more permanent and lasting than fleeting feelings.

## How to Unfreeze a Customer's Decision Not to Buy

We've seen an example of how hypnotists and salespeople can freeze the words and actions of customers. However, what if the customer is already using "Frozen Words" which the salesperson doesn't like? Skilled salespeople "unfreeze" the words. Let's look at an example of how this is done.

Customer:          **"The decision I have made prevents me from engaging in any further negotiations."**

In this case, the prospect, a medical doctor, took a process (decision-making), and turned it into a fixed hard thing: a decision! The salesperson, a top X-ray sales professional working for Toshiba Medical Systems, unfroze the decision by immediately turning it back into a process:

Sales pro:          **"What were the most important factors you considered while you were deciding?"**

When the doctor talked about these factors, he unfroze his thinking. The sales pro took a hard, fixed thing, "a decision," and turned it back into a fluid process of "deciding." A decision is hard to change. "Deciding" is an on-going process. By changing "a decision" to "deciding," the X-ray salesman un-froze the client's thinking.

The physician prospect went on to give the salesman the information needed to get the doctor to reconsider his decision. The doctor talked about what went into his "deciding," and what his buying criteria are. The salesperson learned that the doctor was not totally convinced he had made the right decision. *After the Toshiba salesman learned the doctor's buying criteria, he then showed the doctor how Toshiba could far exceed the doctor's standards and criteria.* By doing this, the salesperson capitalized on the doctor's process of "deciding." Once he got "THE DECISION" out of the way, the doctor was able to consider new information. He got the sale.

We identified dozens of ways he and other top salespeople at Toshiba were able to "unfreeze" words, and actually un-hypnotize doctors who seemingly had already made their minds up. We then organized these and other persuasive messages into sales scripts. These "how to unfreeze decisions" scripts were taught to Toshiba's new X-ray and CT scanner salespeople. *The result was that in a matter of weeks, new salespeople were at a level of effectiveness that had previously taken months to attain.* The new salespeople had mastered the words and strategies of the most successful salespeople.

## Selecting Vague Verbs for a More Powerful Presentation

Hypnotists use "Vague Verbs" when they talk about actions people can take. Let's say you are in a hypnotic trance and that you are seeing two people approaching one another. Rather than specifying that the people "ran quickly" towards each other or that they "slowly walked" towards each other, the hypnotist uses vague verbs and says:

> **"The two people approached one another, and they got closer and closer to one another and . . . "**

The hypnotist leaves all the details up to your imagination. If you want to see them running towards one another, that's what you will see. If you want to see them crawling towards one another, you'll see that. *You will see what is most meaningful to you.*

"Vague Verbs" indicate action, but they do not limit the kind or type of action. They are patently ambiguous and, as a result, they give the prospect the freedom to come up with exactly the specifics he or she most needs. For example, study this sentence used by one sales superstar in describing a sale:

> **"After buying the tax shelter, the man went home, and he went to sleep."**

No information is given as to how the man bought the tax shelter, how he went home, or how he went to sleep. Upon hearing this sentence, a prospect would not be certain whether the man bought the tax shelter in haste or slowly; whether he walked, ran or drove home; or whether he went to sleep quickly and easily or with great difficulty.

Here is another sales sentence used by the sales superstar Pat Knowles. After saying it, he pauses and looks directly into the prospect's eyes:

> **"The man drove to work. He used to hate to drive to work. He hated spending all that money on gasoline. He especially hated it when the price of gas went up. But, now that he owns one of our oil and gas producing properties, he enjoys his drive to work. In fact, he is happy every time oil prices increase. It means he is making more money. Would you like to be happy every time energy prices increase?"**

Pat Knowles used "Vague Verbs" throughout his presentation to give his prospect room to imagine other details. How many "Vague Verbs" can you find in this example? Knowles does not say how the man drove to work. Was it quickly or slowly, or in-between? What kind of car did he drive to work in? He used to hate to drive to work? Why did he hate to drive to work?

Knowles fills in just enough detail to complete the picture and to increase the arousal of the prospect. Then, he is silent. *He lets the prospect tell him exactly how he feels about energy prices. He lets the prospect tell him about the taxes he pays.* Knowles uses this information to craft a solution to the prospect's tax problems. If there is no tax problem, Knowles goes on to another millionaire. If there is a tax problem, Knowles solves it. That is "sales magic," and it is hard to resist.

In our work with AT & T Information Systems, we have found that some of their top salespeople use reassurance statements such as:

> **"This PABX telephone system will fit in perfectly in your operation."**

They make use of many Vague Verbs such as "fit in." *What does it mean to have the system "fit in"?* Will it fit in terms of size, function, price, expandability, color, or some other factor?

Did you notice the hypnotic "-ly word"? *In what ways* will the system "perfectly" fit in? The customer must search through his or her own perspectives to supply this information. The process of doing this mental search makes the sales presentation more personally meaningful. If you deny your customers the opportunity to personally customize your vague speech, you will put limits on their imaginations, and you will put limits on how much you can sell. They will always supply details that are more meaningful than any details you can supply.

You can rest assured that your customer will do a good job of filling in the "missing" information. If he has questions, he will ask them—and you should answer them like a true expert. If she wants more information, she will ask for it. You can then give the customer exactly the information he or she is most interested in. Everyone wins. Everyone gets what he or she wants. Everyone saves time. Communication and excitement are facilitated. You get the sale.

## Secrets of Comparative Hypnotic Words

*Comparative words effortlessly get the customer to make comparisons.* You can recognize these words, whether used by a sales pro or a hypnotist, by their "-er" endings: **faster, slower, fancier, lighter,** and **stronger** are examples. Comparative phrases can also be preceded by the words **"more"** or **"less,"** as in "costs less money," or "makes more units per hour." The words encourage the listener to make an instantaneous and easy comparison. Here's an example from a real clinical hypnosis session:

> "It is **better** to be relaxed than to be tense, and it is **more comfortable** to take a nap than to fight it, and it is **nicer** to float away into the clouds than to worry, and it is **quicker** to close your eyes than to wait for them to close, and it is **easier** to go into hypnosis than you ever imagined."

Notice that the induction begins with an undeniably truthful pacing statement: "It is better to be relaxed than tense." This starts to establish a yes-set of agreement. The next statement, "It is more comfortable to take a nap than to fight it," is also very hard to disagree with and so continues to build a climate of agreement. We next get into "picking up the pace" by using the leading statement, ". . . and it is nicer to float away into the clouds than to worry . . . " The comparative hypnotic words, which are highlighted in the above-example, combined with pacing and picking up the pace, build a climate of agreement, build trust, and move the listener into a more relaxed and free-floating state of mind. *Comparative hypnotic words are building blocks of conversational hypnosis.*

Jim Sweeney is one of the greatest multi-level marketing salesmen in the world. He was the top salesman for Cambridge Diet Foods and later for Genesis. Now, he is the President of his own company, Total Living Concepts. Jim became a multi-millionaire in less than two years through his ability to recruit and sell people on the idea of joining his multi-level marketing organization. *When giving an exciting recruitment speech to an auditorium of people, Jim hypnotically repeats comparatives:*

**"Cambridge is getting bigger, and bigger, and bigger and bigger and better and better and better and better, and why don't you join NOW???"**

Bigger than what? Better than what? People fill in the answers for themselves. What they come up with is more interesting than anything Jim could say. The proof of the effectiveness of Jim's presentations is that he has brought over 7,000 people in his organization! Notice that Jim also makes excellent use of hypnotic repetition and of the attention-focusing word "now" which he stretches out for added effect.


## Demonstrating Confidence through Hypnotic Absolutes

Words such as **"always," "never,"** or **"nothing"** imply that certain conditions are universal and unchanging. *They show self-confidence and confidence in the product.* Absolute Words imply finality. Use Absolute Words only when their use is justified.

Ericksonian hypnotists make skillful use of Absolute Words in inducing and deepening conversational hypnosis:

"It is always better to drop down into a comfortable trance than to resist it."

"There is never any reason to deny yourself the pleasure of exploring your dreams in hypnosis."

People who sit in this special hypnosis chair always find they drop down . . . deeply . . . into a restful hypnotic sleep."

Top salespeople know that the best time to use Absolutes is after they have built a good level of trust with their prospects. Don't open your presentations with Absolute Words. First concentrate on pacing and building trust and rapport. One you have done that, and once you have uncovered the client's true needs, propose your solutions, products and services. When your client has indicated which products or services he or she is most interested in, validate those choices by using absolute words:

"You have made an excellent selection. People are always happy with that model."

"That's a fine choice. You will never regret making this decision."

If you do not use Absolutes, you can induce doubt in the prospect's mind. The prospect will wonder about other products and the options they might offer. Which of these sentences is more persuasive to you:

"You won't find many systems that can do what this one can,"

or

"There is nothing out there that can perform like this system."

Top salespeople not only use Absolutes, they also listen for Absolutes that customers use. When a customer uses Absolute Words, the highly skilled sales professional responds with comments that bring the customer's Absolute back down to Earth. Top salespeople take the "absolute power" away from Absolute Words customers use, if these words might interfere with the sale. The following example illustrates how this is accomplished.

## The One-Step Method to Successfully Handle Customer Absolutes

Andre is one of the top sellers of Sharp photocopy machines in the country. Occasionally, some of the prospects he calls upon use Absolute Words and say, "I would never buy a Japanese product!" What would you say if you were faced with such an absolute statement?

Andre arches an eyebrow, smiles slightly, looks directly at the prospect, and in an exaggerated one-word question says "Never???"

Andre then asks a series of simple questions to un-do the power of the absolute statement.

| | |
|---|---|
| Andre: | "Do you have a camera?" |
| Client: | "Yes." |
| Andre: | "Where was it made? |
| Client: | "Germany, I think." |
| Andre: | "Where was your television set made?" |
| Client: | "OK. That was made in Japan." |
| Andre: | "What kind of car do you drive?" |
| Client: | "A Ford." |
| Andre: | "How about your wife? What kind of car does she drive?" |
| Client: | "A Toyota." |
| Andre: | "Do you own a microwave oven?" |
| Client: | "Yes." |
| Andre: | "Do you know where it was made?" |
| Client: | "The Far East, I guess." |
| Andre: | "And how about your VCR?" |
| Client: | "OK. I see your point." |
| Andre: | "It is an important point. We all use many foreign products each day. We drink coffee made from coffee beans grown in foreign countries. We eat fruit and vegetables grown in other countries. We enjoy wine from |

> France and Italy. Many of our cars, comput-
> ers, VCR's, televisions, stereos, and other pos-
> sessions are made in foreign countries. Lots
> of our clothing and furniture is made in other
> countries. The point I am making is that we
> all use many foreign products. Why, all of a
> sudden, are you applying a different standard
> to my product? Is that fair? Aren't you will-
> ing to take an open-minded look at what
> Sharp photocopiers offer your business?"

Andre knows how to take the absolute power out of Absolute
Words. It doesn't take long before the prospect sees that his "absolute
position" ("I won't buy foreign products") is not so absolute at all. To
be fair, the prospect takes an unbiased look at what Sharp offers in
photocopiers. Andre has undone the power of the absolute word and is
one step closer to making the sale. It is no accident that he has risen to
the top in his sales field.

As a skill-building exercise, write down five Absolute Statements that
prospects use on you. They may be along the lines of:

**"I will never buy from your company."**

**"I will never pay the list price for anything!"**

**"I always get a discount."**

**"I never buy a new model."**

After you have identified the Absolute Statements your prospects
sometimes use to stymie you, write down your script for un-doing these
Absolutes. Practice un-doing these Absolutes now, before the pressure is
on. Craft out your very best responses and then practice those responses.
The next time a prospect tries to use these Absolute Statements on you, you
will have a wonderful persuasive response ready to use.

Remember that one of the very best ways of un-doing Absolute
Statements is to simply repeat back the absolute word to the prospect.
If the prospect says, **"I always get three estimates before I buy**

**anything,"** you can look directly at the prospect and say, **"Always?"** Stretch out the word "always," and raise your voice tone at the end to turn it into a question. Don't be surprised if the prospect has a response like, **"Well, not always, but almost always."** When the prospect says that, ask, **"When was the last time you bought something without getting 3 estimates?"**

You are now well on your way to making that sale. Find out why the prospect did not get three estimates on that previous purchase. Then, replay those circumstances as much as you can. If reassurances were given in the previous sale—give those reassurances if you can. If someone else encouraged him to make the decision to buy without 3 estimates, see if you can talk with that other person.

An excellent way of challenging Absolute Statements is to look for exceptions to the absolute. If your prospect says, "I always sleep on it before making my mind up," ask, "Have you ever made a decision to buy without sleeping on it?" Your prospect will almost certainly answer "yes." Find out how he did that and then replay the same logic or the same circumstances, if possible. This will increase the odds that he'll be able to make a decision today—without sleeping on it.

Whenever you hear an absolute such as "never," or "always" or "nothing," look for the exception by asking, "Has there ever been a time when....you made an exception to that rule?" If you have done a good job of building trust, your prospect will admit there have been times when he has made an exception. When you know how and why he made the exception, you will know how to get him to make the exception again today.

## How to Use Superwords Like a Sales Superstar

Superwords or superlatives can be recognized by their "-est" endings, such as in **"fastest"** or **"strongest,"** and by phrases that include the words **"most"** or **"least."**

When used by the master salesperson or hypnotist, these Superwords *leave out* the information that specifies why or how a product or service or process is the fastest or strongest. The customer goes on a mental search through his own belief system, and fills in the "missing" information based on his needs.

In this example from a session with a top medical hypnotist, we have placed the Superwords in bold type:

"The **easiest** way for you to drop deeply into hypnosis is also the **simplest**: sit deeply in the chair, and imagine that your body is melting, like warm butter melting in a frying pan. All of your **deepest** tensions are melting away, melting, melting away. That is the **fastest** way for you to go down, down, down, into the **best** hypnosis you have ever experienced."

To the patient, this induction fits perfectly with what he is experiencing. This is no surprise because the patient fills in all the missing parts.

In sales, Superwords are equally powerful, but they must not be overused. Never say something you sell is the fastest, the cheapest, or the most reliable—*unless it really is*. If your product or service is the best in some area, make the most of it. Don't assume your prospect knows all the ways your product is the best. Remember, your prospect cannot read your mind! Make the superiority of your product or service clear with Superwords. Master salesmanship is no place for false modesty.

## How to Send Compelling Messages through Hidden Commands

An important part of the persuasion process is the use of *friendly* commands hidden in sentences. This does not mean that the customer is forced to do anything. The command is presented on a more *subtle* basis, and it is not perceived as a command. Instead, *the customer hears it as a powerful subconscious suggestion*. The hidden command may be further emphasized by a shift in the tone of the speaker's voice.

Here are some examples of the use of hidden commands in conversational hypnosis. The hidden action command is highlighted in bold:

"It is very relaxing to, **Tom, close your eyes.**"

"It is simple to, **Mary, begin breathing deeply.**"

Notice that the name of the patient is placed near the middle of the sentence, and directly before the hidden action command. The sentence does not have as much emotional impact if the name is placed elsewhere in the sentence. Compare the following two sentences:

"It is very relaxing to, **Tom, close your eyes.**"

and

"Tom, it is very relaxing to close your eyes."

While these two sentences have the same intellectual or semantic meaning, they hit the listener on different psychological levels. The second sentence sounds like an ordinary sentence, whereas the first sentence, containing the hidden action command, is much more compelling.

When strings of hidden action command sentences are used in conversational hypnosis, a patient can drift into the hypnotic state without any effort or awareness he is doing so.

Hidden action commands work in a similar way in sales. They are "invisible" yet compelling. While the conscious mind does not recognize them, they work on the subconscious mind. In these examples from the field of computer sales, the hidden commands have been placed in capital letters:

"**Just think how much easier all of your work will be if you, MR. JONES, BUY THIS COMPUTER.**"

"**You'll be amazed how much more work you'll get done when you PUT THIS COMPUTER ON YOUR DESK.**"

"**You will see that your employees will be far more productive if YOU, MR. JONES, TAKE ADVANTAGE OF THIS HARDWARE AND SOFTWARE PACKAGE.**"

Notice that you can turn an ordinary suggestion into a hidden action command by either placing the customer's name directly before the hidden command, or by inserting the word "you" before the hidden action command. You can also place both the word "you" and the customer's name directly before the hidden action command, as shown above.

*When properly used, no one ever objects to hidden commands.* Prospects and customers hear them only on a subconscious level, rather than a conscious level. The overall effect is that they feel motivated or compelled to take action, and to make the purchase, without feeling pushed. Try using some hidden action commands later today. You can construct hidden commands by inserting the word "you" or your customer's name in the middle of a sentence, *directly before a suggested action.* Your experience will quickly prove to you that this type of sentence encourages customers to make purchase decisions.

Another fine way of using a hidden action command is to tell a story in which one of the characters in the story gives the hidden action command. If you think back over your sales experiences, you can probably remember a number of sales in which customers made statements which you can now repeat as hidden action commands. Here is an example. Let's say you are selling homes and you want your client to make an offer on a brand new listing. Rather than directly telling or ordering the client to make an offer, you can use a hidden action command in story form by saying:

> "A couple of months ago, I was showing a beautiful home to a young couple. They had been looking at homes for months, but couldn't find anything they liked that was in their price range. When we finally found a home they really wanted, they delayed in placing an offer. The next day, it was sold. We had to keep looking for 3 more weeks until we found another wonderful home that they could afford. This time, the wife looked at me and said, **'Let's make an offer today.'** They made an offer that very day and got the house of their dreams."

As you say the hidden action command, **"Let's make an offer today,"** look directly into your client's eyes. Say the words slowly and with resonance in your voice. It is safe to give extra emphasis to this command because you are not saying it. The character in the story is saying it! However, your client will hear the hidden action command loud and clear on a subconscious level. He might later even think *it is his own idea* to make an offer on the house today.

Action commands that are hidden in stories are one of the most subtle and powerful ways of influencing prospects. You can have a character in a story say things and make suggestions which might be very difficult or impossible for you to suggest directly. Also, you can have different characters in a story give different hidden action commands. The best stories are the ones that are truthful and based on your own experiences. Think back over your many sales experiences and remember the words of customers that you can now use in hidden action commands to get more sales today. The number of hidden action commands you use and the range of hidden action commands you use is limited only by your memory and your imagination.

**Trance Words**: Some words seem to have a special power to induce a trancelike state of focused attention and relaxation in a listener. These include such words as "wonder," "puzzle," "understand," "curious," "amaze," and "awaken." When these Trance Words are pronounced in a deeper, more resonant voice, they acquire extra power. An example from hypnosis:

> **"As you drop into hypnosis, you may begin to wonder how you can better understand the curious sensation of comfort and relaxation you are experiencing more and more."**

And, an example from sales:

> **"When you use this software program, you will be amazed and enchanted at its power and speed ."**

As a skill-building exercise, write down ten mesmerizing sales sentences you can use which contain the trance words "**wonder**," "**puzzle**," "**understand**," "**curious**," "**amaze**," and "**awaken**." Start by putting only one trance word in each sentence. Later, practice working two trance words into each sentence. Here are some examples to get you started:

> **"You may wonder** how we can offer such a sophisticated piece of electronics equipment for so little money."

> **"It is a puzzle** how some of our competitors can stay in business."

"It feels great to be able to fully **understand** how this works . . . "

"He was **curious** about why so many of his business associates had purchased our system . . . "

"She was **amazed** at all the new options we offered . . . "

"This new system **awakened** a new level of productivity in his people."

"They were totally **enchanted** with this product."

"They were **entranced** with this new system."

"I think you will be **hypnotized** by this new car—it is so beautiful!"

As the last three examples show, you can use words directly taken from the world of hypnosis, such as "enchanted," "entranced" and "hypnotized." Upon hearing these words, prospects and customers will begin to experience, on a subconscious level, some aspects of the mesmerization. They may not know why, but they will find your sales presentations fascinating. Few salespeople know how to use these trance words. Use them to add extra sparkle and magnetism to your presentations.

## Using the Element of Surprise to Open a Closed Mind

Putting words together in such a way as to mildly surprise the customer is a very effective persuasion tool. *It is especially effective in breaking the habitual mind sets.*

All of our thoughts and actions, including the decision to buy something, are the products of our frames of mind. And, underlying these mind sets are some strong mental habits. As a result, the ability to alter a person's habitual mind set can mean the difference between making or losing the sale.

A clinical example illustrates the power of surprise in breaking habitual mind sets. Most overweight people are constantly "reminded" by family and friends to lose weight. Unfortunately, these helpful reminders and hints often have the opposite effect. They increase the individual's stress level, and the person ends up eating more to comfort himself and temporarily lower the stress.

When going to a therapist, the overweight person might expect to be again "reminded" of how terrible it is to be overweight, and how important it is to lose weight. However, an overweight patient who went to see the eminent Dr. Erickson would have his or her expectations confounded upon hearing Erickson say, **"Before we can begin treatment, I want you to gain 20 or 30 more pounds. That way I'll know that you truly do have some control over your weight."** This approach can literally surprise the person out of the mind set that has been preventing the weight loss all along.

Sales champions have several approaches that apply a surprise technique to *unfreeze* a client's habitual mind set. The result is that the customer becomes more receptive to the information presented after the surprise. For example, one highly successful door-to-door salesman we know takes two steps backward whenever a prospective client opens the door. This technique is totally surprising to the would-be client, and the reaction is to open the door wider, and even step outside in order to hear what is being said!

A top computer salesman we worked with a few years ago has a very interesting surprise technique. When approached by prospective clients he tells them that he absolutely will not sell them a computer. In fact, that is the first statement out of his mouth!

*This is totally surprising to the customer*. Most customers enter the store with a combination of computer phobia and a fear of spending too much money. His surprising opening statement gets them to relax, and sometimes even to smile. Many will ask, **"Why won't you sell me a computer?"**

His answer is **"I'm not sure that you need one."** With that, the customers typically try to convince him that they do. A conversation is going! He learns about all their needs and wants. He also concentrates on building trust and rapport. When he makes a recommendation for a specific computer or printer, it is likely to be right on target. And since he avoided resistance from the very start of his presentation, he has built a climate of agreement. His refreshing and somewhat surprising way of *opening* the sale contributes greatly to his *closing* so many sales.

## How to Let Your Product Talk and Sell Itself

Hypnotists frequently make use of metaphors, parables, and stories to influence clients and imbed hidden messages. Sometimes they will even have an inanimate object in the story "talk" to the patient. The hypnotist may have a rock, a tree, or a hill "say" something to the patient:

**"And now, as you go deeper and deeper into hypnosis, you will find yourself walking down a trail in a mountain meadow. Up ahead, you can see a tall redwood tree. As you approach this tree, you can hear it talking to you . . . "**

Master salespeople also know ways of literally making their products talk. "Talking Products" is a special technique that is a form of hypnotic surprise. You can also use it to imbed commands.

An example of the Talking Products Technique is given by John Ackerele, a top salesman for Jonathan Forbes Realtors in Northridge, California. John sometimes makes houses talk by telling his client, **"This house told me that it has been looking for a loving family for a long time."** Clients usually smile and warm up upon hearing this statement. And they start to "see" the house as a family home. The fact that a house obviously cannot "speak" or "look" is what gives this sentence its surprise value and its pizzazz.

This type of imagery (a "talking house") will often touch people in a way that ordinary sales presentations can't. A talking product seems friendly and unthreatening. The image is so mesmerizing that it is *easier for the client to recall.*

In addition to making your products talk, you can give them other human qualities. If your prospect fears the technology employed in your product, you can warm him or her to the product by giving it some human characteristics. *Which of the following sentences do you find more compelling:*

**"This computer system is easy to use,"**

or

**"This computer system will hold your hand as you are learning how to use it."**

In addition to giving your product human abilities, you can even give it emotions. You can make it "happy," "sad," "perplexed," "angry," "lonely," or you can have it experience any other emotion that will help you get the sale.

Use the "Talking Products" technique creatively. *If you sound like every other average salesperson, how can you expect to sell more than the average salesman?* "Talking Products" is a fresh, new, unique way of making presentations and of selling. Adding just a few "Talking Products" sentences to your presentation will add sparkle to your speech and will create a lasting positive impression.

## Word Power Revisited

You have just learned some of the most powerful word patterns in the English language. We hope you have found this excursion through the land of hypnotic language interesting and enjoyable. You have met hot words, attention-focusing statements, "-ly" hypnosis words, vague verbs, trance words and many of the other powerful verbal tools of top salespeople. The more you practice using these tools, the more skillful and successful you will become in your business and personal life. This is a great opportunity and we hope you'll make the most of it!

You are now ready to learn how to use sales stories and metaphors—*perhaps the most powerful hypnotic techniques of all.* Stories, metaphors and parables have been used for thousands of years by religious leaders and politicians to influence entire nations and to change human history. While stories and metaphors have been used for many years by top salespeople, this important skill has never been covered in conventional sales training books or tapes. *Why?*

In the past, it was assumed that the ability to tell stories was innate or intuitive. The assumption was, "Some people have it, but most people don't." This assumption discouraged attempts to teach the powerful art of story-selling.

With new tools provided by the science of psycholinguistics (the science of language), many more people can now master the art *and science* of story-selling. You will learn how to develop this wonderful power in the following chapter.

# 6

## Capitalizing On The Persuasive Powers Of Sales Stories And Metaphors

How would you sell someone on the idea of working very hard for many months to build the foundations of a business? Some of your competitors are saying, "Building a business in this field is easy. You can do it. Anyone can do it. It is a breeze. No sweat." Is that appealing?

The people who are recruited sign up with false hopes and expectations. They quit in frustration when the easy money is not forthcoming.

Some of your other competitors take a very different approach. They state flat out, "Building the business is a lot of hard work. Very few people can do it. Of the 30 people in this room, probably only two or three of you could make it in a business like this!" They don't bother to romance people. They try to hit them with the "cold, hard truth." Would this approach work with you? After hearing this, would you want to work for the business?

While it is more honest, that second approach scares most people away. No one wants to sign up. They think they will be one of the failures. What will you do? How will you recruit people to join your organization?

Jim Sweeney, the multi-level marketing genius, faced this challenge. Jim believes in being completely truthful and also in romancing and motivating his people. **He uses sales stories** to encourage hundreds of people every year to start their own multi-level marketing businesses:

> "In order to explain building this business to you, I'm going to draw a building. The most important factor in a building is the foundation. Building a business is just like building a building. Exactly the same kinds of things apply. The hardest work you may very well do on a building is in the foundation. It may even take a good portion of your time, if not most of your time. It's the dirtiest part of the work you are going to do. It's the part that one day will be covered up and nobody will ever see and one day somebody will forget all about it. But, nevertheless, the building stands on the foundation. It either stands or crumbles on the foundation. Let me show you how to build a strong foundation that will stand the test of time . . . "

People know Jim is telling the truth. They trust him. Building the foundation is the dirtiest and hardest part of the work. But, it is also exciting! And, Jim Sweeney shows them how to do it right!

If people ever get discouraged in building that business, they think back to building a building. *They are building a skyscraper!* This inspiring image has given many people the strength to go on. When you can see the goal of the beautiful finished building, the hard work and the struggle seem worthwhile.

Jim has become a multi-millionaire (and he has helped many other people become rich) by using these word pictures. And, stories and metaphors work just as well in selling computers or real estate or cars or factory machinery as they do in multi-level marketing.

## Understanding the Hidden Advantages of Stories and Metaphors

Stories and metaphors play an all-important role in hypnosis and in master salesmanship. The story does not have to be long. *Some of the best ones we have heard are only 4 or 5 sentences long.* We've never met or studied or worked with a true sales champion who did not make extensive use of sales stories, metaphors and analogies.

Metaphors, stories and anecdotes are a very rich source of powerful techniques to influence other people. If well told, *they are inherently enjoyable and interesting to the customer.* **Stories can contain hidden action commands.** A character in a story can make a suggestion that the salesperson might not dare make directly.

In addition, events in a story or metaphor can remind the customer of similar enjoyable experiences that he or she has had in the past. By doing so, they make the message of the story far more interesting to the customer. Stories can artistically incorporate all the most powerful forms of hypnotic selling. By doing all of this, stories and metaphors open up a vast higher level of salesmanship beyond the daily mundane citing of features and benefits.

Stories can help you sell products without talking directly about the products. Hypnotists use stories and metaphors in dealing with delicate subjects that should not be approached directly. Dr. Milton Erickson was famous for his ability to use hypnosis to stop childhood bed-wetting in cases that had defied every other type of treatment. Parents of these children had tried bribing their children to stop the bed-wetting; they had tried punishing their children; they had tried talking their children out of it, and they tried waiting it out. Erickson would build trust with the child and not even talk about bed-wetting. He would then use conversational hypnosis and would make "parallel interventions," using hobbies or other interests in his metaphors.

One of Erickson's patients was a 12-year old boy who had been wetting the bed for several years. Erickson told the parents to leave and then proceeded to have a nice conversation with the young man. He learned that the boy enjoyed playing baseball. This boy had a brother with whom he was very competitive. His brother played football.

Erickson used indirect hypnosis to help the boy achieve a relaxed, light hypnosis state. Erickson then described the fine muscle coordination it takes to play baseball. He contrasted this to the gross muscle movements that are used in football. The boy was fascinated by Erickson's descriptions of all the fine muscle movements that are required to catch a ball and to throw a baseball. When describing the fine muscle movements necessary to catch the ball, Erickson said that the glove has to be open at just the right moment and that the muscles then have to all coordinate to clamp down a split second later. Then, when throwing the ball, it has to be released at just the right time, or it doesn't go where you want it to go. Doing all of this right is something you can take great pride in. And, if you don't let the ball go at just the right time, Erickson said, it can lead to frustration. Letting go at just the right time gets it where you want it to go, and that's what leads to success.

The parents were amazed that their son suddenly and miraculously stopped wetting the bed. He took great pride in the fine muscle control that it took to control one's bladder. Erickson's wonderful metaphor, which never directly referred to bed-wetting, made the cognitive changes in the young man which enabled the physical changes to take place. If you read back through this metaphor, you can see the "parallel interventions" that made it so successful!

This example from Erickson's work clearly has a visual component. It is likely that the young man saw pictures in his mind of baseball, and perhaps also of bedwetting, as Erickson told the story. In a similar way, many sales stories and anecdotes have a visual quality that lets the listener recall them long after the sales presentation has been completed. Good stories can act as long-lasting posthypnotic suggestions.

Are we implying that sales stories and metaphors do more than just entertain the customer? Absolutely.

Stories and metaphors have long been known to be a highly effective means of instructing and informing people. In fact, that's the definition of a metaphor: a story that instructs and informs. Metaphor is from the Greek "pherein," which means "to carry," and from "meta," which means "beyond." A metaphor gives us the ability to carry an understanding or knowledge beyond its original context ... into a new one. A metaphor gives us the ability to carry something we learned in one area to another area of our life. Stories help the listener gain increased **insight** and **understanding** of whatever is being talked about. They help the customer to better understand and appreciate the product, by using knowledge the customer has gained of something else.

Moreover, *the customer tends to mold the story or metaphor* to fit his or her own experiences and needs. *The result is that the story has greatly increased personal meaning and significance.* When Jim Sweeney talks about building a "building," the people in his audience don't see just any building. **They see a building they like and admire!** For some people, it may be a skyscraper, for others a warm cottage in the woods. What kind of building do you see?

The story or metaphor throws a new light on what is being communicated. It may throw a **magnifying** light on something you want the customer to see and understand in greater detail. It may apply a **shadow** to something that you want to stay mysterious and exciting. It may apply a **laser light** on something, perhaps a fear, that you want to destroy!

A machine shop owner who desperately needed some life insurance was complaining about how much the insurance would cost. *Several insurance agents had tried unsuccessfully to sell him low-priced policies.* They had shown him rate cards and explained how insurance costs were based on the life expectancy tables. The prospect still wouldn't buy. Obviously, a fresh new approach was needed. What would you do in this situation?

The salesman who got the business told the following metaphor.

Salesman:        **"When you started your business, *you proba-
                 bly bought the cheapest tools available*, didn't
                 you?"**
Prospect:        **"Yes."**

| | |
|---|---|
| Salesman: | "And, they probably wore out and broke pretty quickly, right?" |
| Prospect: | "Yep." |
| Salesman: | "Then, you had to go out and spend extra money to buy what you probably should have bought in the first place." |
| Prospect: | "That's right." |
| Salesman: | "Well, *life insurance is the same way.* If you don't buy quality and if you don't buy what you really need, you end up paying much more in the long run." |
| Prospect: | "Maybe so." |
| Salesman: | "Also, I've noticed that you drive a Cadillac." |
| Prospect: | "Yes." |
| Salesman: | "You are obviously a man who appreciates quality." |
| Prospect: | "I guess so." |
| Salesman: | "Then, why are you scrimping now?" |
| Prospect: | "What do you mean? You mean on this life insurance?" |
| Salesman: | "It isn't like you to scrimp. That isn't like you. Would you want to go to a lawyer who charged $15 dollars an hour?" |
| Prospect: | "Of course not." |
| Salesman: | "Would you go to a doctor who charged $100 per operation?" |
| Prospect: | "Of course not!" |
| Salesman: | "Well then, why should you buy low quality insurance? Doesn't your family deserve the best protection there is?" |
| Prospect: | "I guess so." |

This life insurance pro used metaphors about: tools, cars, legal services and medical services. These brief story elements got the sale where nothing else had worked.

## Knowing When to Use Sales Stories

When should you use stories? Most top salespeople use them throughout the entire sales process. *Don't reserve your stories for use only at the end of your sales call.* They can serve as powerful openers, as ways of demonstrating product benefits, and as closers.

Let's look at some of the different types of sales stories. By learning the different varieties of sales stories, you'll see how you can use each type more precisely and strategically to influence and motivate people to buy.

## The Ten Most Powerful Types of Sales Stories

1. **Introductory Stories:** Stories about who I am, why I am here, and how I have helped other people and other businesses.
2. **Attention-Grabbing Stories:** To get people to pay attention to you and your products. Dramatic stories. These stories tell them why they should listen to you.
3. **Product-Information Stories:** Instead of simply listing all the features and benefits of your products, you can imbed this information in a fascinating story.
4. **Stories to Overcome Fears:** Show how other people had the same fears the customer has and how they learned there was no reason to worry.
5. **Money-Stories:** Showing people how they can afford your products or services. Show them how your product or service will help them make money or save money.
6. **Ego-Enhancement Stories:** To show how owning your product has increased your customer's self-confidence, pride and self-esteem. Show how other people respect and look up to people who own your product or who use your service.
7. **Improved Productivity Stories:** To show how your products or services have helped companies increase their efficiency, reduce down-time, increase output and decrease errors and flaws.

8. **Family-Togetherness Stories:** To show how your products or services have brought families closer together.
9. **Security Stories:** To show how your products have given people peace of mind, emotional security and financial security. Show how your stories help people get a good night's sleep.
10. **Closing Stories:** To summarize all the benefits of your products, wrap up the sale and get the order!

As a skill-building exercise, write down at least two stories for each of the above categories. Feature your own products or services in the stories. You need at least two of each type of story so that you will have a choice. Also, having a variety of powerful stories to select from helps to keep your work interesting, as it prevents boredom. Who wants to say the same thing over and over again?

Companies such as Shopsmith have powerful script books full of stories for every occasion and every sales step. In selling their expensive wood-working tools, Shopsmith has found that Money Stories, Ego-Enhancement Stories, and Family Togetherness Stories are particularly effective. These are proven stories that have been developed and used successfully by their top salespeople for several years. Shopsmith now teaches these fascinating sales stories to new salespeople as soon as they go to work for the company.

STORIES CAN OVERCOME OBJECTIONS AND UNFREEZE RESISTANCE. They can instruct, advise and imbed suggestions to the customers. Our studies have found that sales superstars place stories and metaphors strategically throughout their presentations. Whenever there is a hurdle to jump, a sales pro has just the story to do it!

Stockbrokers frequently have to deal with customers who procrastinate. The stockbroker has made a well-researched recommendation, and is expecting to get a sale when the client says, "I need more time to think about it." What would you do in a situation like this? Some less skilled salespeople will try to exert pressure at this point, and they are seldom effective. If anything, the high-pressure approach causes the client to show even more resistance.

Instead of the high pressure approach, one stockbroker we trained now reaches into his bag of stories and metaphors. He says:

"Picture yourself in an airport, looking up at the screen that says 'Departures.' You want to fly from New York to San Francisco. There is a flight that leaves one hour from now with a stop in Chicago, and there is a nonstop flight that leaves in three hours. You deliberate back and forth: should I take the early flight or the later nonstop? You walk around and think about it, and before you know it the early plane has taken off. The decision has been made for you—you did not make the decision. Time made it for you. You lost your opportunity!

*"We are in the same situation here today.* If you don't make a decision, *time will make the decision for you*—and you will lose the opportunity. Can't you make a decision today?"

This metaphor makes sense to many prospects. Not everyone buys, but most people are encouraged to make a decision one way or the other. The stockbroker gets more sales, and he saves time because he doesn't have to call customers back nearly as often.

## Understanding More Hidden Advantages of Stories and Metaphors

Metaphors and stories have several other advantages in salesmanship. Since stories are used naturally in everyday social interaction, people are comfortable with them. There is nothing new or mysterious about stories, and as a result, they do not make the customer suspicious. In fact, they do just the opposite—*stories relax customers*.

The second advantage of stories is their entertainment value. When skillfully told, stories develop good feelings in customers. Do you know a great story-teller? Isn't he or she a joy to be around? Think of your best friends. One of the reasons you enjoy spending time with them is that they entertain you and make you feel good with the stories they tell. Stories about their day, about their work, about their weekend, their family, their hobbies.

Movies are video stories. Novels are stories. Television series and situation comedies are stories. Americans spend several billion dollars each year on movies, novels and television. When you develop the ability to tell different types of stories, you have something that people are willing to pay a lot of money for!

We have found that one of the most popular aspects of our sales training programs are the stories we tell. Some corporations have used our services for many years. When we come back to do a "repeat performance," people in the audience will come up to us and say, "I remember that story you told 3 years ago. Whenever I am down, I think of that story and it gives me the inspiration to push on." We've even had some executives hire us to do keynote presentations and seminars based on a "story" they heard from another client. These stories are usually about how much more their sales-people can sell now that they have learned our modern persuasion techniques.

An executive called us recently to schedule a seminar for 18 months in the future. This is a very special seminar that will be held in Bali. He had heard from a competitor that our sales training was very powerful and that we were booked up for many, many months. This truthful story which one of his competitors told, encouraged him to call us immediately and then to send us a retainer check to reserve our time.

We were hired to do a nationwide training for a major annuities company in 1989. We were describing in detail to the senior sales executive how we would do a needs assessment, customize the program, do follow-up to guarantee an increase in sales, etc. when he interrupted us. "I've heard about your great stories," he said. "Use some of those same stories you used with _____ company." He didn't need to hear the rest of our proposal. He trusted us. He trusted our credentials and the research we had conducted. He just wanted to make sure we included the stories and the module on how to master hypnotic story-selling.

Because stories tend to be novel and innovative, they plant a lasting image in the customer's mind. Stories or metaphors can be about almost anything or anyone in the world. *No two metaphors are quite alike.* If properly told, a story can be virtually unforgettable. People who are 80 or 90 years old still remember stories they were told as children. A salesman has a real advantage when he can leave a clear and positive image of his product in the customer's mind. Hypnotic sales stories are the most elegant and powerful ways of doing that.

## How to Use the Seven Hypnotic Metaphor Techniques

Our studies have isolated seven hypnotic metaphor techniques used by sales superstars. Since you are probably already using metaphors and stories to some extent in your personal life, you should find it easy to go a step further in learning these seven specific hypnotic metaphor techniques.

## Motivating Customers through Physical Action Metaphors

One of the shortest and simplest metaphor techniques is the **Physical Action Metaphor.** You don't even have to tell a complete story. You can flash a vivid image that can become a one-sentence story. *Which example do you find more mesmerizing:*

**"You don't build any cash value with term insurance,"**

or

**"You are burning your money up every year with term insurance."**

In the second sentence, "burning your money up" is an example of the Physical Action Metaphor. It uses a vivid physical image instead of a bland, ordinary description. Can you see money burning up as you read this sentence?

The physical action metaphor can be used to shed new light on a product or to intensify benefits or weaknesses of that product. You can also use physical words or phrases to motivate a customer to take action.

Physical phrases do not have to be literally true to be effective. People grant you **"poetic license"** in using metaphors. However, they should be close to the truth and very exciting:

Let's say your prospect has told you he has already made his mind up to buy another product—and, he hasn't shopped around very much. Instead of saying, "Why not think about this decision a little longer?" you can use a Physical Action Metaphor and say, **"You're jumping the gun, aren't you?"**

Let's say your customer is delaying his decision. He is procrastinating. Instead of saying, "Why not make your mind up?" you can use a Physical Action Metaphor and say, **"Let's take the bull by the horns and do it, OK?"**

Let's say your customer wants to feel he is special. He wants a great price or a great deal. Instead of saying, "I can get you a good price," you can use a Physical Action Metaphor and say, **"I can get you a sweet deal!"**

Let's say your customer is hesitating. He is sitting on his hands. Instead of saying, "Why not make your mind up?" you can use a Physical Action Metaphor and say, **"Let's run with it, OK?"**

## How to Use Personal Metaphors to Engineer Agreement

The second metaphor technique, **The Personal Metaphor**, is one of the most frequently used tools of sales superstars. This technique involves a metaphor about the salesperson, his family or friends. Customers are often suspicious of salespeople. Many customers secretly wonder, "If this is so great, why don't you own it yourself." You can handle this issue very skillfully by using the Personal Metaphor:

**"I own this policy myself."**

**"If I could afford it, I would drive this car."**

**"I once lived on this street myself. Those were some of the happiest years of my life. I really love this neighborhood."**

Never say anything that isn't true. If you do own the product, make sure you tell the prospect. However, there is no reason to lie if you don't. The second metaphor above shows you a way of dealing with the issue of your not owning the product. What if you used to own the product, but you don't any longer? Use a metaphor like the third one above. Make sure you mention how happy you were when you owned that product, whether it is a home, computer, car, or any other product.

You can also use the personal metaphor to discuss very delicate issues, such as death.

> **"Say something happened to me, and I couldn't work anymore. What would I do?"**

> **"I really woke up to why I needed tax planning in 1988. The government kept more of my money than I kept. They kept all the dollar bills and I kept all the change. Have you ever felt that way?"**

> **"I know how you feel. I have felt that way many times myself. Do you know what I found?"**

It is interesting to note that Personal Metaphors often contain hidden action commands (which were discussed in the previous chapter):  In saying "I own this policy myself," the sales superstar placed extra emphasis on the words **"own this policy,"** and by doing so, *made a hidden action command to the customer.*

By stating, "Say something happened to me," the sales pro has made himself or herself the center of a story about personal difficulties or a personal tragedy. Without scaring the customer or endangering rapport, he brings up a scary subject. *While the customer might not want to listen to a scary story about himself, he can easily listen to the same story about someone else (the salesperson).* The same points get made in a safe way.

All of the sentences where a salesperson used himself or herself as a metaphor for the customer tend to minimize disagreement and resistance. And, if the customer does show any resistance, the salesperson has an easy and elegant way out by saying, **"I was talking about me; that wasn't about you."**

*An important note:* When telling stories about yourself, keep the stories truthful.

## Using "You Metaphors" to Capture and Redirect Customer Attention

When it is time to use stronger and more direct metaphors in order to lead a customer, call upon You Metaphors. Here are a few examples taken from the work of a top insurance salesman:

"Let's go into the future. The year is 1997, and you have a heart attack. If you have a heart attack, you'll still be able to buy this insurance."

"Let's look at something that happens somewhere in America everyday. You're crossing the street and someone hits you and ruptures your spleen..."

Here is an example of a You Metaphor, a story about the prospect, which was used by a real estate sales professional in Michigan:

"Let's say 2 years from now you want to buy this house and all the prices in this neighborhood have gone up dramatically—what are you going to do?"

The preceding examples were of You Metaphors which dealt with how to avoid or be prepared for *negative* events which might take place in the prospect's life. You Metaphors can also be used to create *positive* short stories the prospect can place himself or herself in:

"How would you feel driving down the street in this new Mercedes Benz, with all of your neighbors turning their heads to see you?"

You Metaphors are very powerful. You Metaphors are very effective tools for use with customers who are bored or who aren't paying much attention to your sales presentation. A "negative" You Metaphor can wake them up and rivet their attention. A "positive" You Metaphor can excite the emotions like nothing else.

## Building Customer Involvement
## through "Other People Metaphors"

In addition to using metaphors about yourself and about your customers, you can use **Other People Metaphors** to convey messages about other customers:

"And then, the farmer said to me, 'I think I need some of this mobile irrigation equipment.' He was right. In the big drought that came, he was the only one who could irrigate all his crops. He made a fortune while some other farmers in his area, tragically, went out of business."

You can even use Other People Metaphors to talk about other sales-people:

"A lot of other salesmen, if they heard me say this, would roll over in their graves."

You can use Other People Metaphors to handle objections. This Other People Metaphor is useful for dealing with *almost any* objection:

"Some of my best customers said that to me at one time. Do you know what they are telling me now? They are telling me that ..."

Other People Metaphors can also be crafted to convey messages about companies:

"Last July, a company like yours bought five of these machines. In August, that company got the biggest order in their history. They wouldn't have been able to handle it if they hadn't bought those five new machines!"

Why use Other People Metaphors? When talking about other people who have had misfortunes, the sales superstar is building the need for the product *in a safe way*. The effectiveness of Other People Metaphors is further enhanced when there is more equivalence between the content of the metaphor and the situation actually faced by the customer. With this "equivalent content," the customer will place himself or herself in the story you tell. *The customer will then have an even greater interest in the resolution of the story, and will be even more interested in the solutions (products and services) that you offer.*

One of the best ways of keeping this notion of equivalence in metaphors is to use a context and cast of characters in the metaphor that is nearly identical to what the customer is currently experiencing. By using your observational and listening skills, you will be able to gather all the information you need on the context and characters to remember the most effective metaphor for this customer.

If your prospect has four children, you can gain equivalence power in your metaphor if you use a story about a man with three, four, or five children. *You would lose equivalence power* if you tell a story about a man with one child. In this case, your prospect might think, "Well, that's different. He only has one child and I have four." You would also lose equivalence power if you tell a story about a man with eight children. Your prospect might think, "Well, that's different. He has eight children and I only have four. What works for his family might not work for mine."

Look for ways you can add more equivalence power to all of your Other People Metaphors. You can add equivalence in almost any variable of the story, including age of the characters, number of the characters, setting, time of year, location, size of business, number of employees, same size budget, etc. Almost any component of the sales story can gain equivalence power by matching it or nearly matching it to experiences or factors in your prospect's life or factors in his or her company.

One of the reasons that salespeople get more and more effective in their story-selling techniques as they gain experience is that they develop additional knowledge and additional memories of "equivalent variables" they can use in their Other People Metaphors. As a skill-building exercise, write down ten equivalent variables you can use in your sales stories to match or nearly match conditions your prospects and customers are facing.

## Increasing Customer Comfort Levels through "Familiar Person, Place and Things Metaphors" (FPPT Metaphors)

As you get to know the prospect better, you can use the fifth metaphor technique: **Familiar Person, Place and Thing Metaphors, or FPPT Metaphors:**

**"I know a man who looks just like you, and he said to me . . . "**

In talking about someone who looks "just like you," a chord of familiarity is struck. The metaphor thus gains equivalence power. You can also use a Familiar Person, Place or Thing Metaphor to draw connections between what you do for your loved ones and what the prospect may want to do for himself:

**"I started my son out with a car like this when he was about your age and . . . "**

**"When my parents were about the same age your parents are now, I bought them an all-expense paid cruise to Hawaii, just like this one. They said it was the greatest vacation they ever took!"**

The "thing," in a Familiar Person, Place or Thing Metaphor can be anything: an insurance policy, a car, a computer, a house, or even a fireplace:

**"Our house had an old brick fireplace like this one too, before we remodeled it. We replaced it with one of the new energy efficient fireplaces, and we are very happy with it."**

The "person," in a Familiar Person, Place or Thing Metaphor should be a famous or well-known person to get maximum effectiveness out of the story:

**"I'm sure you have heard of O.J. Simpson. We are all familiar with him. Well, did you know that our accounting firm does all his tax work? His advisors say we do a better job than any other firm O.J. has used."**

As a skill-building exercise, write down five Familiar Person, Place or Thing Metaphors you can use to sell your company's products or services. Why do FPPT Metaphors work so well? They are effective because people are comfortable with what they are familiar with. The reason we buy Tide detergent instead of brand X is that Tide is heavily advertised. We feel comfortable with it. After seeing hundreds of ads for Tide, when we see the box of Tide on the store shelf, it is like seeing an old friend! We buy it. By contrast, non-advertised brands look strange and unfamiliar. We don't buy them. Capitalize on the power of familiarity in your selling by using FPPT Metaphors.

## How to Use "Other Sales Metaphors" to Eliminate Customer Anxiety

The sixth metaphor technique is called the **Other Sales Metaphor.** It lowers sales resistance by reminding prospects that buying your product is like buying any other product. With Other Sales Metaphors, you create the feeling that since the prospect has bought things before, he can buy what you are selling:

> **"Buying a computer is like buying anything...it is no big deal. Let me show you what to look for."**

Other Sales Metaphors work because *they lower anxiety in customers*. Customers may feel that buying what you are selling is a new, unique or scary experience. You want to take that negative feeling away with an Other Sales Metaphor:

> **"I don't care if you're buying pencils, or penguins or bananas. The same principles apply."**

You can use Other Sales Metaphors to *flatter* the customer and to put him or her in a comfort zone about purchasing your products or services:

> **"You impress me as a smart shopper. You know how to evaluate products and how to buy things. Since you already know how to evaluate products, you won't have any trouble making a decision in this area."**

You can also use Other Sales Metaphors to inform a client that *making the decision to buy will not take a lot of time.* This use of Other Sales Metaphors can help cut down on procrastination by clients. Here is an Other Sales Metaphor used by Kenny Clyde, who is now a vice president for United Resources:

**"You don't have to be a rocket scientist to figure out what a great annuity this is. This will be one of the easiest and best decisions you have ever made, and I respect the fact that you have made a lot of decisions in your life. You can't go wrong. This annuity will guarantee you and your family a happy and secure retirement."**

You can also use Other Sales Metaphors to talk about the unique aspects of your company:

**"You're lucky. Not many businesses operate like we do any more. It used to be, when you went to the gas station, the more gas you bought, the less they'd charge you per gallon. You went to the grocery store, the more fruits or vegetables or meat you bought, the less they'd charge you per pound. Does that happen anymore? Well—in our business—we still offer those volume purchase discounts!"**

Besides telling *your own* Other Sales Metaphors, you can get prospects to tell you *their* Other Sales Metaphors. In telling you about his successful purchase decisions, *the prospect gets himself into more of a mood to buy today.* He remembers how competent he is in buying things. Also, you gain valuable information about his or her decision-making process. You can then use the Instant Replay Technique, discussed earlier in this book, to sell him in the way he has bought in the past. It is almost irresistible.

Here is an example of how one sales superstar, John Moss of Scheduling Corporation of America, gets prospects to tell him how they have made purchasing decisions in the past. John sells management consulting services for SCA, and he is so successful in his sales efforts that he has been single-handedly selling enough consulting work to keep over 70 consultants employed full-time in projects ranging all over America and Puerto Rico! Here is how John Moss uses Other Sales Metaphors to get his prospects to reveal how they make buying decisions:

> **"Tell me about the best decision you ever made to hire manage- ment consultants. How did you do it?  How did you make your mind up to hire them?"**

After listening closely to figure out their decision-making process, John says, **"Well, I think you made a wise decision in that case, but I also think you are going to make an even better decision here today!"** John then goes on to replay their decision-making process and shows them how SCA can solve their management and productivity problems. This approach has helped John bring in multi-million dollar consulting projects from sophisticated banks and insurance companies all over America.

Why are Other Sales Metaphors so effective?  When you get a prospect to think about a good purchase decision he made in the past, you are accessing good feelings. *You are developing an emotional climate that will make it much easier for him to buy today.* You are setting him up to transfer those good feelings from the past to your current sales situation.

Many salespeople make the mistake of asking customers to talk about purchasing errors they have made in the past. They think they can then show the customer how to avoid another such mistake—by buying their product or service. While this can sometimes be effective, it *always* runs the danger of bringing up fears and negative emotions that can be inadvertently transferred to your products. It is usually much more effective to use Other Sales Metaphors to get customers to remember their most successful purchases. These become established points of agreement for making *today's* sale.

## How to Win Sales by Using Competition Metaphors

Many top salespeople also use a seventh technique, **Competition Metaphors,** to talk about competitors *in a friendly way*. Competition Metaphors are also useful in handling criticism that other salespeople may have leveled against your company's products or services:

"They said what about us? Well, I guess everyone wants to take a shot at the fastest gun in the West. Everyone wants to challenge the top dog, even if they're only a little puppy, right?"

Let's say that you are a very large company, and your prospect is concerned that he may not get good service from your huge corporation. Your prospect feels that a smaller company might take his business more seriously and give him more personalized service. You can use the following Competition Metaphor to show how your large company can match or better the service provided by a smaller company:

"It's like taking you and your family on a long voyage across the Atlantic, and you want to get from here to England, and you have a choice of either going on a small tugboat, which is that other company, or on the Queen Mary, which is us. Which would you feel safest on?"

This story has been used for several years by one of the most successful life insurance salesmen in America. When he has been in competition with a smaller company, he has used this "Queen Mary" story to close the sale for millions of dollars worth of life insurance business. We know it works because we have also used it to close sales training assignments when we have been in competition with smaller consulting firms.

What if your company is "the smaller company"? Kenny Clyde has developed a wonderful metaphoric way of dealing with this challenge. While the company he works for, United Resources, is huge, they are number two in size in their industry. And, they constantly have to deal with comparisons with the largest firm in the industry. Kenny Clyde teaches his salespeople the following Competition Metaphor:

"How do you like doing business with your mailbox? If you go with that big company, you will be doing business with your mail box. Their idea of personalized service is an 800 number, and it is frequently busy. If you'd like a real live human being to answer your questions and take care of your account, then we are the company for you."

A great way of using Competition Metaphors is to use short stories or vivid images comparing foods, cars or other products with which people are already familiar:

**"Are we comparing apples with apples or apples with oranges? Is it really fair to compare us with them?"**

**"We are the Cadillac of this industry. Please don't compare us to a Chevrolet."**

**"You know, this is one of the few businesses where you can buy a Chevy and pay Rolls Royce prices, or you can buy a Rolls Royce and pay Chevy prices. *We offer Rolls Royce quality at a Chevrolet price.*"**

One of the great benefits of Competition Metaphors is that, when properly told, they imbue you with great self-confidence. People want to "go with the winner," and Competition Metaphors show your company to be a winner.

A well-told Competition Metaphor eliminates the need, in many cases, to do a detailed item-by-item comparison of what you offer and what the competition offers. The customer is left with such a winning feeling of you and your company that he or she is ready or nearly ready to buy.

Competition Metaphors can help avoid arguments and they can save you a lot of time. They are the verbal equivalent of image advertising. Much advertising today does not give product information, but instead concentrates on creating *an exclusive feeling about a product or company*. Advertisers know that once people feel a product is special and desirable, they will buy it. Facts alone and product comparisons alone cannot create this feeling.

Competition Metaphors give you the ability to develop a "Queen Mary" feeling about what you are selling. Who wants to take their family across the Atlantic on a tugboat when they can go on the Queen Mary for the same price?

Each of these seven metaphor techniques can be used *at any stage in the sales process*, from opening statements to product demonstrations to closing. They can contain all of the previously discussed techniques of hypnotic selling. The richness and variety of sales stories is limited only by your imagination and your experience. You can add to your experience by writing down and practicing each of the seven different metaphor techniques. Craft stories that are customized for your company's products and services and rehearse them in front of a mirror or with a friend. You will find this greatly increases your self-confidence.

For thousands of years, religious leaders, politicians and even parents have influenced generations of people with stories and metaphors. Jesus Christ taught and inspired his followers with stories and parables that are still being re-told. When you master the power of stories and metaphors, you join a select group of the most influential persuaders in human history. The tremendous flexibility and power of metaphor techniques, combined with the enjoyment they bring the customer, have made them a favorite tool of sales superstars.

At this point, you are ready to learn hypnotic questioning techniques used by top salespeople. These probing and questioning techniques will enable you to get the information you need to close more sales. The great philosopher Socrates taught his students by using questions rather than statements. You now have the opportunity to *teach your customers how to buy* through the skillful use of sales questions.

# 7

## Using Hypnotic Sales Questions To Get The Kind Of Information You Need To Close Sales

The best way to open a sales interaction is to ask the prospect a series of questions about what he wants and needs. Right? Wrong! Not unless you want to come across like a drill sergeant.

There are certainly many important *direct* questions that every sales-person needs to ask. However, the beginning of a sales interaction is neither the time nor place to ask them. Top salespeople *first* concentrate on building trust and rapport with the customer. *Then* they use their probing and needs assessment questions to gather the information they use to close the sale.

Why do sales superstars not favor the use of heavy questioning techniques in the beginning of a sales interview? After all, don't most books and tapes on salesmanship tell you that you are supposed to start the sale with needs assessment questions?

Top salespeople know that it does a salesperson no good to have information about a customer if that customer was alienated while the information was being gathered. It is far more important to open your sales interaction by building trust and rapport. If you do this well, the customer will then tell you everything you want to know. Starting your sales call with a string of probing questions certainly fails to build rapport.

Secondly, by avoiding the string of direct questions early in the sales interaction, the salesperson pleasantly surprises the customer. Many customers expect to be "screened" or "qualified" or grilled by salespeople. In fact, many customers anticipate this type of questioning with some fear. It is this type of questioning that gets people to think **"Me-Customer!"** and **"You-Salesman!"** which leads to **"I am going to be on guard!"** Questioning the customer early in the sales call triggers defensiveness.

## Understanding Hypnotic Questioning Techniques

When a client goes to see a skilled hypnotist, the hypnotist does not ask, "Do you want to be hypnotized?" He or she *assumes* the client wants to experience hypnosis.

The hypnotist might start by using an **embedded question** such as, "Can you tell me about your childhood?" This is called an embedded question because of the imbedded command it contains, "*. . . tell me about your childhood.*" This section of the sentence is spoken with extra emphasis and thus comes across as a friendly, invisible command to talk about one's childhood.

As the client talks about his or her childhood, the hypnotist may ask, **"Did you have a nickname as a child?"** or **"What was your favorite game or pastime?"** or **"Who was your best friend?"** As the client gets more and more into discussing his childhood, he begins to experience age regression, which was discussed earlier in the book. The client begins to relive and re-experience the emotions of childhood. Without even realizing it, the client is going into hypnosis.

The hypnotist *deepens* the trance by shifting to a discussion of other trance-like states the client has already experienced. For example, the hypnotist might ask hypnosis induction questions such as:

**"Can you tell me what it feels like to fall into a deep sleep?"**

**"Have you ever experienced wonderful vivid daydreams? Tell me about that."**

If the subject has been hypnotized before, the therapist might say:

**"Can you tell me about the deepest trance you have ever been in? What was that like?"**

**"Can you tell me about the ideal level of hypnotic trance you would like to experience?"**

**"Can you tell me about your favorite experience while in hypnosis?"**

If the person has *never* been hypnotized, the hypnotist might use the following types of questions to begin inducing trance:

**"Can you *imagine* what it would be like to go into hypnosis?"**

**"Can you *pretend* what it would be like to go into a trance?"**

**"Can you tell me about a time when you have been totally relaxed yet fully awake?"**

As the client goes deeper into hypnosis, additional questions are asked:

**"What is happening with your arms?"**

**"What is happening with your fingers?"**

Instead of telling the client, "Your arms are getting heavy," the Ericksonian hypnotist asks a question. No matter what the answer is, the hypnotist reply is something like, "That is exactly what you need to experience to go even deeper into hypnosis."

Recently, one of the authors of this book was conducting a hypnosis session for a company president who was under great stress. When the deepening question, "What is happening to you fingers?" was asked, he replied, "They are tingling." The author then said, "That tingling is exactly what you need to experience to drop deeply into hypnosis." There was no way he could resist. His eyelids closed, his face and body relaxed, he dropped into a wonderful hypnotic trance, and we were able to help cure a sleeping disorder he had.

As the client talks about events in his or her life, or even events in the hypnotist's office, the client might be asked:

**"Did that take you by surprise?"**

When someone is surprised, they are much more likely to be able to go into a hypnotic state. While in a state of surprise, the mind is fluid and is more open to change.

Another powerful hypnotic induction question to ask about almost any event in a person's life is:

**"Can you figure it out?"** or

**"Do you know what that means?"**

If the client has to "figure it out," it implies that there is something more than meets the eye. Properly used, it implies that there is perhaps something going on at another level, perhaps a subconscious level. The hypnotic question, "Do you know what that means?" induces mental doubt which helps to foster the hypnotic state.

An even more powerful version of the above hypnotic question is:

**"Do you really understand what that means?"**

Because it is so powerful, this question should only be used when a high degree of trust and rapport have been established. This question throws doubt on the conscious mind and on its ability to figure things out. Depending upon how it is pronounced, "Do you really understand what that means?" can be an indirect way of saying, "You don't understand what that means." When someone does not understand, they have much more reason to listen to you.

Skilled hypnotists have many other ways of using indirect questions to induce and deepen trance. As you will learn later in this chapter, questions can be used in every step in the hypnotic process. You will even see how hypnotic questions can be used to "read someone's mind."

## How and When to Ask Hypnotic Sales Questions

When questions are properly used in the selling process, instead of feeling he is being grilled by a salesperson, your customer will feel he is being taken care of by a friend. *Since you have first established rapport through pacing, your later questions will get much more truthful and detailed answers.* Your questions are received by an eager "future customer" rather than by a defensive prospect.

Does this mean you can never ask direct questions? No. Quite the contrary! Interestingly, customers are far more receptive to direct questions from someone they like and trust. So, *build the trust first to get permission to ask all the probing questions you want!*

Asking detailed probing questions at the outset tends to create an atmosphere that puts the prospect on edge. Opening with a round of questions can be intimidating, threatening, and confusing for the prospect. The salesperson reminds the prospect of a drill sergeant! Think about it: do you want a total stranger to ask you all sorts of questions before you know that you can trust or believe that person? Most people need to trust someone before they will fully open up. This is a lesson we learn in both hypnosis and sales.

*If you don't have trust, you can ask all the questions you want, but you won't get high-quality answers.* We are am reminded of training sessions we held for stockbrokers in Los Angeles. As a part of this training, the stockbrokers are required to spend three hours per day "cold-calling" new prospects on the phone in an attempt to set up accounts. Another consulting group had been brought in to teach cold-calling. They taught the salespeople how to "qualify" the prospects to make sure they had the money to buy stocks and bonds. The salespeople had been previously taught that they shouldn't "waste their time" on prospects who "didn't have any money."

These stockbrokers had been taught to ask probing questions up front to learn how much money the prospects had to invest. We were surprised to find that very, very few of the hundreds of people who were being called each day had any money to invest. In fact, most of the prospects being called were pleading poverty. Some claimed they were on the verge of bankruptcy!

What made this all so interesting is that we were working in Beverly Hills. We were calling hundreds of people each day in Beverly Hills and the equally wealthy suburb of Bel Air. Prospects were telling us that they were broke. We found this hard to believe, and decided to drive down some of the streets these people lived on (the stockbrokers were making cold calls from local telephone directories and addresses for many homes are listed). Some local real estate agents told us that homes on these streets averaged between $2 million and $3 million each. We noticed that the driveways were lined with Jaguars, Mercedes Benz, BMW's, and even a few Rolls Royces. Yet the prospects were pleading poverty!

It didn't take long to figure out that the prospects who were being called were not giving truthful information about their economic status. The probing sequence the brokers used was turning off prospects. Since there was no pacing and no trust-building, prospects would not give truthful information to the new stockbrokers. We worked with the company sales executives to craft an entirely new sales training program, and the executives decided to scrap the old probing sequence which obviously wasn't working.

The office was soon bringing in dozens of new accounts each week. The only thing that had changed was that we were spending a couple of minutes on hypnotic pacing and trust building with each new prospect. The stockbrokers were selling the same products with the same commission structure they had always used. That didn't change. We found that the trust-building combined with appropriate probes later in the call got more people to open up and give us high-quality information about their investment goals and how much money they had to invest.

Salespeople who use the heavy old-fashioned probing sequences sometimes wonder why prospects lie to them. The answer is that these salespeople trigger dishonesty in prospects by pushing too hard up-front. Some prospects and customers lie because they are afraid of the salesperson or because they don't trust the salesperson. Asking questions without first having built trust is like setting fire to money. You are burning up your list of prospects.

**Have you ever wondered why some prospects or customers don't say much?** *What can we do to get a Silent Clam to open up?* Many salespeople will just ask more and more questions. They push harder and harder on the "Silent Clam," usually without much success. The approach used by superior salespeople, according to the research we have conducted at companies such as AT & T, Paine Webber, and Toshiba, is to first reassure the Silent Clam, make him or her comfortable, and build the basis for a friendship. *When this is skillfully done, you frequently find the Silent Clam opens up all by himself!*

The development of trust comes from using the pacing techniques described in previous chapters, and by showing the customer that you are like he is. Show the customer that he is safe with you, and he will be likely to truthfully answer your questions.

## How to Phrase Direct Questions for a Direct Hit

There is a time and a place to use direct questions in your probing sequence. When are direct questions used by top salespeople? Just after trust has been established, and before a specific product or service has been suggested. You want to ask the direct questions before recommending a product so that you will know *exactly* the product to recommend.

Sales superstars also use direct questions when customer objections begin to surface. Objections are the friend and ally of salespeople because they reveal precisely what is stopping the prospect from buying.

### Key Steps for Using the Questioning Strategies of the Sales Superstars

Let's examine some of the sales questioning strategies used by top salespeople, and what makes these strategies so powerful. Early in the sales call, they will ask questions such as:

**"What features and benefits are you most interested in?"**

It is important to know the prospect's thoughts and value systems *before you begin* your formal presentation. You may think you have the best product or service in the world, but if it doesn't match your prospect's value system, he or she won't be very interested in hearing about it. For example, before presenting the idea for this book to our publisher, we asked what types of sales books they were most interested in. We were told the publisher was interested in a book that stood out from the crowded shelf of ordinary sales books. The publisher was not interested in another book on closing techniques to add to the hundreds of books already written on that subject. The publisher wanted a book on a sales subject that no other authors or consultants had ever written about. When we then proposed our book idea, we emphasized that no one had ever written a book on hypnotic sales techniques before. Our publisher found this, and our credentials in consulting with Fortune 500 companies, to be very interesting.

An excellent follow-up question is:

**"What other products are you looking at in this area?"**

When prospects and customers tell you what they are looking for in a product or service, you sometimes think you have the complete picture when you really don't. Listen to what other products or services they are looking at in your area, and then think about the characteristics, features and benefits of those products or services. Such an examination may reveal product characteristics the customer is interested in which he or she did not mention previously. In some cases, the customer might not even be consciously aware of being interested in these features or benefits.

We were recently working with a home building company that was having difficulty selling some model homes. Prospects stated the features and benefits they were most interested in and this company's new homes seemed to have all of these. However, when we asked what other homes they were looking at, several interesting findings emerged. We learned that these competitive homes had second fireplaces in the master bedrooms and that they had large gourmet kitchens. Many also had larger bathrooms. The development company used this information to make some modifications and additions on its next model homes, and sales started to take off. From that point on, all of the new homes had larger kitchens and bathrooms and second fireplaces in the master bedrooms. It turned out that the entire development sold out in only four months. This was because we gathered the information we needed to customize the homes to give buyers what they really wanted (which was different than what they first said they wanted!).

Another way of asking the question of "what other products are you looking at" is to ask:

**"Who else are you talking to?"**

This questioning technique works especially well with auditory people. Auditory people talk to themselves constantly and they store many of their thoughts in auditory form. You can think of these stored thoughts as similar to recorded sound-tracks. When you ask them who else they are talking to, they will not only tell you, they may repeat some conversations they have had with other salespeople in detail. You will thus be able to gain valuable information about your competition that will guide you in presenting particular features and benefits of your products and services.

Before asking for the order, many top salespeople ask a question like:

**"Do you fully understand what makes our product so unique?"**

This is a very powerful question. It contains the presupposition that your product is unique. Your prospect will start to think about its uniqueness. The word "fully" adds some extra power to the sentence. While a prospect may have some idea of what makes the product unique, it is doubtful that he or she "fully" understands the uniqueness. Whatever answer your prospect gives to this question, you win. If the prospect says he or she does fully understand, they have to explain in their own words what makes the product so unique. If they leave anything out, you can elaborate on other features and benefits.

If your prospect says that he or she does not know what makes it so unique, you also have an opportunity to fill them in on this point. Once the prospect understands the unique features and benefits your product or service offers, this question is an excellent follow-up probe:

**"Is someone else involved in making this decision with you?"**

Always assume that the person you are talking with is involved in making the decision. Don't insult the prospect by saying anything like, "Who is the decision-maker in your household," or "Who is the decision-maker in your company?" If the prospect is not the decision-maker, he or she will inform you of that fact. Until you are so informed, treat your prospect as if he or she is a decision-maker.

Here is a great probe for finding out your prospect's level of urgency on making the purchase decision:

**"Is there anything that prevents you from making a decision today?"**

The answer will identify the barriers you must take down to get the sale. And—if you take down those barriers, you should get the sale because the prospect has implied that those were the only things that prevented him or her from making the purchase decision.

Occasionally in sales, you will encounter the "Silent Clam" type of prospect. They will tell you they want to "think about it." How do you deal with prospects like this? What sales questions are most appropriate? Ask probes such as:

**"Is it only a matter of the money?"**

**"Are you satisfied that we will be able to give you outstanding service?"**

**"Are you comfortable with our financing options?"**

**"Do we have the colors you want?"**

**"Is it the guarantee?"**

You can go through the major objections or questions the prospect may have. These questions hypnotically plant a suggestion in the prospect's mind. They work because some of the questions you raise will match the prospect's thinking. When you hit the question which matches the question the prospect already had in his or her mind, you will get agreement. The prospect will say, "That's right—I was thinking about that." Then, all you have to do to get the sale is to satisfy the prospect on that issue.

Remember, if you don't plant the question, the prospect may not raise it. Don't assume that the "quiet" prospect doesn't have any questions. That's a dangerous assumption to make! Also, don't assume the prospect is not interested! You may call this "uninterested" prospect next week and find he has purchased from another salesperson. He probably purchased from someone who was skilled in using questions to flush out his real objection.

Why do some prospects not ask all the questions they have? Sometimes it is due to embarrassment. They may be embarrassed to talk with you about the price. The price might be higher than they can afford, or than they think they can afford. When you raise the question first, you reduce the embarrassment factor. All they have to do is to simply agree that's what they were thinking about. Then, you can show them how the purchase can be financed, or you can show a less expensive model and you can close the sale.

If a prospect looks puzzled or can't make up his or her mind, ask:

**"Is there something I neglected to *fully* explain to you?"**

Here again, the key word is "fully." Obviously, you didn't explain everything fully to the prospect. That would take a long, long time. When you ask this question, you will flush out the prospect's few remaining concerns. "Well," the prospect might say, "you didn't explain the extended warranty very well. And, I still don't understand the financing options." If you satisfy this prospect on the extended warranty and the financing, you will likely get the sale!

When you start your answer, preface it by saying, "Oh, I am sorry I didn't give you all the details on that . . . " When you start off by saying you are sorry, you put yourself in the "one-down" position. The prospect may say, "Oh, that's OK." At minimum, he or she will not feel threatened by you. You are making yourself human and vulnerable. You come across much more as a friend than as a salesperson. Then, go on to say, "The details are really exciting . . . " You have now moved the prospect into a more expectant state of mind. He or she will expect to hear exciting details, and since we get what we think we are going to get, the prospect will probably find your answer quite interesting.

The information you collect from asking these types of sales questions will help you in customizing your sales messages, which ultimately leads to closing the sale. Since this type of information cannot always be gathered by observation, the direct questions need to be used.

Are we against the use of direct questions? Not at all! We insist that they be used—but, used at the proper time. Failure to use direct questions can actually place the salesperson at a distinct disadvantage when the time comes to close the sale. Direct questions help you to anticipate all the prospect's objections. It is best to anticipate and **disarm** objections rather than to wait for the prospect to bring them up—and then to do battle.

*Salespeople who don't ask direct questions miss opportunities to deal with objections early on, when the objections are easiest to handle.* Moreover, using direct questions communicates self-confidence on the part of the salesperson. It shows that you do not fear anything the customer might say.

It is not our purpose to advertise other books here, but we feel duty-bound to tell you about the best resource available on sales questions. Called **The Sales Question Book**, it is an organized collection of over 400 of the most powerful sales questions ever assembled. **The Sales Question**

**Book,** which is bound in an indexed three-ring binder, is available through Personal Selling Power in Fredericksburg, Virginia. It is the only book we've ever seen that presents powerful specific questions for use in each step of the sales cycle. We recommend it here because many salespeople have told us that it has helped them close sales that brought in thousands of dollars in extra commissions.

## How to Phrase Indirect Questions for a Direct Hit

We have found that as useful as direct questions are, indirect questions are even more powerful. Indirect questions help sales superstars gather the information they need without endangering trust and rapport, as "police detective" direct questions sometimes do.

Indirect questions come in a number of forms. In one form, *the question can be phrased as a statement,* such as **"I don't know what kind of income you have."** Upon hearing this type of sentence, a prospect will often tell you what his or her income is (even though you didn't directly ask for it!). If you directly ask, "What is your income?" you risk having a prospect say, "That's personal," or "That's none of your business." The indirect question enables you to collect information about income and other highly personal matters, without endangering rapport.

Highly skilled hypnotists make frequent use of indirect questions which are disguised as statements:

**"I don't know how deeply you'd like to go into hypnosis."**

Upon hearing this "statement," the patient will frequently respond by answering it as if it were a question. Also note that this indirect question contains the powerful hypnotic suggestion of ". . . you'd like to go into hypnosis." When the hypnotist says this sentence, a special emphasis is given to the words, ". . . you'd like to go into hypnosis," as the hypnotist looks deeply into the patient's eyes. Using these types of techniques woven together many times, it is possible to induce a deep hypnotic state conversationally, without ever asking someone to close their eyes.

Why do indirect questions work so well? Prospects and customers rarely object to an indirect question, while objections to direct questions are actually quite common—particularly when those questions relate to information on salaries, savings, net worth, health concerns, or other personal matters.

Another way to use indirect questions is through the use of a pause, a raised eyebrow, an upturned hand, or some other questioning gesture at the end of a statement. This technique is often found at the end of sentences:

**"This may not interest you . . . but we now offer a 12% interest rate."**

In this case, the indirect question is, "Does this interest you or not?" Typically, after hearing a "statement" like this, a prospect will answer by telling you just how interested he or she is. Here is another example:

**"You probably already know about these special features . . . this laser printer prints 24 pages per minute with magazine quality graphics."**

The indirect question here is, "Do you know about these special features or not?" To make these indirect questions even more powerful, it is important that you pronounce them as questions. That is, raise your inflection and voice tone at the end of the sentence in a questioning manner. This almost guarantees the prospect will "hear" the statement as a question, and that he or she will answer it as a question.

You can also turn a statement, such as the above statements, into a question by raising your hands or by raising an eyebrow in a questioning way as you speak the sentence. This will help to trigger an "answer" from the prospect when he "sees" and hears what you are saying. This use of body language is an elegant way of adding some visual interest to what might otherwise be a simple verbal exchange.

The prospect hears your sentence and, upon seeing your questioning posture, automatically answers the question you never directly asked. This is what we call "sales artistry" and it is one of the skills that separates true sales professionals from average salespeople. The answer the prospect gives you will tell you just how interested he or she is in what you are discussing, and whether you should continue along the same path or switch to a new track in your sales strategy.

## How to Get Positive Results from Negative Questions

When top salespeople do use direct questions early in the sales interaction, they tend to use what can be called negative questions. These special types of questions give the salesperson a gold mine of information on the customer's self-image, self-concept, expectations and needs. This information is then used to custom tailor the rest of the presentation to close the sale.

One very successful life insurance salesman uses the following "negative" question:

"Why do *you want life insurance*?"

This is a surprising and a refreshing question to most prospects. They expect the life insurance agent to "push" life insurance. This successful agent doesn't push at all. He asks the prospect to explain the prospect's own interest. The prospect is then put in the position of having to sell himself or herself.

This "negative" question gains further power because the words are arranged to form a hypnotic presupposition of "...you want life insurance." The salesman adds a special emphasis to these words as he speaks them.

What if the prospect says, "I don't want life insurance"? The salesman follows up with another powerful sales question. He says, "You must have a reason for saying that. Do you mind if I ask what that reason is?" When he finds out "why" the prospect doesn't want life insurance, he learns the objections he will have to deal with to get the sale.

A "negative" question used by a successful computer salesperson is:

"Does your business really need a computer that is this powerful?"

This question is effective because instead of "pushing a product," the salesperson is soliciting the customer's opinion. This "negative" question shows that the sales professional is more interested in learning about the customer's needs than he is in forcing a product on the customer. The answer that the salesperson gets to this question reveals how the customer sees his business and what he perceives his computing needs to be. Frequently, this computer salesman's customers will also answer by talking about growth plans they have for their businesses.

By asking questions that focus on the prospect's self-concept and his concept of his business, the salesperson communicates "*I care about you and your business*." Finding out how the prospect sees himself, and what he thinks he deserves and needs makes it easy to customize your sales presentation to push all his hot buttons.

In addition, the negative question gently *puts the customer in the position of having to defend why he or she wants the product*. In fact, these types of questions sometimes actually put the customer in the position of trying to convince the salesperson to sell him or her the product.

The use of negative questions may elicit surprise. After all, prospects typically expect the salesperson to "push" a product. This sudden "role reversal" is a refreshing change for the prospect. "Negative" questions can put the customer in the role of the salesperson and the salesperson in the role of the customer. It is a powerful way of making the prospect think of even more reasons why he wants and should buy your product. "Negative" questions are also effective because they ask for personal information which only the customer can provide. When the successful insurance salesman asks, "Why do you want life insurance?" only the prospect can talk about his needs and how insurance will address them.

## Building an "Intuitive Link" with Your Customers through Mind-Reading Questions

Most people are uncomfortable dealing with strangers. Top salespeople handle this discomfort by giving the impression they know quite a bit about you, and that they understand you. One of the key ways they do this is with mind-reading questions and mind-reading statements.

*When people feel that their needs, interests, and values are understood, an air of friendship, camaraderie, and trust is far more likely to develop.* Sales superstars have the ability to create an "intuitive link," a special understanding, between themselves and their customers. This link gives the customer the feeling that he or she is truly understood.

Once the intuitive link has been established, it is much easier to influence the prospect. And, with this link, the prospect clearly believes that his or her well-understood needs will be met. Where does this "intuitive link" come from? The answer is mind-reading.

Average salespeople project their own personal needs, wants and interests onto customers. *They assume customers want and like the same things they want and like.* The sales pro does not focus on himself to understand what the prospect wants. Rather, the sales pro focuses outwardly, directly on the customer.

The sales pro establishes an intuitive link with the customer by *temporarily* adopting the customer's views, tastes, and values. The sales pro thinks like the customer thinks, using the intuitive link. By fully adopting the customer's views and thought patterns, sales champions show so much insight into the customer that the customer feels that the salesperson can almost read his or her mind.

Mind-reading techniques give the customer the impression that he or she is intuitively understood by the salesperson. Top salespeople develop *almost psychic skills* in reading their customers. Like psychics or mind-readers, top salespeople collect information through carefully observing the **clothing, hands, face, posture, speech patterns, mannerisms, and gestures** of their clients.

*How can you communicate that you can read another person's mind?* By using statements that are likely to be true of almost anyone. While these statements are generalizations, *if you say them with great feeling and sincerity*, prospects will be amazed at your understanding of them. Examples of mind reading statements used by top salespeople are:

**"I can see that you are a practical person,"**

**"You impress me as someone who tries to take care of his health."**

Most people see themselves as "practical" people. When you use the first sentence above, you will get a nod of agreement and internally, the client will feel you understand him or her. Most people will also feel that the second statement applies to them. Notice that the statement is not, "You take care of your health," but it is "You *try* to take care of your health." Inserting the word "try" makes it applicable to virtually everyone, and if you say it with feeling, people will think you understand every little thing they do to try to take care of themselves.

You can use mind-reading statements that apply to sales:

**"You are the kind of person who won't be talked into buying something you don't want."**

Most people will agree with this statement and they will feel reassured that you know that about them. They will feel they can trust you a little more. They may infer that you won't try to talk them into buying something they don't want. They will let down some of their defensiveness.

One of the most effective ways of using mind-reading statements is to capitalize on truisms. A truism is a statement or a fact that is true for almost anyone. To make truisms into questions, add "... isn't that right?", "... don't you?", "... didn't they?", or any other tag question onto the end of any truism you use:

"You want to have a nice prosperous retirement, **isn't that right?**"

"You try to take good care of yourself, **don't you?**"

"You are interested in saving money, **aren't you?**"

Almost all people will answer "yes" to these questions, and they might be amazed you knew this about them. The best salespeople have hundreds of truisms they use which are based on **stock psychological profiles**. A great source of stock psychological profiles is the daily astrology column in your local newspaper. Even if you don't believe in astrology, you can select and use some of the "meaningful generalizations" from these astrology columns to communicate to your customers that you understand them. These astrology columns and astrology chart profiles are written in wonderful language that *seems to apply just to you* (or just to those born under your sign), but which actually applies to a great many people.

When you use mind-reading questions and mind-reading statements, pronounce them in a confident and knowing tone of voice. Pronounce mind-reading questions as if you have known these truisms about your customer for years. It is OK to use some generalizations, as long as you sound self-confident when you deliver them. When your customer hears these generalities, his mind will automatically customize them and personalize them. Mentally, he will say, "That's me!" as he searches through his memory bank for a more exact understanding. Just as with an astrology column, the customer "fills in the missing details," and you have begun to build that "intuitive link" with the customer.

In addition to building rapport, mind-reading questions can be an excellent method for gathering information about your prospect. The following exchange between a sales pro and customer illustrates how this is accomplished:

| | |
|---|---|
| Sales Pro: | **You are interested in a car that projects an image of success, aren't you?** |
| Prospect: | **Yeah, my ranch is doing really well this year, and I want people to see I'm in the money!** |

Who isn't interested in a car that projects an image of success? If you had absolutely no interest in looking successful, you'd be happy driving any car that was safe. The reason people buy new cars is to communicate a message to other people about who they are and how successful they are.

In this exchange, the salesperson not only used a mind-reading question, but he also paced the customer's visual language. This sales pro observed that the customer uses visual words such as "see," "image," "clear," and "bright." He used the same kind of visual language ("image") in his mind-reading question.

Let's look at the information this mind-reading question produced. The sales pro learned that the prospect has a ranch that is doing quite well. This could be useful to the salesman later in the sales interaction. He might decide to use some words relating to ranching or farming, which would pace the rancher's vocabulary. Another powerful technique would be to tell the prospect about other ranchers who are his happy customers (as described in the "Other People Metaphors" section in the previous chapter).

Some sales pros also use mind-reading statements and questions to learn what actions customers are likely to take in the future. Kenny Clyde, Vice President at United Resources, teaches his salespeople to use this approach by using a generalization followed by a mind-reading question:

**"Many people like to borrow against the money that accumulates in their annuity. Have you been thinking about doing that?"**

If they have been thinking of borrowing against the funds that have accumulated in their annuity (and some clients are surprised that the salesperson knows them well enough to have figured this out!), Kenny will show them their different options and the interest rate they will be paying. He will also have an opportunity to talk about other financial products United Resources and Integrated Resources offer which can satisfy other financial planning needs.

The mind-reading question combines the advantages of mind-reading (showing clients you understand how they think) and information-gathering. Your prospect will either tell you that you're right on track, or he will tell you how to get on track. You can't go wrong with mind-reading questions.

## How and When to Ask Bottom Line Questions

As the sales process moves along, the salesperson wants to know what could **prevent** the prospect from buying his product or service. The sales pro needs to know any fears, doubts, or uncertainties the prospect has that may interfere with the sale.

Bottom-line questions are best used right before you ask for the order. At this point, the salesperson has already established a solid rapport with the customer. While the salesperson is still interested in pacing the customer and in *maintaining* rapport, the questions asked at this time should get more direct and bottom-line oriented:

### "What is the main concern you have left?"

It is interesting to note that this question makes the presupposition that the prospect has only one main concern. This can become a self-fulfilling prophecy if the customer answers the question as it was posed. Even if the prospect says he has two or three concerns left, you still win. You know exactly what issues you have to deal with to get the sale.

Here is a very effective Bottom-Line Question to use when the prospect raises an objection at the end of the sales call:

### "Is that the only thing that is holding you back?"

This question, or a minor variation of it, is one of the most effective of all closing questions. *If the customer's response is positive, the salesperson knows he or she has a good chance of closing the sale.* It means there is only one remaining issue to be dealt with. If the response is negative, the salesperson will learn any other concerns that prevent the customer from buying.

A Bottom-Line Question used by top salespeople in the automobile field is:

### "Tell me, what would I have to do to sell you this car today?"

The answer the customer provides gets right to the bottom-line and lets the salesperson know what kind of chance he or she has of selling the car. If the prospect says, "You have to drop the price you just offered me by $200," the salesperson can get the sale by either dropping the price or perhaps by selling a nearly identical car that doesn't have one of the options. If the customer responds that he or she wants an extra option or a free extended warranty, the salesperson can work on that. Sometimes the customer asks for something that is ridiculous or that can't be done. In this case, the salesperson can inform the customer that his or her request is unrealistic. The customer can either change his or her request, or can leave. Bottom-line questions save both the salesperson and the customer time and energy.

As effective as bottom-line questions are, they should not be used until there is a good bond of trust between the salesperson and the customer. If you ask the bottom-line question too early in the sales call, you are likely to get a lower quality answer. If a customer doesn't know you and trust you, he or she may respond to a bottom-line question by saying, "There is nothing you can do to get me to buy today," even if he or she is genuinely interested in your product or service.

If you haven't been able to consummate the sale, near the end of your sales call, you may want to ask the following bottom-line question:

**"Is there something you haven't told me?"**

This is a very powerful bottom-line question. You want to ask it in a soft, friendly tone of voice. The purpose of this question is to flush out the one major concern that is preventing the prospect from buying—the concern he or she has not told you about yet. If you have built a good level of trust, and if you come across as genuinely friendly and helpful, this question can sometimes get the prospect to reveal his or her "secret agenda." You may find out that there is someone else involved in making this decision. You may find out that they have a relative in the business and they feel they have to buy from that person (even though they would prefer not to). You may find out some other "secret" factor that hasn't been revealed until you ask, "Is there something else going on you haven't told me about?"

It is important to emphasize the fact that the information gathered in the first few minutes and the last few minutes of the sales call is frequently the most valuable. By strategically using Bottom-Line Questions, you will be able to collect exactly the information you need near the end of the sales call to close the sale!

## Knowing Exactly How Many Questions to Ask

Since questioning techniques yield such useful information on the prospect's belief systems and self-identity, a fair question is *"Why not use lots of sales questions earlier in the sales interaction?"*

The answer is that if solid rapport between the salesperson and the customer is not established first, the customer will probably feel uncomfortable giving answers. In fact, if they are uncomfortable, some prospects may actually present a false picture in order to mislead the salesperson.

While the information gathered from using sales questions is obviously valuable, it is not sufficient to close sales. This information is useful only if gathered in a climate of trust and good will. That's why sales champions first concentrate on building trust. Once that is accomplished, the customer will give you all the information and cooperation you want.

## Controlling the Decision to Buy

With the good feelings and trust you have built, and with all the information you have collected on the customer's self-concept, needs, values, and belief systems, you can sell so persuasively it becomes very difficult for the customer to refuse to buy. In fact, the only way that the prospect can refuse to buy your product or service (if he genuinely needs it and can afford it) is to deny all the information he or she has provided! *This is something that is almost impossible for people to do.*

Knock and the door shall be opened. Ask questions and ye shall receive. When you build trust and ask the right questions, your prospects will give you all the information you need to solve their problems and fulfill their dreams. When you build trust and ask the right questions, your prospects will give you all the information you need to close the sale.

8

Developing And Using
Script Books For
Consistently Effective
Hypnotic
Sales Presentations

Jack is a Vice President of Sales for a $2 billion services corporation that prepares payroll for other companies. The United States is broken up into 42 fiercely competitive regions and Jack is the head of one of those regions. When we first met Jack, his division, in La Palma, California, was #7 in the country. Jack was about to launch a sales scripting project, in which the most powerful words ("scripts") used by his top salespeople would be tape recorded, transcribed and indexed in a book. The scripts in this "mastermind" book would then be taught to all of the other salespeople.

Did it work? In 1985, Jack's group became #1 in the USA. They were rewarded with trophies, trips to Hawaii and cash bonuses. Jack says, "I know these proven scripts give my salespeople more power. These hypnotic scripts make it easy for my salespeople to handle any question or objection a customer has."

## Proven Techniques that Enable Anyone to Learn Hypnotic Selling

It used to be assumed that very few people could learn the techniques of the "born salesman" or the master salesman. With the discovery of the linguistic structure of sales hypnosis, the "word magic" used by top salespeople is now available to others.

If you have read thus far, you may be excited about the powers of hypnotic salesmanship. You may also be impressed by the sophistication of these techniques. These are not simplistic sales techniques. How can one learn and master the sales strategies of the superstars?

In this chapter and the coming chapters, you'll learn the best techniques we have found for teaching hypnotic selling: sales script books, interactive video and interactive audio. In this chapter on hypnotic sales scripting, you will learn not only how to use sales script books, but also how to construct one of your own. These sales script books have helped many salespeople double, triple or even quadruple their incomes in relatively short periods of time.

*How would you like to have powerful and persuasive hypnotic sales messages available for immediate use in your sales calls?* How much would your sales improve if you had the most effective ways of handling any objection, stall or resistance? How much less stressful would your life be if you had, at your fingertips, the most hypnotic words ever spoken by the top salespeople in your industry?

You can have this information and the success that goes with it. HOWEVER, it is not available in any book store. It is available in a customized sales script book which only you and your people can develop.

## Introduction to the Sales Script Book

Compared with any other type of book, the sales script book looks lean and mean. It means business. It is, as its name implies, a collection of the most powerful and useful phrases ("scripts") a sales professional can use to counter any objection and close the sale. It is a refinement of *what really works* in a particular sales context.

To be useful, all information must be organized and it must be accessible. *The sales script book is an organized and useful set of the most powerful ways of handling the exact objections and stalls you get in your sales calls.* It enables you to make more sales calls and it helps you close more sales.

It is also important to know what the script book is not. It is not a collection of theories about sales. It is not a set of worn-out overused "power-closing" techniques. It is not a set of tricky words with which you can beat up customers. It is not a book of product information. It is not a book on your company's background. It does not have any fat or theory or background information.

*The world of professional selling is being re-structured in the 1990's.* Companies which previously invested large amounts of money in conventional packaged training programs are now looking for alternatives. Experience has shown that in many cases, the dollars spent on canned or pre-packaged training did not result in increased sales.

Recently, several research groups turned their attention to sales superstars: those sales geniuses who were able to sell 50, 100 or even 1000% more than other salespeople. What distinguished these sales masters? How were they able to earn $100,000 or $500,000 or, in some cases, over $1 million a year in personal income?

A variety of key personality traits have been reliably identified in top salespeople, and tests have now been developed to accurately measure these attributes. However, in addition to these traits, sales superstars were found to have the distinctive forms of verbal communication you have previously read about in this book: the ability to pace to build trust, the ability to tell mesmerizing stories, the ability to use attention-focusing statements and the ability to ask powerful sales questions.

To put it simply, sales superstars don't talk like everyone else! They use special, magical words. They use words which trigger their customers to buy. They don't use the old worn-out cliches presented in off-the-shelf sales training programs. While they are selling the same products at the same prices as their peers, their magic words get more customers to buy. It is as simple and as complex as that.

*Researchers and profit-hungry businessmen began to wonder if there was any way of putting the hypnotic words of the superstars onto the tongues of the less-successful.* Obviously, it wasn't being done by the one-size-fits-all training programs.

The sales script book was re-discovered. Organized sales script books have been known and used by some of America's most successful corporations, such as IBM, Metropolitan Life Insurance, and AT & T. *However, sales script books have largely remained a mystery to many other companies and even to entire industries.*

Those companies that have invested the time and money to develop script books have guarded them zealously to keep them out of the reach of their competitors. How would you feel if your competitors got their hands on the very best lines of your most powerful salespeople? To protect against this possibility, some of the corporations we have worked with have printed their script books in blue ink on blue paper to make photocopying impossible. Jack Tortorice of ADP had his script books printed on special dark red paper that looks black if someone tries to photocopy it!

Some companies hand out script books in the morning and collect them in the evening to lock them in vaults. Two financial institutions we have worked with, Union Federal Savings and Loan, and First Federal Savings and Loan, have assigned special numbers to each sales script book to track where the books are at all times.

Are these moves preposterous or unnecessary? You can decide. At stake is millions of dollars in sales and profits. No one would go to this trouble with ordinary training materials or an ordinary sales book. But, sales script books are different. *They are powerful, and they do work.*

The purpose of this chapter is to shed some light on sales script book development so that readers may begin to profit from this innovative sales tool.

## How *All* Salespeople Can Profit by Using Script Books

Through our studies and work with numerous sales organizations in the USA and abroad, we have learned that even the best salespeople can be inconsistent. We have observed that even sales geniuses have good days and bad days. *On some days, even top people are unable to remember their own best lines.*

Script books help make salespeople consistently excellent. Even if we are tired or fatigued, if we have our very best lines at our fingertips, we can make some additional calls and perhaps close an additional sale or two.

*We at first doubted the power of sales script books.* Shouldn't salespeople be able to memorize all of their best lines? That is impossible. When we saw, time after time, that sales superstars themselves rely on script books, we became convinced of the value of this sales tool. Famous sales trainers such as Brian Tracy, Zig Ziglar and Tommy Hopkins recommend that salespeople write down and practice their very best, most convincing lines. We learned that it was no mere coincidence that highly-successful sales professionals use script books. The script books are, in fact, largely responsible for their success!

*On those occasions when sales superstars misplace their script books, they are invariably less successful.* They are like pro football players trying to play without a playbook.

The script book makes the job of selling much easier and less stressful. Tom Olds, CPA, sells tax-favored investments to wealthy clients in Orange County, California. Using his script book, he is able to make over 100 phone calls per day!

Long after most of his competitors are exhausted and ready to call it quits, Tom is still fresh and has the energy to make an additional 20 or 30 calls. It can be late in the afternoon, and Tom might be hit with any one of dozens of objections, stalls or resistances from a potential client. Tom quickly turns to that section of his script book and glances down at a variety

of powerfully hypnotic ways of handling the objection. While his competitors are racking their brains to come up with a response, Tom has the most
awesome lines in the business at his fingertips.

## How to Use a Script Book Like a Champion

The script book, of course, is not to be read from word-for-word.
Success in sales depends not just upon what is said, but also upon how it is
said. *Even Shakespeare's dramatic words lack power and appeal unless
properly delivered.*

The key to mesmerizing sales presentations is to say your lines with
great sincerity and feeling. *You want the script to "disappear" the way a
script disappears when a great film star delivers it.*

For this reason, we coach salespeople in acting and voice-change
techniques. While this training is a lot of fun, it has a quite serious purpose.
Research has shown that we trust people like ourselves. We trust people who
sound like we sound. Sales champions know this intuitively. They match their
voice to the customer's voice. They will speak slowly to someone who speaks
slowly. They will speed up their speech rate with a faster talker. Research shows
top salespeople will speak softly with people who speak softly. They speak
more forcefully with people who have strong voices. When you speak the way
the other person speaks, the effect is hypnotic. They trust you because they trust
themselves—and you are talking the way they talk.

These voice-matching techniques can now, for the first time, be taught.
We have had great success in helping salespeople deliver scripts in a most
convincing manner. *No prospect or customer knows scripts are involved.*
All they know is that they want to buy!

**These same voice-matching techniques can be used in face-to-face
selling**. Script books are not just for telephone sales. They can be a very
useful memory enhancer for personal sales calls. Here is how they work in
face-to-face sales.

Suppose you are going to make your next face-to-face sales call on a
physician. From your first phone call, you know that his major objections
will be: price, your service contract and equipment reliability. You drive
out to see him and you park outside his office. Before you go in, you look
at the following sections of you script book: **"PRICE," "SERVICE CON-**

TRACT," and "EQUIPMENT RELIABILITY." There, at your finger-tips, you find the most powerfully hypnotic lines you or any other salesper-son has ever uttered on these subjects.

You glance at these scripts to recharge your memory. They are now on the tip of your tongue. You walk into the doctor's office totally relaxed and self-confident. *When he brings up these objections, you handle them effortlessly.* You make the sale.

Some of our clients do face-to-face selling almost exclusively and they find script books are indispensable. They use them everyday. One client calls his script book **"the brains on the front seat of my car."**

You obviously can't read a script book when you are directly in front of a customer. However, reviewing the book before you see him or her is the best investment of five minute's time you can ever make.

## How Script Books Trigger Creativity

People who do not understand script books sometimes think they will lessen creativity or spontaneity. That has not been our experience. In fact, *we have found that salespeople who do not use script books are much less creative than those who do use them!*

We have found that most salespeople suffer from insecurity about their persuasive skills. WHO HAS EVER FELT THAT THEY WERE JUST TOO PERSUASIVE? No one. *Who has ever felt that it was just too easy to make lots of money in sales?* Probably no one. This insecurity leads many salespeople to give up too early in sales calls. When they find a line or approach that seems to work, they use it over and over again. This insecurity in salespeople leads to a loss of creativity.

Some salespeople become superstitious about a few sales lines. *They become like robots who are programmed to say the same thing (the same lines) again and again.* After all, that's easier than thinking up new lines.

The sales script book encourages creativity and spontaneity because instead of having just two or three ways of handling an objection or question, there are 15 or 20 ways. If you want a soft, friendly approach, it is at your fingertips. If you want a stronger approach, it is there. If you want to answer the prospect's question with a probing question of your own, there it is. And, there will be over a dozen other proven approaches.

With all these approaches and sales styles to select from, salespeople don't get bored and they don't burn out. They find their work fresh and challenging. There is always a new or creative way of *combining* powerful sales responses to increase your chances of getting the sale. You can use this script here, combine it with that script there, and weave in this other script later on. The combinations are endless, and are limited only by your imagination and the needs of the customer.

Some of the lines in a script book can be funny or a little surprising. These enhance creativity, they can be a great joy to use, and they are also very effective. **Some prospects can withstand tremendous pressure, but if you get them to laugh, it will break them wide open.**

If you think of anything especially new or creative or dazzling, you can include it in your script book. When used with the powerful voice-change and voice-matching techniques, the sales script book is perhaps the greatest tool for increasing sales creativity and innovation. The bottom line is that it adds up to more sales and more profits for you.

**Think of your script book as your cue cards.** When a highly-skilled professional actor is reading from cue cards, you never know he is reading. You are totally caught up in the drama. In exactly the same way, no prospect or customer will ever have any idea that you have professionally prepared using a script book. *All they will know is that they trust you and that what you say is convincing.*

## How to Build Your Sales Script Book

The sales script book is a business art form. Like all forms of art, it takes some discipline and training to master. The masters of this art are much in demand and are well-rewarded for their expertise.

Some of the best script book writers in the world can command over $100,000 for researching, writing, editing and producing a mastermind sales script book. *Is this too much?* Are they over-paid? Apparently not to the corporations that retain them. The corporation may make well over $1 million in increased profits through the additional sales they get with the script book technology—in some cases the corporation makes much, much more. *The corporation can make ten dollars in profit for every one dollar they expend on developing a top quality script book for their salespeople.*

There are few business investments with as substantial a return on investment as the sales script book.

*While it takes time and training to become a master at writing powerful sales script books, almost anyone can develop a basic book.* Even a basic sales script book can substantially increase sales effectiveness and profits.

**A good sales script book does not have to be long to be effective.** One of our clients, an oil and gas investment company, uses a book that is less than twelve pages long. Some of our clients in the banking industry have script books that are over 125 pages long. **The book only needs to be long enough to get the job done.** Remember, your book will contain no sales theory and no general company background information. It will only contain powerful mesmerizing sentences ready for immediate use.

If your book is going to be more than twenty pages long (and most are), it should be divided into sections. The sections should be separated by heavy sheets of paper with index tabs sticking out. *The name of each section of the book should be written on the tabs so that any desired section can be instantly located.*

So that you can develop an in-depth knowledge of how script books are developed, we have reproduced below the exact sections of a script book used by a major savings and loan in Michigan. This script book was developed for the purpose of selling this company's stock to the public. The president and several vice presidents, including David Hamilton, were involved in developing this script book with us. The sections in the book are:

1. **Features and Benefits**
2. **Why Are You Going Public?**
3. **How to Make the First Phone Call.**
4. **Getting through the Secretary.**
5. **I'm Too Busy to Consider It.**
6. **I Need More Facts.**
7. **It's Too Complicated.**
8. **It's Too New.**
9. **I Want My Investments Insured.**
10. **My Money Is All Tied Up.**

11. **I Don't Want to Pay Commissions.**
12. **I Want Liquidity.**
13. **It Is Too Risky.**
14. **Bank Stocks Haven't Been Doing Well.**
15. **I Don't Have Any Money.**
16. **I Only Invest in Real Estate.**
17. **It Is Not Guaranteed to Go Up.**
18. **I Am a Saver, Not an Investor.**
19. **I Want to Think About It.**
20. **I Need to Talk to My Spouse.**
21. **I Need to Talk to My Accountant.**

No matter what objection or stall a potential investor brought up, we had a dozen or more proven ways of dealing with it. Some of the sales scripts were soft and friendly and supportive, because that is the way some people are most comfortable selling. Some were stronger and more direct, because *some customers prefer a more direct approach.* Some were highly logical. Others were more emotional. The book contained scripts **everyone** could use. The salespeople were so well prepared, there was no objection they feared.

You will notice, though, that this mastermind script book contained more than just ways of handling objections and stalls. The third section showed a number of effective ways of making the very first phone call to a potential stock purchaser. In fact, a number of companies today are primarily using the sales script technology not to deal with objections, but to prepare for the very first sales call. They script out and rehearse the very best ways of opening each sales call. This type of scripting is working out quite well for Patterson Capital in Century City, California, which now has over $3 billion under management in its pension and fixed income funds.

**Did the script book work for this Michigan-based savings and loan?** In one month, using its own employees (not professional stock brokers) the savings and loan sold over 1,760,000 shares of stock to the public and brought in nearly $14 million dollars! *Many of these new salespeople had never sold anything before in their lives.* All were trained with the mastermind sales script book.

W. David Hamilton, the Marketing Director, wrote a letter to us which said, "We actually *exceeded our estimates* of community stock sales, saving a good deal in commissions which would otherwise be paid to underwriters in the national offering." The script book made these sales possible. The stock, by the way, has done very well, and investors have earned over 50% profit in less than a year.

# 9

## Customizing Your Script Book To Meet Your Needs And Those Of Your Customers

The sections in your script book, of course, will be different than those shown in the previous chapter, which brought the savings and loan over $14 million dollars. You'll probably have some similar sections, since nearly all of us in sales have to be able to skillfully deal with objections and stalls like, **"I Want to Think About It,"** and **"I Need to Talk to Someone Else About It."** However, even though you might have some of the same sections, the exact scripts that work best for you will be different than those that work best for another company.

## How to Strengthen Your Script Book

The reason script books are so effective is that they are totally customized. If you don't sell real estate, your hypnotic script book will contain no lines or strategies on how to sell real estate. If you don't sell computers, your script book will contain no lines on how to sell computers. It will only contain the best proven lines of top producers in your company or industry, boiled down to their essence.

To be effective, a script book must be based upon research. Sitting in your arm chair and dreaming up ways of handling objections and challenges may be fun, but it is unlikely to produce a high-quality sales script book. The reason that most canned or pre-packaged training programs lack long-term effectiveness is that they lack industry and company-specific sales scripts.

**The best way to build your sales script book is to watch and, if possible, tape record your company's sales superstars in action.** Make a note of all the major questions, stalls, objections and resistances you encounter in your sales work, and then carefully study how your sales pros handle these potential stumbling blocks. When you have captured the hypnotic words of the sales superstars, you have something worth more than its weight in gold. Organize these scripts, and index them in your book. *You will then be able to reproduce the proven techniques of top salespeople.* Your sales script book will contain knowledge, insights and techniques not available in any book store or library.

It will take some time and energy to develop a strong sales script book. Be patient. The rewards, both financial and in terms of increased self-confidence, will be great. *Remember: Even a brief, organized sales script book is better than none at all.*

## Sample Pages from a "Mastermind" Script Book

To aid you in building your own hypnotic sales script book, we will here present several pages of a "mastermind" sales script. By "mastermind," we mean that these are some of the best lines of top salespeople we have worked with in a variety of industries. We are certain that *after you have customized these scripts*, they will also help you and your salespeople to become even more successful. Pages 174-77 show how lean and mean and bottom-line oriented a real sales script book is.

## "I'M NOT INTERESTED"

**17.1 There is no reason on earth** why you should be interested in our product until I can show you how it can help you make money, increase productivity and solve some of your problems. CAN I SHOW YOU HOW WE CAN ACCOMPLISH THAT?

**17.2** (Prospect's name), 70 business executives have bought this product over the last 2 weeks and they **all** began by saying they were not interested.
They only bought because they found it would save them money and cut down on their headaches.
Would you like to learn what they learned?

**17.3** May I ask you to **consider your company's interests** for a moment?
I believe that my product will help you produce extra cash.
I would appreciate your looking at the evidence and then I'll leave it to your judgment, of course, to decide whether or not you want it.

**17.4 May I ask why?**

**17.5** This is a calculated call.
We just installed a system in a company like yours.
They are now saving money and sleeping better at night.
**Isn't your main interest in saving money?**
Can I show you how we help companies save money?

**17.6** *I would be interested in your reasons why you aren't interested.*
Did I say something that offended you?

**17.7 You are not interested in making money???**

**17.8** You are not interested??
**We very rarely hear that!**
Could you explain to me how you could not be interested in saving money and making money?
I THOUGHT THAT IS WHY YOU WERE IN BUSINESS.

# "I ONLY BUY AMERICAN PRODUCTS"

11.1 HOW ABOUT COLUMBIAN COFFEE, FRENCH WINES AND JAPANESE
STEREO EQUIPMENT?
Do you use any of those products?
Chances are, you do.
The point is, we live in a world economy.
**We all use products from many different countries
everyday.**
Why, all of a sudden, are you singling out our product, just
because it is not made in America?
*Is that fair??*
Does that make sense?

11.2 **Do you feel that the U.S. government is anti-American?**
The government makes money on every single product we
sell here—twice.
First on import duty and second on sales tax.
If it weren't profitable to the U.S. government, we
wouldn't be allowed to sell these products here.
Our sales benefit every American!

11.3 *Have you ever wondered why so many people wear sweat-
ers from Hong Kong, watches from Switzerland and cam-
eras from Japan?*
The reason is very simple.
They've got great products, and they've got great prices.
We are one of those companies with the best products and
prices.
It is really not important where our products are made.
Aren't the most important factors the quality and price of
what we offer?

11.4 *Did you know that any foreigner who has been in this
country for a certain period of time can become a U.S.
citizen?*
Well, the same is true with our product.
We have been here so long, we are practically American.

11.5 Our company employs over 500 able Americans.
We pay thousands of dollars in taxes.
We're producing 20% of all of the parts we use here in America.
DON'T BE FOOLED BY OUR FOREIGN-SOUNDING NAME.
*We are more American than most "American" companies!*

## "THERE ARE HARD TIMES AHEAD"

14.1 That's exactly the reason why we recommend buying now, so that you will be able to meet the hard times head-on with increased productivity.

14.2 **If you were the captain of an ocean liner, you wouldn't stop sailing just because you saw a little storm cloud on the horizon, would you?**
Well, your company is like that ocean liner.
Are you going to stop leading and managing your company just because there might be some difficult times ahead?

14.3 You know what they say about the success rate of economic forecasters?
They accurately predicted nine of the last two recessions. (Say this with a smile in your voice.)
**Are you absolutely sure a depression is ahead?**
Even if there is, it may be smart to do what many of our clients do and give us a large order now to have materials on hand if times get tough.

14.4 **Hard times call for a harder look at lower costs and higher profits.**
Luckily, you'll get both with our product.
*Why not place an order today?*

14.5 **Is it just a matter of money?**
If so, I am certain we will be able to extend you credit to pay this off conveniently.
Shall we look at our credit terms?

14.6 **Why** do you expect hard times ahead?

14.7 **Who told you** there will be hard times ahead?
*Does he really have a crystal ball?*
Can anyone, besides God, really predict the future??

## Updating Your Script Book for Fast Action

Notice that there is an index tab on the side of each page which identifies which stall or objection is being handled. In an actual sales script book, you only have this index tab on the first page of each section. The tab enables you to immediately go to any section of the book you desire. Your very best hypnotic words are at your fingertips!

**Whenever you have the opportunity to hear a sales superstar in your industry give a presentation, seize the chance.** Take accurate notes on his or her most successful sentences. By adding these phrases to your script book, you will be acquiring the power of that sales superstar.

Start your script book by customizing and adding to the scripts we have provided for you here. Then, start new sections for the special objections you encounter in your industry. Have brain-storming sessions with your fellow top salespeople to get powerful new scripts. As your script book grows in completeness, your self-confidence and your sales will soar! You will fear no objection!

How is it possible that some salespeople are able to consistently earn $100,000, $200,000 or even more per year in personal income, while others selling the same product and working just as many hours flounder? What is the sales superstar an expert in?

He or she is not to be distinguished by product knowledge, as product knowledge is easy to come by. *Any high-school kid can memorize product brochures.* The sales superstar is distinguished by an expertise in people and an expertise in motivating people.

How does this "people expertise" show up? It shows up **in the ways they use words to influence and persuade other human beings.** It is their special skills in using words which makes them so richly successful. **And, this is precisely what your sales script book contains.**

When you are doing your sales work over the phone, leaf through your book for outstanding ways of handling any objections you hear. If you are hit with an objection or stall you can't handle, it simply means it is time to start a new section of your book! As your book gets richer and more complete, you will find your closing ratio increasing dramatically. *One of our clients recently invested 3 hours doing cold calls with his new hypnotic script book and had a 100% success rate in getting people to come in for a sales presentation!*

## Keeping Your Script Book Safe and Secure

Also as your script book gets stronger and more complete, you will want to protect it. After seeing how well it works for you, the last thing in the world you would want is for a competitor or another salesperson to get their hands on your very best lines and scripts. ALWAYS KNOW WHERE YOUR SCRIPT BOOK IS! A good script book is worth more than its weight in gold. With it, you can make enough sales to buy perhaps a hundred pounds of gold.

If one of your competitors got their hands on your finished sales script book, their sales could take off and yours might decline. It is the very effectiveness of the sales script book that leads many sales executives to have their script books numbered and registered. One of our corporate clients, a Vice President of Sales for a Fortune 500 company, knows where every one of the 41 copies of his division's script books are at all times. Also, the dark red paper and black ink they are printed with comes out nearly black on most photocopying machines. It is no accident that his sales force has retained their #1 position in this highly competitive company for several years!

## How to Find Script Book Writers

Just as very few companies today do all of their own legal work or advertising work, few would try to tackle a full-blown script book project. It is more expensive and more time-consuming to produce a comprehensive script book in-house than it is to delegate it to outside experts. Moreover, an in-house produced script book is usually not as effective as one produced by full-time sales scripting experts.

The only thing worse than having no script book at all for your sales team is having one that doesn't work, or one that contains outmoded or ineffective lines. We have been called in numerous times to "clean-up" existing script books, and have found that, in most cases, it is wiser to start from scratch than to try to patch up a poorly-conceived and poorly-written script book.

In selecting writers or consultants to help you develop a script book, experience is all important. Check references carefully. Make certain your script book consultants have a library of at least 10 to 20 master sales script books to draw upon, because no matter how good your best people are, there will be ways of handling objections they have never thought of. These can only be gleaned from the master-mind script books of other sales superstars. That is why the script book library is so important.

Make sure that your script book developers study your top salespeople before they start writing the script book. They have to be willing to travel with your best salespeople to capture their most powerful ways of selling and of handling objections. They must be willing to meet with your top people in groups to brainstorm the script book. The consultants must be keen observers and listeners. They must be willing to work hard at the research. If they tell you they will write the scripts from their own home office, or "customize" an existing program, or if they tell you that research will be minimal or unnecessary, you should probably look for other script book writers. We have never seen a good sales script book that was not based on extensive research of sales superstars in action.

If you select the right sales script book developers, they will make the process of building a script book almost effortless for you. Once the script book is installed in your sales force and once your people are taught how to skillfully use it, your salespeople will become **systematic sales geniuses.** They will be able to quickly master all of the powerful forms of hypnotic salesmanship contained in this book because these forms of persuasion will be built-in to the scripts!

## How Script Books Help Make Every Day a Great Sales Day

With a powerful sales script book to work from, your salespeople will no longer have "good days" and "bad days;" every day should be a great day. A strong sales script book is one of the greatest aids to "positive thinking" ever devised. *Without a proven set of scripts, your salespeople have a right to be depressed.* Depression is the appropriate mental state for an unprepared person doing a tough job. With a fine set of scripts, they can't help but have a more positive outlook on the world and on the profession of selling.

At some point in the future, most of the companies in your industry may have sales script books. However, right now, only a fortunate few probably do, and they are likely to be profiting handsomely from the use of this scientific sales tool. Start building your script book today and have this advantage before one of your competitors gets it. If you are sincere about making more money by increasing your sales, developing a powerful sales script book is one of the quickest ways of achieving that goal. Hypnotic sales script books are working in many of the most successful companies in America, and they can work for you.

# 10

## Mastering Sales Hypnosis Through State-Of-The-Art Training Technology

Now that you know what sales hypnosis is and how it works, how can you master it to increase your own sales? Not just learn it—but truly *master* it?

The answer is found in the new high-technology sales training systems that have recently become available. Whether you are a sales professional, a corporate sales trainer, a Vice President of Sales, a Vice President of Marketing, or one of the tens of thousands of business consultants in this country, you'll find many advantages to the new interactive video and interactive audio training systems. They can dramatically increase sales skills and, thus give you a major competitive advantage. And, they can do this while lowering your costs of sales training.

It is widely accepted that the most effective way to learn verbal techniques and verbal material is through interactive practice with feedback. This is also the best way to build *comfort* and *self-confidence* in using new verbal material.

**The most effective interactive *training* technique is known as role-playing.** Of all the corporate trainers and training departments we have worked with, we haven't yet encountered a trainer who said that role-playing doesn't work. We have found that it works in teaching sales hypnosis and it works in teaching virtually *any* sales or management skill. However, while the power and utility of role-playing have been recognized for many years, role-playing has been under-utilized in most business, sales and training environments.

In this chapter, you will learn about some of the **challenges** that conventional role-playing presents. After reading about each challenge, *you will learn how breakthroughs in interactive training technology (interactive video and interactive audio) have successfully addressed that challenge.* You will learn how forward-thinking individuals and businesses are getting a competitive edge over others by combining this new technology with sales hypnosis.

You will learn how results-oriented companies are training their employees more thoroughly and more expertly, in a shorter time period, and at lower cost than they ever imagined possible by utilizing this new training technology.

**Interactive video training and interactive audio training together make up a $1 billion industry.** Despite the exponential growth of this new industry, it is still not well-known to many of the 14 million people in sales. That is rapidly changing. In the coming decade, the interactive learning industry is expected to more than double in size and to replace many old-fashioned sales training and management training programs.

If you want to be on the cutting edge of exciting new developments in human psychology and exciting training techniques, then interactive high-technology instruction is where you want to be. Due to the youth of the field and due to the effectiveness of this learning methodology, a great many new jobs are being created in this field. Consultants with expertise in interactive learning systems are much in demand and developing your expertise in this area will make you a much more valuable member of your corporate sales team.

## Moving Into the 21st Century with Interactive High Technology Training

**Interactive video** training employs a compact video disk player, computer and keyboard. Hundreds of thousands or millions of images can be stored on the video CD (compact disk) and the trainee can interact with customers and prospects he sees on the video screen by typing responses in through the keyboard. **Interactive audio** is based on a dual-cassette stereo dubbing deck which is equipped with headphones and a tiny microphone. The trainee using interactive audio can *directly* talk back to and interact with customers and prospects on audio tape. Since interactive audio does not require the use of a keyboard, typing skills are not required.

The key to the effectiveness of interactive video and interactive audio training is that they enable the salesperson or trainee to practice and refine sales skills by directly interacting with customers presented on video or audio tape. You don't just sit back and passively listen to or watch a tape of a customer—you interact with and talk back to that customer! In doing so, you quickly find out how much you know (or don't know) and you practice and strengthen your most important sales skills, including pacing, sales stories, and the other techniques you have learned about in this book. It is an exciting way to learn that really helps you internalize the techniques you are learning.

Both interactive video and interactive audio learning systems can be programmed with an unlimited variety of software, *an unlimited variety of types of customers,* and an unlimited number of customer objections or questions. In teaching sales hypnosis techniques, these systems are especially useful because the trainee can be taught not just the words, but also how to say the words.

Interactive video and interactive audio training enable the salesperson or trainee to gain all the benefits of role-playing without the necessity and costs of assembling a group of people to do the role-playing. This is because these new training methods are based on individual SELF-PACED instruction. The trainee interacts directly with the interactive video compact disk or the interactive audio machine and progresses at his or her own rate. Role-playing can thus now be done on an individual basis.

## The Unique Advantages of Interactive Video and Audio Training

Interactive video and interactive audio training combines the ability to create custom material to meet virtually any imaginable learning scenario with an interactive device that allows the salesperson or trainee to learn that material.

In other words, YOUR trainees can learn YOUR company's most powerful sales scripts and sales presentations in an interactive format.

Most important of all, they can learn your company's material and the expert presentation **at their own rate, without the constant attention of a training specialist.** In addition, they can learn all of these techniques and sales presentations in a much shorter period of time.

How can interactive high-technology training save you money? Many trainees receive a company draw or salary during their training. By shortening the amount of time training takes, less money needs to be invested in each trainee before it is determined whether or not he or she will "make the grade." By monitoring the trainees' progress on high-technology training, the trainer or coach is able to evaluate attitude and skill level *early in the probationary period* and judge whether the trainee is likely to "make it" before investing heavily in further time, effort and expense.

Using interactive video and interactive audio, your salespeople or trainees can expertly learn sophisticated sales presentations at less expense and with less effort than was ever dreamed possible. Sophisticated sales techniques such as hypnotic story-telling, which can take many, many hours of personal one-on-one coaching to teach a trainee, can now be largely self-taught with interactive video and interactive audio. This is an exciting breakthrough in sales training.

Interactive video and interactive audio training is flexible in its design and is adaptable to the demands of the user. For instance, in many cases, the reaction time of the student will be important. If you are teaching salespeople how to speak slowly to hypnotically match the speech rate of slow-speaking customers, you can adjust the video or audio player to allow a slower reaction time. If you are teaching them to speak quickly to hypnotically match the speech rate of rapid speakers, you can set a faster reaction time.

Using interactive training systems, questions or objections can be presented at anything from a leisurely pace to a very rapid one. The beginning student can be given more time to formulate a response. The more advanced student can be tested for his or her ability to rapidly "think on his feet." This is accomplished through an adjustable threshold for trainees' reaction times. An immediate response can be requested or the trainee can be given some time to formulate an answer. This special feature adapts the learning software to meet the needs of all levels of trainees.

Interactive video and audio training also has the capability of handling student responses of different lengths. Some salespeople and trainees will have short responses and others will respond at greater length. High technology training systems accommodate all response lengths. In teaching sales hypnosis, you want the trainee to be able to put together as many interconnected sentences as is effective. Interactive video and interactive audio adjusts for this need.

In the 1990s, it is likely that a majority of companies will be using interactive video and interactive audio training. For now, those companies using these high technology training systems have a significant competitive edge. Utilizing interactive video and interactive audio training in your training department or your consulting business enables you to train more people, more thoroughly and at lower cost.

## The Four Skill-Building Benefits
## of Interactive Video and Audio Training

Interactive video and interactive audio training allows the learning, training, and rehearsing of hypnotic sales techniques to be carried out in a *planned* sequential manner. This insures that the salesperson will steadily and progressively move through the important steps of skill development. The benefits to the salesperson include:

Initial familiarization with the full body of knowledge on hypnotic selling and familiarization with the Expert Model of master salesmanship can be done at a pace suited to the individual.

An unlimited number of exercise sessions may be repeated with the same material or different lessons, without drawing upon the time and energy of a live trainer.

The amount of time given to the trainee to react to a question or inquiry is adjustable. This time requirement may be progressively reduced to prepare trainees for real life conditions. Reaction time may be preset by the instructor or reset incrementally by the trainee based on his progress.

The student can repeat the lesson and review his or her efforts until he has recorded a result that is ready for evaluation by the instructor. Thus, the instructor does not need to spend time reviewing work in progress but rather can concentrate on evaluating the final results.

Major companies all across the United States, Canada, Australia and Europe are investing tens of millions of dollars in these new training technologies. Why all of the excitement? *Why are companies moving away from the tried and proven method of live role-playing to these new high-technology training systems?*

Despite its popularity, *conventional* role-playing presented an almost overwhelming number of challenges and problems which have only now been solved with interactive video and interactive audio training.

## The Seven Major Advantages
## of High Technology Training Systems

*1. Conventional Role-Playing Is Time Consuming*

In a typical corporate classroom environment of 15 to 20 students, each role-playing exercise can take a couple of hours if each trainee demonstrates his skills and gets individual feedback. Without this demonstration of skills and without the feedback, role-playing is much less effective than it could be. Teaching hypnotic selling techniques and other sales techniques in a group setting takes a significant investment of time. Another hour or more can be spent on analysis of each role-play and on playback of tapes, if video is used.

Despite its time-consuming nature, many competitive companies did invest days in role-playing training because it increases skills far more than simply reading training manuals, listening to audio tapes, watching conventional (non-interactive) videos or attending lectures.

This challenge is solved by interactive video and interactive audio, because these new training methods do not require that a group of individuals be assembled for training to take place. Since this high-technology training is based on the proven methodology of SELF-PACED INSTRUCTION, each trainee can progress at his or her own rate. A slow learner won't hold up the rest of the group, and a fast learner won't get bored by a slow pace. If a student wants to repeat a lesson to deepen his or her understanding, this is easily accomplished because the high-technology learning systems allow learning to be done on an *individual* basis.

Interactive automated training can be used during *non-peak business hours*, or whenever convenient. Skill development with high-technology interactive training does not interfere with business hours or on-going sales efforts. Since it is based on self-paced instruction, high-technology training saves the time of the instructor for its highest and best use. The instructor or trainer can monitor his or her students' recorded responses when it is most convenient for the instructor.

## 2. Conventional Role-Playing Can Be Tedious for the Instructor

Role-playing is a form of a drill. It increases skills by repetitively taking the students through several real life challenges. *As the salespeople practice their skills again and again, and as they receive feedback, they improve.* However, it can be boring for an instructor to take new trainees through the same sales lessons time after time. The instructor, of course, has long since learned all of these lessons and may find little intellectual excitement or stimulation in going through them so many times with group after group.

This challenge is solved by high technology interactive training systems because such systems never get tired. They are as fresh and effective at 7:00 p.m. as they are at 6:00 a.m. If the trainee wishes to go through a lesson again and again, interactive video and interactive audio oblige where a live instructor could not or would not. For example, in teaching hypnotic pacing or matching techniques to build trust, we have found that many students need extensive practice to master voice rate and voice volume pacing. These lessons can easily be repeated with the high-technology training systems so that the trainee masters these important skills.

High-technology training is thus consistently excellent and insures a predictable high level of competency in those being trained. While all instructors occasionally have a bad day, high-technology interactive systems never have a bad day.

### 3. Conventional Role-Playing Is Expensive

Because it takes so much time, role-playing can be expensive. For example, if each employee's time is worth $10 an hour, a two day program for 20 employees costs the company a minimum of $3,200, plus the cost of the instructor and the cost of the training facility.

There are also many other significant costs which are more difficult to quantify. Chief among these is the cost of lost business. While employees are in a training program, they are not bringing in business for the company. If the cost of lost business is quantified, it will be discovered that for many companies, the true cost of a role-playing training program is at least $5,000 per day for each small group trained. Multiplied over the course of a year, this dollar amount can become very significant. Yet, companies continue to train their employees with role-playing because role-playing is so much more effective than either listening to tapes or watching conventional videos or going to lecture-based seminars.

Whereas conventional role-playing always costs money, automated interactive training can quickly become a profit generator. High-technology training pays for itself very quickly through a rapid return of the original investment and then through increased profits. *For example, we have found that a mere seven hours of interactive video or interactive audio training in sales hypnosis can significantly increase sales closing ratios.* This cannot be said for seven hours of listening to sales lectures or watching conventional (passive) sales films.

With automated interactive training, transportation costs and lodging costs are reduced or non-existent. High-technology training can be economically installed in branch locations of a business to insure constant on-going reinforcement of lessons learned without the necessity of traveling back to headquarters. Since trainees can learn on automated training systems during non-peak business hours, there is minimal interruption of on-going business.

The master tape modules of high-technology training systems can be designed to deliver or reinforce lessons in 30-minute to 90-minute segments. Sales hypnosis topics you have read about in this book can be presented and demonstrated and practiced in a step-by-step manner in 30-minute learning modules. Therefore, the need to take entire days off work for training is dramatically reduced or eliminated.

There are significant cost differences between interactive video and interactive audio systems. The initial purchase price of interactive video equipment is similar to that for interactive audio systems. However, the interactive video *software* is much more expensive than its interactive audio equivalent. Many companies find interactive video software is prohibitively expensive to develop in-house.

The amount of equipment and technical expertise required to produce interactive video software puts such production out of the range of all but the largest corporations. Therefore, most training departments are limited to buying "off-the-shelf" generic software for their interactive video training programs. With interactive audio, customized master learning tapes can be affordably prepared in-house and can be updated as needed.

### 4. Some Instructors Don't Like to Do Role-Playing

Some instructors and trainers don't use role-playing as much as they should because they would rather be in front of an audience than a member of an audience. It may be a part of human nature to prefer to be a"star" rather than a "star maker." Consequently, many trainers spend too much time talking and not enough time letting their people talk and practice skills.

Another challenge with conventional role-playing is that it is difficult for anyone to listen for hours to the presentations of other people. It is tiring to listen to a multi-hour presentation of even a *highly*-skilled speaker. It is especially difficult to listen for hours to the presentations of new trainees. It takes great patience and a very high energy level to do extensive role-playing training. Moreover, many trainers and instructors have numerous other job responsibilities which limit the amount of time they can invest in role-playing training.

Despite the fact that some trainers don't like to do role-playing, virtually all trainers admit that role-playing is the most powerful training method available. Nothing can substitute for role-playing—not books, not lectures, not training films or ordinary audio tapes. Those who have studied the research and findings on adult learning know that adults prefer to learn by doing, and they learn best by engaging in tasks that closely approximate real life situations. We have found that in teaching sales hypnosis there is nothing more effective than role-playing and interactive practice.

Automated training systems solve this challenge by making real-life learning simulations possible *without the constant attention of a live trainer*. In teaching sales hypnosis, trainees can practice their choice of hypnotic words and the delivery of those hypnotic words over and over until they have achieved mastery. Students thus get the experience they need in dealing with customers and prospects without taking such large amounts of the time and energy of corporate trainers. The trainer or instructor can then concentrate on his or her highest and best uses in instructional design and in coaching those being trained.

### 5. Some Salespeople Don't Like to Do Role-Plays

The reason some salespeople or trainees don't like to do role-plays is that participants are on public display. Other people can see how skilled *or unskilled* they are. There is no way to hide. By contrast, in a conventional seminar, participants merely talk about ideas or talk about techniques. *Simply talking about techniques is much easier than actually showing what you can do*. It is the difference between talking about brain surgery and actually doing brain surgery, the difference between talking about hitting a home run and actually hitting a home run. Most conventional sales training is "talking about" rather than "doing."

Since a role-play reveals just how skilled or unskilled a person is, **preparation must take place**. Salespeople must work to become good at the skills being tested. The learning process requires high quality involvement from the trainee, and that is what makes it so effective. However, trainees who are shy or insecure do not like the public nature of *conventional* role-playing. If students haven't been given enough time to prepare for the role-play, those with high standards or who are perfectionists will probably not be satisfied with the results they are able to display .

This challenge in conventional training is solved by interactive audio and interactive video training because salespeople and trainees can **practice in complete privacy** with these high technology learning systems. Practicing with some privacy, trainees are uninhibited and unselfconscious and thus can fully concentrate on the skills to be mastered. Their mastery of these skills leads to increased self-esteem, increased self-confidence, and better presentations in front of groups. In addition, interactive video and interactive audio have many of the characteristics of games. Since the process of using these interactive systems is inherently enjoyable, trainees practice *more* and thus rapidly increase their skills.

The newest interactive audio systems, which are called "roleplayers" are especially exciting for teaching sales hypnosis. By listening to their own presentations and by listening to their own interactions with customers, trainees are able to *self-correct* and rapidly improve their performance. This continual feedback is almost never present in conventional training. Auditory feedback is also lacking from most interactive video training because interactive video systems use keyboard interface rather than verbal interaction.

Many professional trainers and consultants feel that verbal interaction is a closer approximation to real life situations than is the use of a keyboard. We have found that since word pronunciation and phrasing are especially important in hypnotic selling (and in all selling!), interactive audio training has a significant advantage over interactive video. In the future, we expect that new, more powerful computer interfaces will be able to combine interactive audio and interactive video into one complete simulation of all real life sales situations. However, due to the incredible complexities inherent in programming computers to recognize and process words spoken with different accents and speaking styles, this next generation of learning technology probably won't be seen until the 21st century.

While salespeople and trainees can use high-technology training systems with privacy guaranteed, there are also add-on devices which permit the trainer or instructor to listen in or monitor as many as ten trainees working with interactive systems. *The instructor can then give individualized feedback and coaching to each trainee in privacy.* This unique feature combines the best of personalized, private self-paced learning with the efficiency of group instruction.

### 6. Role-Playing Requires Special Skills

Not all competent, qualified instructors possess the special skills required to do role-playing. To be outstanding and inspiring at role-playing, the instructor or coach must be able to present an expert model of what a top performer should do. For example, in teaching sales hypnosis, the trainer should be highly skilled in using the techniques (not just talking about them!).

Trainees who do not see expert models in action do not have a clear idea of the level of performance they are aiming for. A trainee who hears a lecture about hypnotic pacing and matching techniques but does not see and hear them demonstrated will not have a clear idea of exactly what he or she should do. Without this clear goal his movement towards an ideal performance is non-systematic, happenstance and slower than it should be. Some instructors cannot do role-plays well and so avoid them. When this happens, the company suffers and salespeople do not gain the skills they need.

*Conventional lecturing only requires the ability to memorize material.* This is much simpler than knowing how to present skills in a true-to-life simulation (role-playing). Instructors who can't do it avoid role-playing, not because there is a better way to develop skills, but because of their own personal limitations.

Interactive video and interactive audio training addresses this challenge by **empowering** individual sales professionals, sales trainers and business consultants. High-technology training makes it possible for almost anyone to offer a consistently high level of outstanding instruction. *Since the expert performances are on video or audio tape*, the instructor does not have to be an actual expert in doing such demonstrations. He or she needs only to possess skills as a facilitator and coach. With expert demonstrations on interactive video and interactive audio, there is no longer any reason for instructors to avoid role-playing and the skills it develops.

Salespeople using an interactive training system have an idealized performance, or several different idealized performances, from which to model their own behavior. They then interact with customers and prospects and can immediately practice the skills they just learned. This creates an optimal learning environment as there is no time gap between the learning of ideas, principles and techniques *and their practice.* We have found that in teaching sales hypnosis, it is absolutely essential that trainees practice the hypnotic techniques as soon as possible after they have heard about them. This insures internalization and ownership of the techniques learned.

### 7. Role-Playing Can Be Boring for Some Trainees

Many salespeople are fascinated by role-playing *when they are doing the role-play*. It can be fun and challenging to be on center stage—especially when you are using sales hypnosis. However, it can get tedious or boring to watch trainee after trainee go through the same presentation or sales call in front of the group. The boredom factor alone can account for a significant *mental* drop-out rate among participants in multi-day role-playing training programs. We have found that salespeople, especially, are action-oriented and that they are particularly easily frustrated by having to watch many other people practice. They don't want to watch other people do, **they want to do!**

High-technology training solves this problem by utilizing self-paced instruction, and thus the trainee is seldom, if ever, bored. He or she can progress at his or her own rate. More ambitious, energetic or brighter students can progress at a faster rate. Other students can repeat lessons as necessary. We have found that in teaching sales hypnosis, interactive video and interactive audio training enables the "slower" more methodical trainees to actually achieve just as high a skill level as the faster "quick study" trainees. Since trainees don't have to "wait for their turn," each trainee learns more in a shorter period of time through constant high-quality involvement and interaction with the learning software.

## Additional Applications of High Technology Training

Conventional role-playing has been used extensively in training and business because it does work and because no alternative training method produces equivalent results. However, with the advent of automated interactive training systems, the role-playing can occur without the constant attention of a live trainer. Interactive video and interactive audio training also solve many of the challenges inherent in role-playing. High-technology training is thus, in most cases, less expensive, less time-consuming and more effective than live role-playing training. High-technology training helps the salesperson or trainee achieve a level of skill and self-confidence that lectures and conventional audio tapes and videotapes cannot provide.

There are applications for automated interactive training in many fields including sales training, management training, public school education, foreign language training, law, and the performing arts. Students training with high-technology learning systems have the advantage of a skilled tutor that is ever ready to coach them.

If you are a sales professional, a sales executive, or a business consultant, you will find interactive video or audio training the most valuable addition you can make to your training program this year. Automated interactive training frees you up from the most tedious aspects of training and consulting—and it insures the transfer of knowledge and skills.

Interactive video and interactive audio training, combined with software based on the skills of sales champions, enables you to teach and test the most important hypnotic sales skills and closing skills. Let's examine a real-life application to see how this is accomplished.

## How to Increase Telemarketing Effectiveness
## through High Technology Training

Telemarketing is one of the most rapidly growing areas of employment in the United States today. According to McGraw-Hill Research, a typical face-to-face sales call now costs approximately $248—when all costs of the car, gasoline, travel time, presentation time, etc. are factored in. *The average telemarketing sales call costs less than $10*. Businesses simply can't afford the old door-to-door sales call of the past. Consequently, telemarketing is the wave of the future.

While telemarketing saves money, there is no guarantee it will bring in sales unless the telemarketers are highly trained. Telemarketing is a sedentary job that has many stresses. Due to the high level of rejection telemarketers get, turnover is a fact of life. Some telemarketing sales managers have 100% turnover every year! Thus, new salespeople must be constantly hired and trained, which takes a great deal of time and energy. Interactive high-technology training to the rescue!

A skilled telemarketer can be just as effective as a sales- person out in the field. To develop telemarketing skills, salespeople must be trained to handle customer questions, objections, opinions, reactions and complaints. They must also know how to use what we call ICR's or Interest Creating Remarks. When you call someone on the phone, you are almost undoubtedly interrupting some other activity. Unless you have a compelling Interest Creating Remark or unless you can offer a strong benefit, they won't want to listen to you.

In training telemarketers, the prospects opinions, needs, questions, and objections are presented to the trainee. The trainee practices making an appropriate response to further the conversation, uncover the buyer's needs, and close the sale. Using conventional training methods, this is a very time-consuming, energy-consuming, and money-consuming process!

Due to the high turnover in telemarketing and the limited time trainers have to spend with new employees, *many telemarketers are not trained as thoroughly as they should be*. Consequently, poorly-trained or half-trained new telemarketers are let loose on the buying public. As a result, telemarketers are held in low esteem by the general public—and sometimes even by the executives of their own companies.

Using interactive video and interactive audio, telemarketers can be trained in friendly yet powerful methods of hypnotic selling. As the sales-person goes through the program several times, he or she has an opportunity to practice hypnotic pacing, delivery style and verbal emphasis—some of the most important skills of telemarketing. Interactive audio training records the student's responses and by listening to his or her taped responses, and in practicing the material again, the student self-corrects and improves the presentation.

## Success Stories of Companies Using High Technology Training

Do interactive video and interactive audio training actually work in teaching telemarketing skills? The results produced by GTE Interactive Video are impressive. This new division of GTE has used interactive video to teach pacing techniques and other powerful presentation techniques to *dozens* of major telemarketing companies around the United States. Documented increases in sales due to this training total in the tens of millions of dollars.

International Trading Group, Inc. was one of the first companies to train its telemarketers with the new interactive audio system known as RolePlayer. Teaching both pacing and leading techniques with RolePlayer, the telemarketers at International Trading Group have been able to take away market share from their competitors in a highly competitive industry.

History is now being written by the ambitious pioneers who are training their salespeople with interactive video and audio. Recently, United Resources, the second largest annuities company in the nation, began using RolePlayer to train their salespeople in interactive verbal skills. Their ambition is nothing less than to become the largest annuities company in the nation! Those who have reviewed the expert model United Resources has built of its sales superstars are saying that this goal is attainable. Kenny Clyde, a Vice President, has publicly stated, "We wanted to develop the best sales training program in the industry. Now we have it."

Interactive video and interactive audio training rapidly get the salesperson in a comfort zone of safely practicing powerful sales techniques. *Actual customers are very valuable resources in most businesses, and it can be dangerous to have new employees "learn on" them as guinea pigs.* It is much safer to practice on model customers stored on interactive video or interactive audio. In businesses such as real estate, stocks, bonds or commodities (in which a license is required to sell the product), the future sales pro may practice and gain substantial skills using interactive video and interactive audio training *before* getting his or her license. Such unlicensed new employees obviously cannot practice with real customers, but interactive video and interactive audio gives them the opportunity to interact with taped simulations of those customers they will soon be encountering.

A testing program to measure what the salesperson has mastered can be implemented by using alternate learning program software that presents different opinions, reactions and objections of customers—or that presents the previously learned material *in a different scenario* or in a different order.

In summary, by allowing the trainee to perform the repetitious—but all important—*skill-building* portion of the sales training process on his own using interactive audio and interactive video, the effectiveness and efficiency of the instructor and the learning process are significantly increased.

## How Customized High Technology Training Programs Facilitate Growth

Custom programs can be created for interactive audio and interactive video whenever the need arises. When your company introduces a new product or service, a new master interaction tape or video can be developed to teach salespeople how to sell it. *When your company expands to a new geographical area, a new master learning program can be created to teach employees how to gain accounts there.* Thus, high-technology training provides obvious advantages for any growing company that is introducing new products or expanding into new territories.

New tapes or videos can be created to teach sales hypnosis quickly and thoroughly, with reduced or minimal effort from the live trainers or instructors. Master learning tapes, known as the learning software, can be produced in-house or by outside vendors. Every year, hundreds of new high-income jobs are being created for people who know how to create master learning tapes for interactive video and interactive audio. It is one of the most exciting new frontiers of adult education. These master learning tapes are replacing books and workbooks as the means by which sales knowledge is transferred in corporate America today.

We are proud to have had the opportunity to have worked with many outstanding companies in creating expert models of sales superstars. The need is so great for software developers and expert model script writers that the consulting companies existing today cannot meet it. Trainers and script writers with motivation, creativity and new ideas are needed in ever increasing numbers in the interactive video and interactive audio training industries.

## How to Protect Your High-Technology Training Software

Since high-technology interactive video and interactive audio training is so effective, some companies are taking special steps to guard the security of their learning software. On machines such as the interactive audio RolePlayer, master learning tapes can only be made or modified by people possessing a special key to the machine. Any salesperson can use the machine as a trainee and thus improve his sales skills, *but only authorized software developers or approved in-house trainers are given the key that enables them to develop the expert model software.* This helps insure that an unauthorized person will not change the messages on the master learning tapes.

As another means of protecting their valuable learning software, other companies are locking this software in vaults each night. They don't do this with ordinary old-fashioned sales training manuals and ordinary seminar workbooks. The power and effectiveness of customized company-specific hypnotic selling programs seems to beg for such protection. The nightmare these sales managers have is that a competitor will get their hands on the powerful sales techniques that their top producers have used and perfected.

## Capitalizing on the Benefits of High-Technology Training

Since an unlimited variety of training software can be developed in-house or by outside vendors for automated interactive training systems, virtually any business or sales subject or skill can be taught rapidly, professionally, thoroughly, and at low cost using high-tech training systems. Training lessons, expert models, sales skills, sales hypnosis, product information, and company procedures—all now captured on interactive audio tape or interactive video discs—can be easily and rapidly updated. With interactive video and interactive audio, there is no longer any need to put up with old or outdated training materials. The state of the art, the "unteachable" hypnotic skills of sales superstars, can now be systematically taught using interactive video and interactive audio training.

# 11

## Unleashing The Power Of Self-Hypnosis

There is another *crucial* element in the sales hypnosis formula, but instead of using hypnotic states with the client or customer, it is focused on ourselves. This element is self-hypnosis.

Self-hypnosis occurs frequently in everyday life and can be found in such diverse activities as day-dreaming, jogging, prayer, reading, listening to music, meditation, or even driving the freeways. Once in the self-induced hypnotic state, suggestibility is greatly heightened. Psychological barriers and defenses are lowered, and the person's unconscious becomes more receptive to new programming. *This offers a unique opportunity for the sales professional to give himself or herself positive messages that will impact on later thinking, attitudes and behaviors.*

Self-hypnosis can be used to overcome problems and concerns such as fear of cold calling, anxieties about a competitor's product or pricing, reluctance to ask for the order, high levels of stress, nervousness, or concerns about self-image. *Self-hypnosis can even be used to transform many of these fears or concerns into strengths.*

In self-hypnosis, resistance is minimal to nonexistent because the person is *voluntarily* engaging in the self-programming.

There are a number of easy, practical ways to practice self-hypnosis without having to sit in a darkened room, perhaps with a candle flickering on the desk, and stare at a shiny gold watch that swings rhythmically from a chain. Those props are not necessary because any set of words, thoughts, suggestions, visual images, or auditory messages, *when repeated over and over again*, develop the ability to mesmerize.

## How to Use Repetition to Trigger Self-Hypnosis

In sales and marketing, Madison Avenue has long used advertising techniques based on self-hypnosis, or, as it is sometimes known, "autohypnosis." A famous saying in advertising is, "**Nothing sells like repetition.**" Advertisers know that a message repeated again and again can sink into the *deepest* subconscious levels of a person's mind. Consequently, the movement in advertising now is for *relatively simple messages* presented continuously over a period of time. In radio advertising, for example, spots are not sold individually, but in groups of 25 or 50 or 100 or more to each client company.

Why is the *repetition* of a message so effective in triggering autohypnosis? The first time we hear something, we might doubt it. It might even shock or surprise us. By the fifth time we have heard it, it has become "old news." After we have heard it fifty times, it is a part of our subconscious minds. We might even find it difficult to remember a time when we didn't like Tide detergent or Palmolive soap or Ritz crackers. *We like and trust what is familiar* and familiarity is bred through continuous presentations.

In some cases, autohypnotic messages may even seem to acquire a life of their own. Have you ever found yourself humming an ad for MacDonald's hamburgers or for Juicy Fruit chewing gum? You heard the ad so many times, it became a part of your subconscious programming.

In the same way that Madison Avenue advertises to us through repetition, *we can create our own ads and advertise to ourselves.* However, instead of selling ourselves a product, we can sell ourselves on powerful thoughts and powerful actions. If we program ourselves with these powerful thoughts on a regular basis, we internalize them and believe them.

Many top athletes use forms of autohypnosis. Some repeat phrases such as, "I am relaxed and strong," or "I am full of energy," hundreds of times. They also visualize perfect performance. They see themselves effortlessly gliding over the hurdles, swimming through the water like a dolphin, or giving it that last kick in the final mile of the marathon. Gradually, these messages are *internalized* as part of the athletes' unconscious—part of their personality—and, as a result, show up in their behaviors during competition.

These athletes realize that the human mind is never a vacuum and that *we are always thinking of something.* Knowing this, they have decided to actively take control of their thinking by programming their minds with positive thoughts and images of perfect performances. It is a powerful hypnotic process that gives a competitive edge.

## Using Self-Hypnosis to Transform Negative Thoughts Into Positive Action

Competition is also the hallmark of most sales jobs, and it is essential for salespeople to be relaxed, strong, full of energy, and motivated.

Take the case of Jay, a stockbroker for one of the major brokerage houses. After the crash of October 19, 1987, Jay found that he was having difficulty making cold calls. For the first time in his brokerage career, he felt paralyzed when he attempted to cold call new prospects. As his stomach tied up in knots, he looked for anything else he could do to avoid making cold calls. He re-read the *Wall Street Journal*, he straightened out his files, he re-organized his desk, he even typed letters. He did anything and everything except make cold calls.

Jay found that he had been negatively hypnotizing himself with the following self-talk:

**"Cold calls are worthless."**

**"No one wants to talk with me."**

**"This is a waste of time."**

**"No one wants to buy stocks anymore."**

**"Why did I ever go into this business?"**

Jay had *unwittingly* re-programmed himself with thoughts that destroyed his ability to make cold calls.

We then taught Jay how to use some new methods of self-hypnosis which are specifically designed to substitute positive thoughts and expectations for negative ones. Here are some of the autohypnosis affirmations he used:

**"I am a skilled cold-caller."**

**"Cold calling is easy for me."**

**"I am a pro."**

**"I am a skilled sales professional."**

**"People like to talk with me."**

**"I make good investment recommendations."**

As Jay repeated these self-talk messages about 100 times a day, day after day, he began to internalize them. They became part of this thinking, orientation, and self-image. In relatively short time, he was back making cold calls. And, he was back to making money.

## How to Use Positive Images

Like the successful athletes who visualize perfect performances, top salespeople picture themselves communicating effortlessly with prospective customers, persuasively answering questions, skillfully uncovering needs, and smoothly moving towards the close.

Through positive imaging, people can picture the way they think various situations will transpire, whether picturing an evening with the in-laws, a discussion with the auto mechanic, or a sales call. And, the positive imaging can become a self-fulfilling prophecy, with the situation unfolding as it was visualized. *This occurs because people behave in a way that makes the inner "mental" reality become outer "real world" reality.*

As with all great powers, autohypnosis has its negative as well as positive forms. It is quite revealing to look at how negative self-hypnosis can be turned positive to increase sales.

Picture a runner who keeps seeing the third hurdle in the race as a major problem. As he or she approaches that third hurdle, it will look like the Great Wall of China. The runner is very likely to hit this third hurdle.

What about golfers and the word "shank"? A shank is a low, grass-eating dribbled shot that skids off sideways. Any golfer will tell you that you should not even think of a "shank," and never, ever say that word on the course. Golfers believe that if they say it, their next shot will be one.

Let's look at a case history from sales where positive hypnotic imagery was beneficial. Lou sells X-ray equipment and CT scanners for a company we do sales consulting with. He had been earning over $100,000 a year, but entered a sales slump recently. What changed? He still had the same high level of product knowledge. He was still honest, energetic, and helpful.

After several interviews with him and after traveling with him in the field, we learned *he had fallen into a habit of visualizing failure.* As he drove to see a prospect, a doctor at a major medical center in California, he would imagine being kept waiting for an hour to see the physician. Then, he would hear himself speaking to the doctor with anger in his voice. He imagined the doctor showing no signs of interest in the company's medical equipment. Then he would imagine the doctor cutting the appointment short. Lou repeated these scenarios endlessly in his mind.

He hypnotized himself to expect the worst and made his expectations self-fulfilling prophecies. In a word, he expected to go into his sales call and "shank it." When he walked into the doctor's office, he was already three-quarters defeated.

We gave Lou new methods of autohypnosis. We showed him how to substitute positive images for negative ones. Here are some of the **autohypnosis visualizations** that helped Lou break out of his sales slump. Lou ran these images through his mind again and again, particularly as he drove to see clients:

"I see myself enjoying sales."

"I see myself selling with ease."

"I see myself working well with doctors."

"I see doctors smiling at me."

"I see doctors valuing my opinions."

"I see myself relaxed and self-confident with doctors."

## Four Essential Characteristics of Effective Self-Hypnosis Messages

Notice that these autohypnosis images and the previously described autohypnosis affirmations have four characteristics in common: they are **short, unambiguous, clear,** and **positive.** Let's look at each of these characteristics of successful autohypnosis affirmations.

**Short and unambiguous:** It does little good to say, "I *sometimes* like to sell *when* people are nice to me and *if* I have a lot of energy and *if* I am getting a lot of sales." There are too many conditional statements such as "sometimes," "when," and "if." Successful self-hypnosis is built on short, clear, unambiguous statements. It is far more effective to say: "*I like to sell.*" "*People like me.*" "*I like people.*" "*I enjoy selling.*" If you repeat these short unambiguous autohypnotic affirmations enough times, you will actually re-program your own unconscious, and these beliefs will become a viable part of your personality.

**Clear:** You want that positive image to be crystal clear in your mind. *Turn up the brightness, see all the colors and details. Zoom in for a close-up shot. See it in three dimensions.* The more vivid and intense the mental image is, the deeper it sinks into your subconscious mind. And, the more power that image carries.

**Positive affirmations:** Instead of saying, "Selling is not hard for me," say "*Selling is easy for me.*" Eliminate words such as "not," "never," "can't" and "impossible." These words create mental strait-jackets which severely limit your actions. Remember: Your dominant thoughts, whether positive or negative, will become your reality! Henry Ford said, "If you think you can or can't, you are right." Think you can—and you will be able to do it!

*When positive affirmations ("positive self-talk") are combined with positive images, the impact is even greater.* Not only did Lou repeat his positive messages over and over, he also visualized clear images in his mind of how he wanted his sales calls to go. Instead of picturing himself sitting in a doctor's waiting room staring aimlessly at his watch or an outdated sports magazine, he pictured himself meeting successfully with the doctor. He pictured himself greeting the receptionist warmly and being ushered in to see the doctor. He pictured himself pacing the doctor's body language and pacing the doctor's thought processes. He pictured himself anticipating every one of the doctor's toughest objections and saw himself answering it with ease due to his professional sales preparation. And, he could picture himself and hear himself close the sale. *With that positive self-image and a positive sound track he was bound to succeed.*

### Using Self-Hypnosis at Night to Get a Running Start in the Morning

In addition to using self-hypnosis while making your sales calls, there is another time it is extremely effective—just as you are about to fall asleep.

When people are about to fall asleep, just at the point of dropping off, there is a "Twilight Zone" between sleep and wakefulness. During this time, there is a window into the unconscious. Some of the normal barriers, defenses and filters are dropped, and this offers a great opportunity to plant positive messages and images.

This Twilight Zone time is the *optimal* moment to visualize successful sales presentations and to program yourself with positive self-talk. You are maximally open to these healing and motivational messages. See yourself confidently greeting people, see them warmly responding to you, see yourself making fascinating presentations, effortlessly answering questions and filling out the paperwork to close the sale. Hear yourself complimenting your prospects and customers and hear them complimenting you and your products or services.

Just as you are falling off into sleep, your final self-hypnosis message should be, "*I will sleep soundly and deeply and tomorrow morning I will wake up refreshed, energized, fully-rested and ready to go!*" "*I am a winner and tomorrow is going to be a great day for me!*" Creating these belief systems virtually guarantees that you will sleep more soundly and that you will wake up feeling refreshed and invigorated.

We have worked with some of our clients to make cassette tapes of various positive images and positive messages. As the sales professional drifts off into sleep, these wonderful hypnotic messages are effortlessly slipping into their belief systems. We normally use just a short ten or fifteen minute taped hypnotic message. The sales pro wakes up the next morning recharged, enthusiastic and ready to go! His or her sales personality has been boosted with some strong psychological vitamins.

## How to Use the Classical Steps of Self-Hypnosis

In addition to using positive imagery and positive affirmations, there are classical steps that can be used to rapidly induce states of self-hypnosis. You should find a quiet and private setting where you will be uninterrupted for 10 or 15 minutes. If you have succeeded in hypnotizing yourself and the phone rings or someone enters the office, you'll be pulled out of the hypnotic state.

The first step is to sit in a relaxed position, lean back, and place your arms on the armrests or on your lap. Next, take a couple of deep, healthy breaths. As you breathe, tell yourself:

"I am breathing in clean, healthy air."

"I am breathing out tension and stress."

"With each breath, I am becoming more and more relaxed and sleepier."

Then say:

"I am looking forward to going into hypnosis."

"I am beginning to enter hypnosis."

"It feels good to go down into hypnosis."

"Nothing can disturb me."

"Nothing can disturb my peace of mind."

"Nothing can disturb my focus."

You are now entering a state of increased suggestibility in order to plant positive messages and images.

Now, pick a focal point. It can be any object at all, although it should be rather neutral in terms of its meaning to you. So, your focal point should not be an award, an appointment book, or a picture of a family member. Rather, a light switch, a corner of a picture frame, or a drawer handle will do nicely. What you are trying to do is to totally clear your mind and focus only on that object.

Having selected it, concentrate on the focal point and on nothing else. Now, while you continue to breathe slowly and deeply, *repeat the word "relax."* Over and over and over again, say the word "relax" to yourself.

You can now tell yourself the following:

**"I am very relaxed."**

**"I am in a state of self-hypnosis."**

**"I am going to give myself some important suggestions."**

**"I can feel my eyes relaxing, my shoulders relaxing, my stomach, my legs, and my feet relaxing."**

**"I am totally relaxed."**

**"I am going deeper and deeper and deeper into hypnosis."**

Repeat these words over and over again for a few minutes.

To check to see if you are actually hypnotized, you can tell yourself that your right hand will lift automatically, with no effort by you whatsoever. If you feel it start to move and slowly rise all by itself, you know that you have entered a hypnotic state. Now, you are ready to program yourself with positive affirmations and positive images. You are in a hypnotic state.

The hypnotic affirmations and positive images you program in should be repeated a number of times, and should be *short, clear, unambiguous, and positive:*

**Say:** "I am a great closer," and see yourself effortlessly closing sales.

**Say:** "My products are superior," and see customers who are very happy with your products.

**Say:** "I love to prospect," and see yourself warmly meeting and interacting with new prospects.

**Say:** "I have extra sales energy," and see yourself making one extra sales call each day.

In addition, you can also program yourself to be relaxed, self-confident, poised, gracious, knowledgeable, and helpful. *You can use self-hypnosis to program in virtually any productive behavior or positive attitude you desire.*

You can even program in **post-hypnotic suggestions.** These are suggestions that call for a specific action to take place after the hypnosis. For example, another stockbroker who was having problems making cold calls gave himself the post-hypnotic suggestion to associate making a cold call with looking at the ticker tape. During the hypnotic session, he programmed in himself, "Each time after I look at the ticker tape, I will pick up the phone and make a cold call." And, that is exactly what he did. He almost effortlessly made more cold calls and picked up additional clients.

When you feel ready, whether after a few minutes or even a half-hour, you can easily "wake up" from self-hypnosis—although you are not technically asleep at all. As you begin to feel the need to come out of hypnosis, it is best to give yourself a message like:

**"When I count to three, I am going to leave the hypnotic state."**

*"The messages I have heard and the positive images I have seen in hypnosis will be a permanent part of my thinking and my actions."*

**"When I wake up, I will feel rested, positive, and refreshed. One, two, three."**

Now, you may want to slowly stand up, stretch, take a few deep breaths, and then get on with your day with a positive attitude.

It is important to note the fact that *the effects of hypnosis do not last forever.* While you can give yourself powerful messages and positive images in hypnosis, there are other factors at work in society that can program in negative beliefs and fears. Sometimes, even other salespeople or a sales manager can program in negative thoughts!

To maintain and increase the positive benefits of self-hypnosis, it is best to practice it on a regular basis. For some people this may be once a week. If everything is going very well for you, and you are exceeding your sales quotas, you may only need to use self-hypnosis once a month. During stressful times, you may want to use the benefits of self-hypnosis on a daily basis.

## How to Manage Stress through Self-Hypnosis

There are numerous methods to manage stress, such as time management, assertiveness training, life change analysis, exercise, and diet. You have undoubtedly noticed that each method works some of the time for some of the people. What you may not know is that the effectiveness of each method is dependent primarily upon the attitude of the person using it. And, self-hypnosis can give you the positive attitude and positive expectancy that is necessary to make any stress management technique *maximally* effective. Also, self-hypnosis itself is one of the most powerful stress management tools we have.

MOST SALES JOBS, BY DEFINITION, EXPOSE A SALESPERSON TO SOME OF THE MAJOR SOURCES OF JOB-RELATED STRESS. Read any detailed description of a sales job and you will see these stress-causing factors. Called "**stressors**," they include: dealing with obstacles placed in front of goals; dealing with unreasonable demands; dealing with conflict; dealing with differences of opinion; time deadlines; frequent travel; lack of privacy; dealing with strangers; and long work hours. In fact, many sales jobs contain almost all of these stressors.

Maryanne, a successful salesperson, had been kept waiting for over an hour for what should have been an easy sale. This made her upset to begin with. And then the presentation went poorly—there were several telephone interruptions, she didn't have all of the necessary figures, and the customer indicated that he wanted to do some more checking with her competitors.

Maryanne left the meeting dejected, frustrated, and physically tired. She drove a long way to get to the meeting, and could have made several other sales calls instead. Riding in bumper-to-bumper traffic, her white-knuckled fists clenching the steering wheel, she had a choice. On the one hand, she could fume. She could sit in the car, and focus on how unfair it was that she had to deal with all these frustrations, how terrible it was to have to deal with this kind of prospect, how she could have made other sales calls, how slowly the freeway was moving. . . .

If she pursued this option, what would Maryanne really be doing? She would be making herself the target of all of this stress, and the stress would be internalized. Prediction: Maryanne would arrive at her *next* meeting with a headache, a bad attitude, or upset stomach, or a backache, or increased blood pressure—or some of all of the above.

Fortunately, she knew she had another choice. She could use self-hypnosis even as she drove on the freeway. She did this by taking a few slow deep breaths and then repeating some positive affirmations to herself. These affirmations dealt with the sales situation she had just encountered, and were designed to lower her stress. They included:

**"I can feel my shoulders and neck relaxing."**

**"I can feel my back, arms, and legs, relaxing."**

**"I am a careful, alert, relaxed driver."**

**"I am still a winner."**

**"I have positive expectations."**

**"I feel my energy increasing."**

Many people *naturally* fall into hypnotic states while driving. This is called "highway hypnosis." People skilled in the use of self-hypnosis know how to guide and use these hypnotic states to their benefit. They enter into *positive* highway hypnosis. People who don't understand how subconscious programming works fall into *negative* highway hypnosis. It is important to remember that whenever you are driving you should program yourself with the message, "I am an alert and careful driver."

While sitting in her car, Maryanne also accessed some positive visualizations. *She saw pictures of her many happy customers.* She saw the faces of people who were grateful she had helped them in the past. She also saw positive images of great sales she had made. These positive images and the affirmations helped her to quickly drain off the frustrations of the earlier sales call. She soon returned to her normal cheerful, high-energy persona. She was able to close two sales that afternoon.

There are many other images that Maryanne could have used to drain off the stress. She could have used the **"mental vacation tech-**

nique" to go to a wonderful tranquil place. We strongly suggest you use this technique in your home or office, but never in your car. Using the mental vacation technique, you can go into self-hypnosis and rest deeply in a beautiful vacation spot such as a trip to New England while the leaves are changing colors in the fall, or a ski trip to Aspen, or a trip to Hawaii. She could have visualized a long walk along the shores of a favorite lake, with the waves slowly lapping at the shores and receding back to the deep blue depths, over and over. She could vividly imagine the colors, the sounds, and the smells of that place, and how deeply relaxed and rested and peaceful her whole body would feel. In drawing on these images, she could again repeat the affirmations: *"Relax; relax; relax; I am a winner; I have always been a winner; I will always be a winner."*

You have unlimited freedom in what you can program into your mind during self-hypnosis. You can program in messages and images to improve your marriage, to improve your relationship with your kids, to get more exercise, to be more relaxed or to sell more. Each person can select the positive images and messages he or she most needs at that moment. You are the director and the star of the most important movie in the world—the movie that is going on all the time inside your mind!

If you practice self-hypnosis as Maryanne and thousands of other top salespeople do, you will easily be able to handle the inevitable frustrations of selling with grace and dignity. *You will be able to draw on your hidden inner strengths.* Upon arriving at your next sales call, instead of having to pry your hands from the steering wheel and force yourself to make the call, you will be eager and enthusiastic to make a sale. You will be relaxed, comfortable, and confident. You will be a winner.

## How to Treat Stress-Related Ailments through Self-Hypnosis

Not only has self-hypnosis been found to be effective in reducing stress, there is evidence that it can be helpful in dealing with ailments that emanate from stress as well. Self-hypnosis is frequently used today to deal with complaints of headaches, backaches, neck aches, nervous stomachs, and many other disorders.

To see just how effective self-hypnosis can be in this area, let's take a look at the case of Adam. He was a very successful telemarketer in the insurance and financial services business. However, he was finding that he was getting serious neckaches by mid-afternoon. At first he thought it was the way that he was holding the phone or positioning himself in his chair or at his desk. He made a few equipment changes and body posture changes, but it was to no avail.

A medical check-up indicated what he already knew: His neck muscles were tight and were holding in a great deal of tension. This was placing excess stress on his spinal cord and brain stem. He tried chiropractors, massages, and even special vitamins. But his problem literally and figuratively continued to be a pain in the neck.

When virtually every other treatment had failed, Adam decided to try self-hypnosis. He used the classical steps and, in time, was able to induce a fairly deep hypnotic sate. He then repeatedly gave himself one key suggestion: his left hand has the power to relax his neck muscles. Over and over again he told himself of the healing powers of his left hand. He told himself that if he rubbed his aching neck with his left hand, the pain would subside. He told himself that his left hand, when rubbed over his neck, would warm up his neck, increase the blood flow, and relax all the muscles in his neck. He planted this message deep in his unconscious.

From that point, when his neck ached at work, he would rub it with his left hand, while holding his lightweight telephone in his right hand. The result: his neck felt better. Was it perfect? Not yet. *He next imagined warm blood flowing up and then down every artery and vein in his neck.* He imagined the warm blood brought nutrition and oxygen to every muscle and every cell in his neck. He was able to see rivers of healthy blood washing through his neck. He told himself that this blood was washing away all of the remaining tension.

His neck began to feel soft and supple and relaxed. Adam began to experience whole days, and then weeks, with no pain. The pain does, however, occasionally, return. Whenever it returns, Adam uses self-hypnosis to melt the pain and tension away. Adam also uses self-hypnosis not just as a treatment for his stress-induced ailment, but also as a preventative measure. He has found that by regularly using self-hypnosis, he can actually prevent the painful neck condition from arising.

## Using Self-Hypnosis to Become a Better Learner

We live in a fast-paced and rapidly changing society. What we learn in high school and college is not enough to last us for a lifetime. To be successful in our modern society calls for continual learning. The most successful salespeople and business executives are "lifetime learners." How can salespeople develop an attitude that makes them eager and enthusiastic lifetime students?

The classical steps of self-hypnosis are very effective in mastering the learning process. One of the reasons many salespeople don't get much out of conventional sales training is that they have never "learned how to learn."

*Learning, or knowledge acquisition, is strongly dependent upon your self-image and attitude.* If you tell yourself, "This is going to be difficult for me," or "I am going to have a hard time learning this"—you will! On the other hand, you can program yourself with positive images and positive self-talk which will virtually guarantee an increase in your ability to learn and master new material.

Here are some powerful self-hypnosis messages you can use to program yourself to be a good learner:

**"I love to learn."**

**"I find it easy to master new material."**

**"I can easily remember new ideas."**

**"I am an intelligent and creative person."**

**"I find it easy to put new ideas into practice."**

**"To earn more, I will learn more."**

Next, visualize yourself using the new ideas and techniques you have learned. See yourself using the classical steps of self-hypnosis. See yourself hypnotically slowing your voice down with slow speakers. **See** yourself speeding your voice up with fast talkers. **See** yourself using powerful unforgettable sales stories. **See** yourself writing down your most powerful sales scripts. **See** yourself using all of the other tools of sales hypnosis you learned in this book.

Using these affirmations and positive images will insure that you will learn and internalize this material. We have found that using self-hypnosis to learn and internalize the powerful techniques of hypnotic selling will increase your sales power and your income.

If you have children, you might want to use these techniques to develop in them a positive attitude towards learning. By having them repeat affirmations such as, "*I enjoy learning,*" and "*Learning is fun and easy for me,*" they will become much more open to the learning process. With a healthy attitude towards learning, they will be far more likely to get "A's" in calculus, chemistry and other subjects that many students have "negative" attitudes about. Positive hypnotic affirmations about learning will help your children throughout their entire scholastic careers. Giving your children these positive mental programs about learning is one of the greatest gifts you can bestow.

## How to Profit from Self-Hypnosis *Today*

Our last suggestion is to give self-hypnosis a try today. There is a great deal of scientific documentation regarding the effectiveness of self-hypnosis, and it is safe, easy and free. How many products can make a claim like that?

Where should you start with self-hypnosis? What part of yourself or your behavior should you work on first with self-hypnosis? Look carefully at yourself as a salesperson. Where is your Achilles' heel? None of us is perfect and we all have some weakness in sales. What is your weakness? Are you anxious about cold calls? Are you afraid to close? Are you overly nervous about the competition? Are you experiencing stress-related ailments? Is your self-confidence slipping?

Why not turn these weaknesses into potential strengths? Self-hypnosis is not a miracle cure, but it is a proven method of using the power of your subconscious mind to give you an extra edge in everything you do. Self-hypnosis using affirmations and positive imagery can definitely give you a competitive edge and a self-confidence edge in your next sales presentation.

You have been introduced to the most powerful elements of modern salesmanship and persuasion. By mastering the combination of sales hypnosis and self-hypnosis and hypnotic sales scripting, you will always know the most powerful thing to say to interest any prospect, you will know how to say it, you will be able to program yourself to make a self-confident presentation, and you will have mesmerizing scripts to close the sale. By practicing with the new tools of interactive video and interactive audio, you will rapidly develop and strengthen your skills. *Using hypnotic selling techniques, you will be able to help more people and make more sales.* You will have unlocked the most powerful formula for sales success in existence today: programming yourself and effectively communicating with the customer on a very deep level. And, you will gain much self-knowledge and self-esteem in the process.

# 12

## Developing And Implementing Your Action Plan For Sales Success

*Is it possible to bring in multi-million dollar sales with brief, mesmerizing sales presentations?* Joseph Patterson thinks so. Joe is the Chairman of the Board of Patterson Capital Corporation, a highly-respected money management firm. Joe and his team manage over $2 billion dollars for their clients across the United States and they obtained many of their multi-million dollar accounts from sales presentations that are less than one hour long!

After two relatively brief sales calls, a pension fund prospect turned into a client by giving Patterson Capital $15 million to manage! We had the honor of helping Joe and one of his associates prepare extensively for those two important meetings by going over most of the techniques in this book, by practicing those techniques and by videotaping the practice sessions. In this chapter, we will share with you the secrets of "perfect practice" that have worked so well for Patterson Capital and many other companies.

How does Patterson Capital consistently bring in multi-million dollar accounts with brief presentations? In addition to being tremendously skilled money managers and pension fund managers, Joe and his team constantly hone and perfect their sales and presentation skills.

Joseph Patterson and his staff are a good example of how people can systematically master the techniques of mesmerizing salesmanship. If you have read this far, you may be overwhelmed at the number of new ideas and techniques you have learned, from pacing speech rate and volume, to using sales stories to scripting and using interactive audio. In this chapter, we will pull it all together and help you develop an action plan to use and profit from what you have learned.

The first thing to point out is that you shouldn't try to do everything at once. When you wake up tomorrow morning, **don't** tell yourself that you must pace all of the verbal and non-verbal behaviors of everyone that you meet; that you must tell dazzling sales metaphors; that you have to script every word, and load in must-do statements, can-do statements, hot words and sales questions throughout. That is not how Joe Patterson mastered this material and it won't be how you will do it!

If you try to do everything at once, you will simply overload yourself, get discouraged and maybe even give up! The formula that we will give you in this chapter will help you master these powerful sales and persuasion techniques in a **step-by-step** way that is enjoyable and self-reinforcing.

## Identifying the Key Areas
## where Sales Training Is Needed

After we had built some trust with Joseph Patterson and his staff, we did what we do with all of our clients: **a Needs Analysis.** When it comes to sales training, we don't believe in selling anything "off-the-shelf." We have found that "one size fits all" sales training simply does not work in the long run. No matter how nicely it is packaged or how many fancy workbooks or videotapes it has, sales training will not work unless it is based on satisfying real needs and unless it is customized.

Your first step, then, in mastering this material is to *ask yourself what you most need in the sales and marketing area.* We sometimes ask our new clients, "If we had a magic wand and could give your salespeople any skill or ability, what would you want?" Ask yourself that same question.

Do your salespeople need to know how to build trust and rapport very quickly? If so, concentrate on the pacing techniques to build trust. Do they need to know how to gather information that is reliable and accurate and revealing? If so, start with the material on sales questioning techniques.

Let your needs and the needs of your people dictate which techniques you start with. That way, the material will have your full and immediate attention. *It will be maximally relevant.* Also, it will probably yield the quickest rewards in terms of increased sales.

There is no "best-place" to start in mastering this material. The "best place" for AT & T may be the "worst place" for IBM. Or, they may be one and the same place! It all depends on your needs. We therefore encourage you to do a needs assessment that is extensive and honest.

*Ask yourself:* what are the strengths and weaknesses of our sales team? How do our customers perceive us? Do they see us as boring? If so, you may want to concentrate on sales stories and metaphors and hot words. Do they not believe us? Concentrate on building trust with pacing strategies. Take an honest look at yourself and your sales team, and you will know exactly where to start in mastering this material.

## The Seven Steps to Learn Anything in Life

The strategy we will give you for learning mesmerizing salesmanship is one you can use for learning anything in life. It is from the laboratories of learning psychologists and from top real-world consultants like Jerry Richardson. Do you want to learn a new foreign language? This system will work! Do you want to learn how to use computers? This strategy will work! Do you want to learn to become a better parent or spouse? This system will work! We hope you will start by using it to master the techniques of win-win salesmanship we have shared with you in this book.

### 1. Start with Something You Are Really Interested In.

Your motivation is highest to learn what you are most motivated in. Dave Del Dotto, the well-known television personality and real estate expert, was most motivated to learn story-selling techniques. His new half-hour television specials are full of mesmerizing success stories from students who have purchased his real estate investing courses. Dave's viewing audience and his sales of real estate education programs have been growing every week since he started using the half-hour television specials we helped him script. The hypnotic sales stories are the keys to the program's effectiveness.

In learning mesmerizing salesmanship, start with what you or your people need most, based on your needs assessment. Don't try to learn something just because someone else said you "should." Your motivation will be low and you probably won't succeed! The reason people drop out of law school or medical school or any other kind of school is that, in many cases, they never really wanted to go in the first place!

### 2. Take One Thing at a Time.

Don't try to master everything. You will just overwhelm and frustrate yourself. Tell yourself, "Today, I will just be my regular good self. But, I will try to pace the speech rate of everyone I meet." At the end of the day, you will probably be pacing speech rate automatically and effortlessly! You'll probably remember how to do this for a long, long time. The next day, take just one other technique, say using hot words. Practice using hot words extensively. The following day, practice one other technique.

At the end of a few weeks, you will have mastered many of the techniques presented here. Doing just one thing at a time keeps your stress level low and your energy level high. And, if you concentrate on learning each thing *thoroughly*, it practically guarantees success.

### 3. Overlearn It.

Practice, practice, practice. Do it again, again, and again, and it will become part of you. **Don't** tell yourself you will practice pacing speech volume for five minutes, and then go on to something else. You will never master it!

You have to "overlearn" each thing you want to learn. Practice it so much that it becomes part of you. Practice one skill at a time, but practice it all day—in every sales call that day.

Then, three weeks from now, practice that same skill for half a day. Three weeks after that, practice that same skill for a few more hours. Overlearn it. You will never forget it. It will become intuitive and part of you. The great coach Vince Lombardi once said, "Practice does not make perfect. Perfect practice makes perfect." To practice perfectly, you have to practice a lot. Overlearn it.

### 4. Set Time Aside for Practicing.

If you don't take it seriously and if you don't set the time aside to do it, it may not get done! As busy as Joseph Patterson and his staff are, they set the time aside week in and week out for training sessions. The results have been tremendous, but they had to pay the price of disciplined practice.

There is no short-cut to great results. Multimillionaire sales superstar Jim Sweeney told us, *"Many people don't recognize opportunity because it goes around disguised in work clothing."* If you come across a sales training program that promises instant results with no effort, you should be suspicious. You may be dealing with charlatans. Remember, the time to practice for the marathon is not the night before the race. You have to practice often, and the best time to start practicing is now.

Don't pull this book out the day before the most important sales call in your life and expect to be a top-notch sales professional! Set the time aside for some daily or weekly practice.


### 5. Make It Fun!

How, you may ask, can I set this time aside for practice? Remember, we always find the time to do the things we enjoy doing. Right? We always find the time to watch TV, go fishing, golf, go to restaurants, play with our kids, garden, etc. *Make learning sales hypnosis fun, and you will find the time to practice.*

Many of the corporations we work with schedule their training programs in wonderful resort locations. We have conducted sales hypnosis workshops in Bali, in Australia, in the Philippines, in Switzerland, in beautiful resort locations all over the United States, and in the most glamorous hotels in our biggest cities. If you can, schedule your training sessions in a beautiful location. Work your people hard, but also give them an opportunity to relax and have fun. If they associate learning with having fun, they will develop a very positive attitude towards learning and attending workshops.

You have a big head start with this material in that many of the techniques of sales hypnosis are already fun. It is enjoyable to tell sales stories and metaphors. You will enjoy telling them and your customers will enjoy hearing them. It is fun to hypnotically pace other people. They may not know consciously what you are doing, but they will feel more relaxed with you and will enjoy your sales calls more.

As you see the positive responses that come from your use of these techniques, you will get more and more enjoyment from mesmerizing salesmanship. You will also find that the more skills you develop in hypnotic selling, the more you will want to learn. Our clients tell us that the two major reasons they want their people trained in hypnotic selling are:

1. It works. It helps them sell more.
2. Their salespeople find the training fun and motivating.

## 6. Use these Techniques in Your Personal as well as Your Business Life.

The more uses you find for hypnotic selling techniques, the more you will believe in it and benefit from it. The trust-building techniques and story-telling techniques and probing techniques presented in this book will serve you very well in many other areas of your life besides salesmanship. They will help you make more friends, avoid arguments, and get along well with almost everyone you meet. A technique that works with human beings either works all the time or it doesn't work at all. *These are not just sales techniques*. These are techniques for successful human relationships!

## 7. Combine these Techniques with what You Already Know.

When you started reading this book, you were not a blank slate. You already knew a great many things and had many ways of successfully interacting with people. You don't have to give up any of that to successfully use the hypnotic sales techniques we have shared with you.

These strategies are not a new religion or a new belief system. You don't have to give anything up to benefit from using mesmerizing salesmanship. In fact, what you will learn from using these techniques will make the techniques you have used all along even more powerful. So, combine *all* that you have learned here with what you already know. Rearrange the techniques of hypnotic salesmanship and customize them and **make them all your own** to get the greatest benefits!

After doing a needs assessment with Joseph Patterson and his staff, we learned that what was most needed was sales scripting. Joe and his people have a somewhat complex message to get across and not very much time to do it. Joseph Patterson uses his two million dollar computer system to track and analyze every stock sale made on the New York Stock Exchange every day. *How can you explain the complexity of what Joe and his staff do in just a few minutes?*

In their relatively brief presentations, *every minute counts*. Joe sometimes has only twenty minutes to make a proposal to manage over $20 million dollars! He knows what he is going to say in minute one, in minute seven and in minute nineteen. And, it is different for each client! It is totally customized, based on the client's needs.

Joe Patterson and his staff know every objection and stall that a client could bring up. They have scripted out dozens of their most powerful responses, and handling these objections has become much easier for them and more successful. Joseph Patterson, Chairman of the Board, has become a master of using scripts.

We used opinion-pacing techniques, objection-pacing techniques, sales questions, sales metaphors, and hot words in developing the sales scripts. To Patterson's prospects, it all sounds as natural as a conversation between two close friends. However, it took many hours of work to make it come out that way. With tens of millions of dollars on the line, all the preparation was justified.

Once we had the scripts developed and polished to a high gloss, we did another needs assessment. Needs assessments should be on-going, because needs do change—especially as organizations grow and develop. From this needs assessment, we found that the team members now needed to know how to deliver the message in a mesmerizing way. We therefore next focused on teaching techniques to pace speech rate and volume.

In practicing using pacing techniques, we videotaped Joe and one of his associates delivering the customized sales presentation. We studied and analyzed the tapes together and came up with many new ways Joe could modulate his voice, change his body language and control his pacing to grab the attention of his prospects, to quickly build their trust and level of interest, and then to move self-confidently to the close.

The tapes revealed dimensions of behavior and pacing we had not yet been aware of or analyzed. Once we understood these dynamics and carefully considered the thought processes of Joe's customers, we were able to weave in more mesmerizing sales techniques to strengthen the presentation.

Finally, we did another needs analysis. From this analysis, we learned that Joe and his staff had to learn how to collect more detailed information on prospects *before they even made that first visit*. We utilized all the probing techniques described earlier in this book and even developed customized information-gathering forms that have proven very useful in prospecting.

Here is a philosophy we share with every sales professional we train:

**"The more I know about the customer, the more I control the sale."**

We believe *a sales professional can never know too much about a client.* We believe information is power. And—how you use the information can be just as important as the information itself. Joe and his team have gotten so good at probing and information gathering that they now know much more about their prospects than they ever thought was possible. And, *all this is done before the first visit!*

How much time did all this take? Not as much as you might imagine. We would spend two to three hours a week with Joe and his staff. Joe and his staff practiced the techniques and strategies on their own. We did this for about six months, with a few follow-up visits afterwards.

From day one, Joe and his team were able to use this material. They put it into immediate service on sales calls they were doing that week, and every week. We followed all of the steps in the learning sequence provided above. We concentrated on doing one thing at a time: whatever was most needed. Joe and his team members then over-learned the material, we all made it fun, and we combined it with what they already knew.

The rewards and benefits were immediate and have been long-lasting. In the past year, Joe has signed up police departments, pension funds, cities and towns, and even banks and savings and loans for his company's expert money management services. Joseph Patterson and his staff manage several billion dollars for their clients, and they do it very well.

Not many people reading this book will be able to bring in the kinds of dollars that Patterson Capital has brought in. However, everyone can significantly increase their sales by using the hypnotic techniques of sales champions presented here. Follow the formula for learning we have just presented, concentrate on learning one thing at a time, over-learn it, make it enjoyable, combine it with what you already know, and you shall enjoy the rewards that come from being a mesmerizing sales professional.

## How to Make Sales Training Work for You

*Does sales training really work?* Good training works, bad training doesn't. Good training, training based on scientific research on what sales superstars really do, does work.

However, we'll sometimes say just the opposite: "**Training doesn't work.**" We've told that to executives of Fortune 500 companies on our first meeting and they look shocked. *"What?,"* they ask, *"I thought you guys were here to sell us training. Why are you saying that training doesn't work?"* And, then we say, "Training does not work; **reinforcement works!**"

*Anything that is not reinforced, we tend to forget.* If you studied Spanish in high school, you won't be fluent in it today or five years from now unless you practice and reinforce your skills. This is something that Cloe Madanes calls the **"German Shepherd Phenomenon,"** because if German Shepherds are not constantly reinforced in what they have learned, they will forget it. Don't get caught by the German Shepherd Phenomenon. Reinforce your skills, reassess your needs and go back through this book several times to practice the hypnotic selling skills we have presented, and you will be amazed at how you can multiply your persuasive powers and your self-confidence in many areas of your life.

Techniques don't work all by themselves. It takes people to work the techniques. If you work these techniques, they will work for you! Practice perfectly, as Vince Lombardi suggested, and you will be richly rewarded for your efforts. If you can, use the new interactive video and interactive audio technology to intensively practice the techniques of mesmerizing salesmanship.

If you have read this far, you must be a highly ambitious, education-oriented professional. You are one in one thousand in the field. *Now, you have the winner's edge.* Now, you have seen the opportunity. We invite you to take full advantage of the opportunity, and to use the powers of mesmerizing salesmanship to set new sales and income records.

We'd like to hear from you, and to learn about the success you are having from using these techniques. When we write the sequel to this book, we'd like to be able to add your name and your story to the honor roll of sales superstars that includes Joe Patterson, Tom Olds, Jack Tortorice, Kenny Clyde, Bob Torre, Gerhard Gschwandtner, John Moss, and hundreds of other top producers all across the United States and in many foreign countries.

You now know the secrets of hypnotic sales presentations. It is our hope that you will use these powerful techniques to help other people and to help yourself!

# 13

## Using
## The Sales Magic
## Of Ed McMahon

Ed McMahon, known to millions of Americans as the television celebrity on *The Tonight Show* and *Star Search*, is a sales superstar. We know one when we see one. We've had the opportunity to work with some of the best salespeople in the country—people earning $500,000 to over $1,000,000 per year—and we believe that Ed McMahon could be their match, or better them in the selling profession. If he wasn't in the entertainment business full time, we bet Ed would be a sales superstar. His intuitive skill in using hypnotic sales strategies is phenomenal.

His autobiography, *Here's Ed,** contains a fascinating, detailed account of how Ed McMahon uses his awesome sales powers. The scene is the Atlantic City boardwalk. The time is just after World War II ended.\*\*

The range and sequencing of Ed's hypnotic sales techniques is impressive. Few people could resist his charm, his wit, his surprises, his honesty. While the setting was the Atlantic City boardwalk, it could have been anywhere. People are people. The hypnotic persuasion principles Ed used have universal application.

We have here reproduced, with permission, Ed McMahon's magic words. You will find many principles, techniques, and phrases that you will be able to adapt to your sales. On the left side of each page, you will see Ed's exact words. On the right, we will take an X-ray look at the hypnotic powers carried in these phrases and sentences. This is the great art of hypnotic selling as performed by one of its greatest practitioners.

## Ed McMahon's Word Magic

| TRANSCRIPT | ANALYSIS |
|---|---|
| *"You are familiar, ladies and gentlemen, with the famous Western Fountain pen . . . a familiar object in the vest pocket of every successful business- man."* | At the time, people were famil- iar with this pen. By making this statement, Ed got the lis- tener into a "Yes Set" of minor agreement. He paced or matched the listener's experi- ence. All the listener could do was to nod his head in agree- ment. This undeniably truthful statement started the building of a climate of agreement. When Ed says that this fountain pen is *". . . a familiar object in the vest pocket of every successful busi- nessman,"* he is using a hyp- notic absolute in the word "every." |
| *"You are familiar, too, with the way this pen operates."* | Another undeniably truthful pac- ing statement, which leads to more minor agreement. The more minor agreements Ed gets, the easier it is for him to get major agreement (the sale) later on. |

## TRANSCRIPT

*"Let me show you. You just
pull this lever down, insert the
point of the pen in a bottle of
ink, let the lever go, and you
are ready for many uninterrupted hours of writing pleasure."*

## ANALYSIS

Ed predicts what he is going to
do, which is pacing the future.
Then, when he does it, he creates more minor agreement.
The prospect thinks, "He said
he was going to do it, and now
he did it." This helps to further
build the "Yes Set" of agreement. Ed then uses *visual involvement* with the prospect.
The pen functions like a shiny
watch or a pendulum to help
focus the client's attention. Ed
next uses hypnotic leading.
After pacing the client (telling
the client what the client already knows or has seen), Ed
*leads* the client by introducing
some new information. In this
case, the leading statement is
*"you are ready for many unin-
terrupted hours of writing pleasure."* Ed leads the client by
telling him that he WILL experience writing pleasure.

*"Now you have seen how this
pen operates. . ."*

This is an undeniably truthful
hypnotic pacing statement. The
prospect has just seen how the
pen operates. Since it is impossible to disagree with, it helps to
deepen the "Yes Set."

## TRANSCRIPT

*". . . and I am now about to shock you . . ."*

*". . . by announcing that I am not selling this expensive article for two dollars. Not for one dollar. Not for fifty cents. No. I am giving this pen away, ladies and gentlemen, absolutely free, to every man, woman and child who buys one of these absolutely necessary gold-finish pen points without which it is impossible to use any fountain pen."*

*"Now, friends, I can hear you saying to yourself, 'He's giving us the fountain pen, but he's making us buy the point in order to get it.' "*

## ANALYSIS

This is an Attention-Grabbing Device that breaks the client's ordinary mind-set. This also makes Ed stand out from ordinary salesmen. Have you ever heard a sales professional say he was going to "shock you"? (A word of warning: this technique should only be rarely used. If overused, it loses its effectiveness).

This is a suspense-building technique. Ed then ends the suspense by saying that he is giving the pen away. This fulfills his promise that he would "shock" the prospect. With this promise fulfilled, he has deepened the "Yes Set" of minor agreement. The word "absolutely" in "absolutely free" is a hypnotic "-ly" word. He uses still another hypnotic "-ly" word when he says the pen point is "absolutely necessary."

Here Ed McMahon skillfully uses hypnotic mind-reading. He says out loud what the prospects are quietly thinking to themselves. This also shows a lot of self confidence, because Ed is *pacing an objection* and is bringing it out into the open (where he can deal with it).

## TRANSCRIPT

*"This is not true, my friends. But show me a man who does not buy one of these fine, durable gold-finished writing pen points at the miniscule price I am offering them today and I'll show you a man who doesn't recognize a good deal when he sees one, a man with no business sense whatsoever, and I know there are no such men in this gathering."*

*"You can see, friends, that this pen I am about to give you already has a point in it . . . "*

*"So why should you buy this point I'm offering?"*

## ANALYSIS

Ed introduces the hot words "my friends." As the presentation continues, you will see how he uses these hot words again and again as an anchor to bring up good feelings. Ed now deals with the objection he just raised and he used two more hypnotic absolutes ("no" and "whatsoever") when he refers to ". . . a man with no business sense whatsoever. . ." He then uses the hypnotic leading conjunction "and" to add the phrase *"I know there are no such men in this gathering."*

Ed uses the hot word "friends" again to fire off good feelings. Ed draws the prospect's attention back to the pen. He is pacing an observable when he says, *"You can see, friends, that this pen . . ."* As they see what Ed is referring to, more minor agreement is created.

Ed uses hypnotic mind reading again. He states the question that has been going through the listener's mind.

| TRANSCRIPT | ANALYSIS |
|---|---|
| *"What if you are about to sign an important contract and you drop this pen and bend the point? What if you get hold of some bad ink that clogs the fine point of this pen beyond repair? What if you're forced to write on rough paper that wads up and wrecks the point? What will you do?"* | Ed uses hypnotic mind reading again. He states the question that has been going through the listener's mind. |
| *"You will not be able to sign the contract. You will not be able to use the pen unless you have with you an extra point such as the one I am offering you now for only fifty cents."* | Ed uses two hypnotic "can do" statements when he states that the prospect will not be able to sign the contract and will not be able to use the pen (in this case, the "can" is a "can't"). This deepens the need. Ed goes on to fulfill the need with the pen points he is selling. |

## TRANSCRIPT

*"Now, friends, who will be the first one to buy one of these extraordinary gold-finished pen points for only fifty cents and get this guaranteed fountain pen absolutely free?"*

## ANALYSIS

Ed uses the hot word "friends" again to bring up the good feelings that have become associated with that word throughout his presentation. He uses a long, rhythmic hypnotic sentence structure (rather than using several short, choppy sentences). Ed uses a hypnotic presupposition when he assumes that someone will be the first to buy a gold-finish pen point. He doesn't even leave the possibility open that no one will buy. He then uses a hypnotic "-ly" word ("absolutely" free) to close the sale! It is no accident that Ed McMahon was so successful in selling pen points in Atlantic City. His presentation was so fascinating and factual you had to pay attention. It was mesmerizing.

### Ed McMahon's Attention Grabbers

Ed then went on to face on of the greatest selling challenges ever. *How can you sell empty boxes?* Read this transcript and the analysis and you will learn Ed's secrets.

You will also learn some techniques you can adapt to sell your company's products or services. If these powerful techniques will sell empty boxes, you can use them to sell almost anything.

| TRANSCRIPT | ANALYSIS |
|---|---|
| *"That's right, friends! You there with the pretty young lady in red, you heard me right."* | Ed starts his presentation with the hot word "friends." He will use this word several times in his presentation to anchor good feelings. By using the attention grabber statement, *"You there with . . ."* he reaches out and grabs both attention and prospects. Ed doesn't wait for the prospects to come to him. He then uses flattery power by making reference to "the pretty young lady . . ." |
| *"I'm about to sell ten of these empty boxes."* | Ed creates excitement and arouses interest by making the surprising statement that he will sell ten empty boxes. This is slightly disorienting to the listener, who begins to wonder how this is possible. The need to understand this situation compels the prospect to stop and listen, which is exactly what Ed wants. He has reached his first goal in the sales presentation: to attract the prospect and hold his attention. |

| TRANSCRIPT | ANALYSIS |
|---|---|
| *". . . just exactly ten . . . the specially selected ten I have piled up right here on the counter . . ."* | Ed here uses the "-ly" hypnotic words "exactly" and "specially." He is also pacing observables. As the prospect sees there are 10 boxes on the counter, he begins to build a "Yes Set" that what Ed says is true. This also starts to build a climate of agreement. |
| *"I'm about to sell these ten boxes only to ten lucky buyers at only one dollar each."* | Ed uses hypnotic repetition and repeats what he has just said. He also paces the future and shows self-confidence by predicting that he will sell the ten boxes for one dollar each. |
| *"Now, I hear you saying, 'Who's going to pay a buck for an empty box?'"* | Ed uses hypnotic mind reading and voices the inner thoughts of his listeners. He is also pacing an objection by bringing it out in the open. |
| *"That's a good question."* | Ed uses the power of flattery ("good question") to compliment his prospects for their thought—which he just mind-read. |

## TRANSCRIPT

*"Not your staid, conservative, solid unimaginative man with no romance in his soul."*

*"But those of you who know that there's often more to a thing than meets the eye . . . those of you can become fascinated, intrigued by an idea . . . those of you who wonder why a man would stand up here before you and offer an empty box for a dollar . . . "*

## ANALYSIS

Ed uses a hypnotic absolute in saying that only an unimaginative man with "no romance in his soul" wouldn't buy one of the empty boxes.

Like a skilled hypnotist, Ed uses the power of vague, non-specific words to trigger the power of the human imagination. He doesn't say what this "thing," is—he only says there is more to it than meets the eye. He then uses three trance words in succession: "fascinated," "intrigued" and "wonder." Ed then uses a hidden action command in saying, ". . . *wonder why a man would stand up here before you and offer an empty box for a dollar . . . "*

This subliminal technique gets the listener to wonder about that question. Since Ed is undeniably standing up in front of them and is asking a dollar for an empty box, this statement is also an example of pacing observable things in the environment. If you read Ed's words again, you will see that he is also seducing and romancing the prospect with flattery statements.

## TRANSCRIPT

## ANALYSIS

*"You will say to yourself, 'There must be more here than meets the eye.'"*

Ed skillfully combines hypnotic mind reading and pacing the future by telling the prospect what he WILL be telling himself later. This is a quick-acting post-hypnotic suggestion which the listener immediately acts on by saying to himself, *"There must be more here than meets the eye."*

*"But there is a limit to the number of these empty boxes that I can sell at the price of just one dollar."*

Ed uses another slightly confusing statement to mildly disorient the listener. The listener wonders, "How can there be a limit on the number of empty boxes he can sell?" or "Why is there a limit on the number of boxes he can sell?" As the listener searches his mind seeking an explanation for this puzzling statement, he must stay to hear the answer. Thus, Ed is guaranteed of the prospect's continued interest in the boxes.

## ANALYSIS

*"Here they are. I will count them for you . . . one, two, three, four, five six, seven, eight, nine, and ten! That's the limit."*

Ed uses an undeniably truthful statement, as he counts the boxes in front of his prospects. This is an example of pacing ob servables in the environment. This also guarantees visual involvement as he counts the boxes one by one. It focuses the viewers' attention much as does a shiny watch or a pendulum. Throughout all this, his listeners are still wondering, "Why only ten empty boxes?"

In his book, Ed then comments, *"At this point, I would pick up one of the boxes, look knowingly inside it, and smile provocatively at the crowd as if I wished they could see what I saw."* This is another highly skillful visual involvement device.

*"Now, ladies and gentlemen, I say . . . I say . . . these boxes are empty. That's what I say."*

Ed uses hypnotic repetition by saying, *"I say . . . I say . . . That's what I say."* He also makes the intriguing statement that the boxes he is selling are empty. His prospects continue to wonder how and why he can sell empty boxes. They have to stick around to hear the answer

| TRANSCRIPT | ANALYSIS |
|---|---|
| *"But I wonder if there are ten ladies and gentlemen among you out there who believe that I would actually presume to sell you an empty box."* | Ed uses the hypnotic trance word "wonder." He then uses the hypnotic "-ly" word "actually." |
| *"So this is what I'm going to do."* | Ed now paces the future and tells the people what he is going to do. |
| *"As each of you steps forward to buy one of these little jewelry boxes . . ."* | Ed now leads the prospects with the hypnotic leading statement *"As each of you steps forward to buy one of these . . . "* This also functions as an assumptive close: Ed assumes they WILL buy. |
| *". . . I'm going to put one—the one you buy—on top of your dollar. When I have ten dollars covered by ten boxes, I'm going to ask each of you to step up here, open the box you bought and find out if I told you the truth when I said the box was empty."* | Ed continues to use future pacing to predict and describe what he will do. Since he knows what he is going to do, this is guaranteed to create a "Yes Set" of agreement in his listener. |

| TRANSCRIPT | ANALYSIS |
|---|---|
| *"Remember, I say these boxes are empty. Do you or don't you believe me?"* | Ed uses the power of hypnotic repetition in saying, *"Remember, I say these boxes are empty."* He then challenges and provokes the listeners to take action by asking, *"Do you or don't you believe me?"* |

Ed would, in almost no time at all, have ten boxes on top of ten one dollar bills.

### Ed's Secrets of Group Selling

| | |
|---|---|
| *"Now then, folks, I want each of you to step up here, open your box, and show everyone here exactly what you bought."* | Ed uses hypnotic leading to tell his customers what to do next. Ed started by predicting his own future behavior, and now he is predicting the future behavior of his customers. |
| *"You bought an empty box, exactly as I told you you would. Very well, ladies and gentlemen, what does that prove? It proves that I am an absolutely honest man."* | Ed confirms what he has been saying all along: that he is indeed selling empty boxes. This confirmation deepens the "Yes Set" of minor agreement. Ed then capitalizes on this minor agreement by saying it "proves that I am an absolutely honest man." Notice the use of the hypnotic "-ly" word "absolutely." While Ed could have simply stated that he is an honest man, it is much more powerful to prove it! |

## TRANSCRIPT

*"So you must believe me when I tell you that the very greatest item I have ever been authorized to offer here on the board-walk of Atlantic City is this handy Morris Metric Slicer which . . ."*

*". . . I have here in my hand."*

*"Forget the two dollars these great little gadgets were made to sell for."*

## ANALYSIS

Ed uses a hypnotic "must do" statement when he says that ". . . *you must believe me when I tell you that . . .*" He then uses a hypnotic superlative when he refers to the next item he will sell as "*very greatest.*"

Ed is pacing observables in the environment by stating the obvious: that he does have the slicer in his hands. This adds another "yes" to the "Yes Set." As he holds the slicer in his hand, he focuses the listener's attention in the same way a hypnotist focuses attention with a shiny watch or pendulum.

Ed triggers the power of human curiosity when he asks the listener to "*Forget the two dollars these great little gadgets were made to sell for.*" The listener wonders, "Why should I forget it?" He or she has to stick around to hear the answer.

| TRANSCRIPT | ANALYSIS |
|---|---|
| *"I'm cutting the price in half. Just look at the way it slices these cucumbers, ladies and gentlemen."* | Ed uses a clever physical metaphor when he says he is *". . . cutting the price in half . . ."* He is selling something that cuts and he is cutting the price of it in half. As he slices the cucumber, he is using the slicer as an attention focusing device. This adds visual involvement to his sales presentation. |
| *"Is that great or is that sensational?"* | Ed here skillfully uses two superlatives ("great" and "sensational") in a forced choice format. No matter which superlative the listener chooses, Ed wins. |
| *"With a machine like this, you can slice anything so thin, you could get a job with a tobacco company slicing calling cards into cigarette papers."* | Ed here uses the power of story selling. He creates a wonderful hypnotic word picture of cutting calling cards so thin they could be used as cigarette papers. |

**TRANSCRIPT**

**ANALYSIS**

*"And I'm about to give this lit-
tle machine more use and
abuse in the next two minutes
than you would give it in an entire lifetime."*

Ed paces the future by telling
his prospects what he will do
next. Since he knows what he
will do next, this is guaranteed
to create a "Yes Set" of agreement when he does what he
says he was going to do. Ed
also triggers the power of absolute words when he says he will
give the machine more use and
abuse than anyone else would
give it in an *"entire lifetime."*

*"It's guaranteed not to rip,
rust, bust, split in the back or
smell bad in warm weather."*

Ed knows that the word "guaranteed" is one of the most persuasive in the English language.
He also triggers some good feelings by making the humorous
statement that it is guaranteed
not to *"smell bad in warm
weather."*

*"Just a minute, what was that I
heard? Did someone say cabbage? Thank you. Perfect
stranger. Get a load of how
this remarkable little machine
handles your cabbage problems."*

Whether or not someone would
say "cabbage," Ed would mention cabbage. He knew someone in the crowd was thinking
about the difficulty of cutting
up cabbage. He used hypnotic
mind reading to bring their
thought out into the open.

| TRANSCRIPT | ANALYSIS |
|---|---|
| | This is also an example of pacing objections, as Ed is bringing up the objection (*"your cabbage problems"*) early in his presentation on the slicer. |
| | In describing cabbage as a "problem," Ed is drawing attention to a need. The listener is compelled to watch how Ed solves this "problem." |
| *"For coleslaw, hot slaw, sauerkraut, or anything that may constitute your cabbage pleasure. Could I hear it for this coleslaw, ladies and gentlemen."* | Ed now does a demonstration of making coleslaw which guarantees the visual involvement of his prospects. He transforms the "cabbage problem" into "cabbage pleasure" with the Morris Metric Slicer. |
| | Ed then asks to "hear it" for the coleslaw—not for himself. It is much easier to ask the crowd to applaud the slicer, or the man operating the slicer. The crowd yells its approval. Ed knows that while the crowd thinks they are applauding the coleslaw, they are really complimenting him and the slicer. |

## TRANSCRIPT

*"But wait a minute, that's not all!"*

*"Did you ever see a lady slice a tomato? She takes a poor defenseless tomato and plunges at it with a butcher knife. And the poor little tomato dies of a hemorrhage before it ever reaches the table."*

## ANALYSIS

Ed builds suspense by stating *"that's not all."* The prospects have to stay a minute longer to see what is going to come up next.

Ed uses the power of story selling and paints a humorous picture of someone trying to cut up a tomato with a butcher knife. The humor and the word picture trigger good feelings in the listener. They like Ed. They want to hear more.

Ed uses a variation of the "talking products" technique and imbues his tomato with human-like qualities. He calls the tomato "defenseless" and then says it "dies of a hemorrhage." If he wanted to, he could have taken this a step further and could even have had the tomato yell out, or say something to the prospects.

| TRANSCRIPT | ANALYSIS |
|---|---|
| *"Now watch as I show you how this wonderful little invention handles your tomato problem."* | Ed predicts his own behavior when he tells people what he is going to do. This is hypnotic pacing of the future. He also hypnotically repeats the vegetable "problem" theme, this time applying it to the tomato. |
| *"Look at those slices, ladies and gentlemen. Each one is so thin, it's no wonder stingy people adore this little machine."* | Ed uses visual focusing of the audience's attention to keep their minds from straying. He adds humor and good feelings by saying that *"stingy people adore this little machine."* He also included the trance word "wonder." |
| *"Why I sold one of these to a lady in Bayonne, New Jersey, and it made one tomato last her all summer long."* | Ed repeats his use of Sales Humor. People are laughing so much now they can't help but like Ed (and his product). |
| *"Look at those slices!"* | Visual Focusing of audience's attention. |
| *"And . . . wait a minute, ladies and gentlemen, that's not all!"* | Suspense-building statement. This holds the audience's attention for another minute. |

| TRANSCRIPT | ANALYSIS |
|---|---|
| *"Today and for today only I'm including with each and every sale of this remarkable slicing machine a rotisserie cutter invented by the famous dean of the Parisian School of Potato Surgery. It was he himself who taught me how to use it."* | With the use of the hypnotic "-ly" word "only," Ed triggers scarcity thinking. He also layers on more sales humor by referring to the *"famous dean of the Parisian School of Potato Surgery."* |
| *"Any child can learn."* | Ed here uses the hypnotic absolute word "any," in making a psychological reassurance statement. |
| *"Look at this!"* | Attention-focusing statement. |

At this point, Ed McMahon spins a potato on the rotisserie cutter in such a way as to produce a springlike spiral of potato that he'd pull out and let snap back.

## How to Use Humor to Close the Sale

| | |
|---|---|
| *"When company comes to dinner, spread it out. When they go home, let it snap back together again. One potato could last you a lifetime."* | Ed uses a hypnotic story image and some intoxicating sales humor when he explains how *"one potato could last you a lifetime."* At this point, the audience is laughing so much and feeling so good they'd buy almost anything from Ed! |

*"And in addition to the slicer and the machine for performing miracles with a potato, I'm adding the juice-o-matic . . . here it is folks . . . all for one dollar."*

*"Plunge this handy little juice-o-matic into an orange, a grapefruit, or a watermelon like this."*

*"Take it with you on your way to work and drink the juice right out of the fruit on your way downtown."*

*"We don't supply the vodka."*

## ANALYSIS

Ed uses the leading conjunction "and" to connect up his previous statements to still another product, the juice-o-matic. He injects a little more sales humor with his reference to *"the machine for performing miracles with a potato."*

Ed uses Visual Involvement and Attention-Focusing.

Ed uses the power of hypnotic story telling combined with hidden action commands. He paints a picture and in the picture tells the people what they will do: *"drink the juice right out of the fruit on your way downtown."* This also sells the audience on another benefit of the juice-o-matic.

Ed uses still more sales humor to anchor the good feelings.

## ANALYSIS

*"Stick this into a lemon and you have juice for a salad, a little lemon for your Tom Collins, and some for Mary and Jane Collins, too. There's enough for the whole Collins family."*

Ed continues using sales humor and paints another hypnotic word picture. Ed has us laughing so much, we have forgotten many of our day-to-day problems.

*"And wait till you try it on a grapefruit. Take this number two grapefruit. With this juice-o-matic, you get enough juice to float the USS North Dakota."*

More sales humor with his reference to getting enough juice out of a grapefruit that you could *"float the USS North Dakota."* At this point, I like Ed so much, I'd like him to be my son-in-law!

*"Who'll be the first to raise her hand and say 'I'll be the first to give you a dollar for those three marvelous kitchen innovations?' "*

Ed uses a hidden action command and a presupposition that someone WILL say, *"I'll be the first to give you a dollar for those three marvelous kitchen innovations."* Through the use of hypnotic suggestion, Ed even tells them exactly what to say.

*"Lady over there? Thank you very much, my dear. And there's a man who wants two. He's obviously leading a double life, the sly old fox. Good luck to you, sir. And thank you all for your enthusiasm."*

Ed uses sales humor to the very close when he suggests that the man who orders two is *"obviously leading a double life, the sly old fox."* Notice the use of the hypnotic "-ly" word "obviously."

## TRANSCRIPT

*"You have made this sale a success for both of us."*

*"And to those of you who didn't buy, I hope you won't regret the mistake too much in the future when you might want to become a little cutup."*

## ANALYSIS

Ed displays win-win thinking and gives the audience the credit: *"You have made this sale a success for both of us."*

You can't help but like Ed. He uses humor up until the last second. Here he uses a play on words: "cutup" (which is what his product does).

### Using Salesmanship as Your Passport to Financial Freedom

As the crowd dispersed, Ed would start his presentation again. He always began with the empty boxes to show his truthfulnesss. No one ever complained because Ed was completely honest in telling the audience exactly what he was going to sell them. Ed made 400% profit on everything he sold, plus the dollar on the empty box, which was almost pure profit.

It was a wonderful summer job and Ed earned enough to register at Catholic University in Washington, D.C., to study drama. The rest is history and Ed McMahon has become an international celebrity. Sales and Ed's intuitive understanding of hypnotic language techniques made it all possible.

As we stated earlier, while the setting was the Atlantic City boardwalk, it could have been anywhere. You can customize these and the many other powerful techniques you learned in this book to sell more of your products and services with less effort. The hypnotic persuasion principles Ed used have been used by thousands of others. The number of applications these principles have is limited only by your imagination.

We invite you to use sales hypnosis to help yourself, to help your clients and customers, and to help your company. You now have the tools of success that Ed McMahon and other powerful communicators have possessed for many years. If you use them wisely and enjoy them, the tools of sales hypnosis will bring you riches.

# Epilog

## Sales Hypnosis: The Key To Lifelong Sales Success

Our findings on the hypnotic powers of top salespeople interested so many people in business and the media that, as a result, we've been invited to do interviews on dozens of radio shows and more than a few television shows. During the course of the interview, we are usually asked something like, "Is hypnotic selling a fad? Will it be around next year? Will it stand the test of time?"

We answer by explaining that hypnosis has been used for thousands of years by healers, religious leaders, politicians, and other influential people. Carvings on stone walls in Ancient Egyptian "sleep temples" document the use of hypnosis, as do two thousand-year-old writings from Greece. Hypnosis is not likely to go away. Ignoring it will definitely not make it go away. Hypnosis can be a force for much good, if you know how to use it. Those trained in the use of sales hypnosis can utilize it for what we call "win-win selling." That's where the salesperson wins, and the customer wins.

The story we'd like to leave you with dramatically proves the power of sales hypnosis. It illustrates how sales hypnosis can be used over the course of an entire career for *sustained* sales success. This example shows that sales hypnosis will not be a passing fad, but will continue to make a powerful and lasting contribution to the fields of sales, marketing, and persuasion.

In the late 1970s and early 1980s, word of our research studies on top salespeople began to slip out. People from around the United States and several foreign countries contacted us to request additional information. Some of these people mailed us stories of how they had been using hypnotic principles for many years in their own sales work.

## Use Sales Hypnosis to Get into the Million-Dollar Round Table

In late May of 1981, we were deluged with phone calls and mail. *The Wall Street Journal* ran a front page story on May 29 about Seymour Frank, an insurance sales superstar who proudly claimed that much of his success in sales derived from his use of hypnotic communications techniques.

Seymour Frank is not a Johnny-come-lately. He has been able to sustain his success over a 25-plus-year career in insurance sales. In several of those years, he was a member of the Seven Million Dollar Forum, which is an elite group of approximately 200 insurance agents who annually sell over $7 million in policies. *In his career, Mr. Frank has sold well over $100 million worth of insurance.*

Mr. Frank is a performing hypnotist as well as one of the best insurance sales professionals in the country. The *Wall Street Journal* quotes him as saying, "Hypnosis is the power of suggestion and so is selling."

During World War II, Seymour Frank toured throughout the United States and the South Pacific entertaining the troops with a hypnosis revue. After the war, he worked with Milton Berle, who still holds Mr. Frank in high regard. Mr. Frank used hypnosis to eliminate Milton Berle's mother's sinus headaches. "He was excellent, terrific," The *Wall Street Journal* quotes Mr. Berle as saying.

When he entered the insurance sales field, he enjoyed even greater success. After qualifying for membership in the exclusive Million Dollar Round Table year after year, the organization finally gave up and named him a *Life Member* of the Million Dollar Round Table in 1963.

## The *Wall Street Journal* Reports on Sales Hypnosis

Some of his clients even know he is a trained Master Hypnotist. Does that interfere with his success? It doesn't seem to. The Wall Street Journal quotes one of Mr. Frank's clients, Arthur Abramson, an accountant. Mr. Abramson confronted Frank and said, "I know who you are, and I want to know something: Did you hypnotize me?" Mr. Abramson had just purchased a $100,000 insurance policy, which was a larger policy than he had planned to buy. Abramson said he did feel a little mesmerized by Frank's voice. The Wall Street Journal quoted Abramson as saying, "It gets you into a state where you're completely relaxed; your attention is right to him. Whatever objections I had disappeared; everything he said seemed so right."

The power of Seymour Frank's presentation comes from the persuasive language he used. Mr. Frank has an extra edge in that he has formally studied hypnosis. From reading this book, you too now have that competitive advantage. You now know the techniques of sales hypnosis.

*The Insurance Conference Planner* magazine quotes Frank as saying, "I do know, from my experience as both a professional hypnotist and a professional insurance salesman, that the two have much in common—from the opening to the close of their performance. And what combination is more logical? Hypnotism and sales have much in common because they are both forms of persuasive communication. Hypnotism is persuasive communication, and persuasive communication is salesmanship. In addition, hypnotism is the selling of an idea to a subject to get the subject to do what you want him to do. In sales, you have to present an idea that's satisfactory to the prospect so that he'll part with his money to buy what you are selling. And, in both instances, the presentation is everything."

Mr. Frank goes on to say, "The hypnotist and the sales person both introduce their topic. They explain it, make the other party comfortable, and condition and cajole their 'subject' to do what they wish. They parry and thrust and, ultimately, when they're good, they 'close.'"

## Success Secrets from a Sales Hypnosis Superstar

Seymour Frank notes that both hypnosis and salesmanship are based on a competence and self-confidence that generates others' trust in you. This Lifetime Member of the Million Dollar Round Table also believes that hypnosis and salesmanship both require "careful preparation and a step-by-step progression toward the close." That's why we have included chapters in this book on sales scripting. Our corporate clients across America, Canada, and Australia have told us that careful scripting using hypnotic language patterns is the best way in the world to improve sales presentations quickly.

*The Insurance Conference Planner* magazine reported on some of Seymour Frank's techniques for using the power of suggestion to increase the persuasiveness of your sales presentations. Here are some tips on sales hypnosis from the master hypnotist and sales superstar:

Your initial goal is to get the appointment. You must put the prospect or subject in a frame of mind ready to accept your suggestion. To the hypnosis subject, offer a way to get eight hours of sleep in just five minutes. To the sales prospect, offer a way to save a lot of money in only twelve minutes.

Think of yourself as a problem-solver, not just a salesman. You must understand your prospect's needs and then attempt to meet them. Once you lose your power of concentration on his needs and think of your own, you won't be able to solve his problems, and you will lose the sale. The professional hypnotist is trained to focus on solving the client's problems.

Attitude is everything. Be confident. You must believe in yourself before you can sell others. Believe you are the world's greatest salesperson and then act like one. Who says that Seymour Frank is the world's greatest theatrical hypnotist? He does!

Resistance is the initial hurdle which both the hypnotist and the salesman must overcome. When Frank encounters a new subject or a new client for the first time, he reports that their initial reaction is often skepticism, distrust, and even fear. Frank avoids alienating his subject or client by avoiding any type of high pressure. "There is no way you can make people fall into a hypnotic trance by threatening them," Frank explains. He also observes that it is ineffective to try to use any kind of force to get customers to sign on the dotted line.

Seymour Frank is a great believer in qualifying the prospect, whether he is a hypnotic subject or a potential customer. He notes that the hypnotist can't hypnotize everyone and that a sales professional should not try to sell everyone. The hypnotist can't hypnotize an uncooperative subject, and the sales professional should never try to sell if the prospect does not have the need or does not have the money.

A tip that Seymour Frank always gives in seminars is that both the sales professional and the hypnotist need to plan and rehearse their presentations. Even after 25 years as a sales champion, Mr. Frank still rehearses his script. And, after an even greater number of years using hypnosis, he still rehearses the hypnotic inductions he will use. Mr. Frank notes, "Remember, you've heard your presentations 735 times. The prospect hears it once."

Seymour Frank is a master at using rhythm, pace, and cadence in both hypnosis and sales. These are verbal tools to make the subject or prospect feel comfortable and secure. If a salesman says, "Mr. Jones, do you want to buy this program?" he will fail, according to Mr. Frank, because he has "shifted gears too quickly and has broken his pace." In this book, you have learned that the ultimate pacing technique is to match and mirror the customer's voice to communicate subliminally, "I am like you are." Since we trust and like people like ourselves, matching your client's speech qualities will make your client feel more comfortable with you.

## How to Use Salesmanship and Hypnosis to Offer Benefits

Both hypnosis and salesmanship are based upon offering benefits. Successful salesmanship and successful hypnosis both offer peace of mind. The positive motivators are what make hypnosis and selling—sales hypnosis—so successful. Always stress the benefits of what you are offering. While the benefits may be crystal clear to you, don't assume they are clear to the client. It is your job to make these benefits clear to him or her.

Seymour Frank, one of the top life insurance salesmen in America, is a great believer in asking questions which will elicit a "yes" answer. In this book, we have shared many powerful methods of using the "repeated yes" technique. Mr. Frank reminds salespeople to *never disagree* with a client. This makes it more likely that the prospect will then disagree with you—and then you might lose the sale.

Mind-reading is a key to success in both salesmanship and hypnosis. And, skilled mind-reading is based on being a good listener. Seymour Frank tells us to stop talking and let the other person speak, "even if his lips barely start to move." He elaborates by stating that what the client says is "infinitely more important than your thoughts for it will provide you with the key to his problems." Remember, you get the sale by solving his problems and addressing his needs.

Another useful tip offered by Seymour Frank is to make your presentation *simple, direct,* and *understandable.* "Use power phrases, in the right order, with the right gestures and with confidence and a positive attitude to gain trust."

## Giving Suggestions Gives You Power!

Both the sales professional and the hypnotist earn their livelihoods by giving suggestions. While Mr. Frank says you should never disagree with the client, he also notes that you should not be afraid to give suggestions.

For example, let's say that you have to deal with a client who has constant phone interruptions during your sales presentation. What do you do? After building trust and rapport, *suggest* to your client that his phone calls be held. Or, *suggest* that you meet outside the office, perhaps at a restaurant. Be gracious at all times. And, show the client the benefit to him in not having these interruptions. Seymour Frank has a powerful script for dealing with such phone call interruptions. He says, "Mr. Jones, it is not fair *to you* if I make the presentation under these conditions."

Seymour Frank says, "I believe there is nothing stronger than the power of persuasive communication. Remember, hypnotism is persuasive communication, and persuasive communication is salesmanship. Be a salesman with this knowledge, and the ability to deliver a presentation well and success will be yours." These are the words of advice from a sales champion who is one of the top 200 life insurance agents in the country (out of over 900,000).

Seymour Frank has been hired by dozens of major corporations to teach sales hypnosis. These progressive corporations recognize that Mr. Frank's long career of Olympic-caliber sales success is a testament to the power of sales hypnosis. The many corporations for which we have done research and sales training have also discovered that sales hypnosis gives their people an awesome competitive edge.

We wish you the greatest success in using hypnotic pacing techniques, hypnotic trust-building techniques, hypnotic leading techniques, hypnotic story selling techniques, hypnotic sales scripting, and all of the other strategies and tactics of sales hypnosis we have shared with you in this book. Sales hypnosis is different from most other conventional approaches to salesmanship in that it is effective, and it does work. We hope that, by using these techniques, you may become the next Seymour Frank. When it comes time to write the sequel to this book, we'd like to include you and your great sales hypnosis success stories!

# Index